7/05

Frontispiece. Paul Balluriau's illustration for Ferdnand Mazade's "Le Sphinx," Gil Blas, 1895.

BOOK OF THE
Sphinx

Willis Goth Regier

University of Nebraska Press : Lincoln

Library of Congress Cataloging-in-Publication Data
Regier, Willis Goth.
Book of the Sphinx / Willis Goth Regier.
p. cm. – (Texts and contexts)
Includes bibliographical references and index.
ISBN 0-8032-3956-4 (cloth : alkaline paper)
1. Sphinxes (Mythology) 2. Sphinxes (Mythology) in
literature. I. Title. II. Series.
BL820.S66.R44 2004   203'.7–DC22   2004002523

For the Sphinx of Nebraska

Contents

List of Illustrations ix

Preface xv

1. Phix and Horemakhet 1

2. Secrets 19

3. Confrontations 39

4. Riddles 69

5. Body 89

6. Eros 113

7. Mind 135

8. Symbol of Symbols 151

9. Exit 197

Acknowledgments 213

Notes 217

Bibliography 253

Index 287

Illustrations

Frontispiece: Paul Balluriau's illustration for Ferdnand Mazade's "Le Sphinx," *Gil Blas,* i

1.1.
Photograph of Horemakhet, 1899, 2

1.2.
Phix and Oedipus, circa 470 BC, 4

1.3.
Photographers at the Great Sphinx, circa 1910, 7

1.4.
"When Wakes the Sphinx!" cover of *Strange Tales,* 1959. © 2004 Marvel Characters, Inc. Used with permission, 9

1.5.
"The Power of the Sphinx," cover of *Fantastic Four,* 1979. © 2004 Marvel Characters, Inc. Used with permission, 9

1.6.
Engraving of Horemakhet, 1870, 11

1.7.
Postcard view of Horemakhet, circa 1910, 11

1.8.
Precursors by V. Kortabinsky, circa 1910, 13

1.9.
Sphinx stamp, Israel, 1966, 13

1.10.
L'énigme by Gustave Doré, 1871. Musée de Orsay, Paris. Copyright Réunion des Musées Nationaux / Art Resource, New York, 14

1.11.
Sphinx on the cover of *Life,* 1909, 17

2.1.
Sphinx in Los Angeles Public Library,
23

2.2.
Engraving of Giza, 1679, 25

2.3.
Engraving of Giza by Sharp, 1735, 25

2.4.
Engraving of Giza by Benard Direx,
1752, 26

2.5
Colossal Sphynx's Head by T. Wallis,
1804, 26

2.6
Engraving of the Sphinx by Page,
1807, 27

2.7
Engraving of Horemakhet, 1822, 27

2.8
Engraving of Horemakhet, 1831, 28

2.9
Emblem of Horemakhet, 1893, 28

2.10
Engraving of astigmatic Horemakhet, 1857, 28

2.11
Die Ausgrabung der Sphinx by Ernst
Koerner, 1880, 30

2.12
Horemakhet, 1895, 30

2.13
Stereograph of Horemakhet by H. C.
White, 1901, 30

2.14
Postcard of Horemakhet by H. H.
Stratton, circa 1910, 31

2.15
Secret of the Sphinx by Elihu Vedder,
1863. © 2003 Museum of Fine Arts,
Boston, 32

2.16
*Secret of the Sphinx (Homage to Elihu
Vedder)* by Mark Tansey, 1984.
Courtesy of Gagosian Gallery, 33

2.17
Ida Rubenstein as the Sphinx, 1924,
35

2.18
Panel from "Priestess of the Sphinx,"
Chilling Tales, 1971, 35

2.19
Helmeted Sphinx on Celto-Iberian
coin, circa 50 BC, 36

3.1
Le repos en Égypte by Luc Olivier
Merson, 1879. © 2003 Museum of
Fine Arts, Boston, 49

3.2
La Vierge by Amédée Vignola, 1896,
50

3.3
Egypt stamp, 1867, 52

3.4
Mali stamp, 1971, 52

3.5
Horemakhet on casino token, 2000,
53

3.6
Crown Prince Wilhelm of Prussia
and Crown Princess Cecilie at the
Sphinx, 1911, 53

3.7
Horemakhet stamp, Egypt, 1872, 54

3.8
Horemakhet stamp, Egypt, 1888, 54

3.9
Horemakhet, circa 1880, 55

3.10
Tourist at Giza, circa 1900, 55

3.11
Photograph of Horemakhet by Bonfils, 1878, 56

3.12
Keystone stereoview, 1899, 57

3.13
Detail of Keystone stereoview, 1899,
57

3.14
Roman funerary Sphinx, first century, 57

3.15
Sphinx on Athena's helmet, detail
from Greek banknote, 1939, 58

3.16
Postcard of Horemakhet, circa 1905,
59

3.17
Horemakhet on Egyptian coin, 1957,
59

3.18
Complaint by Rozenfeld, circa 1910,
61

3.19
Postcard of prayer before Horema
khet, circa 1918, 61

3.20
Napoleon and the Sphinx by Jean-
Léon Gérôme, 1886, 63

3.21
Masthead of *The Sphinx,* 1932, 64

3.22
Les deux Sfinxs by W. Kossak, 1918,
65

3.23
Russian postcard of Napoleon and
the Sphinx, 1907, 65

3.24
Teddy Roosevelt as the Sphinx, 1908,
66

3.25
"Big Game to the Last," 1910, 66

3.26
The Sphinx and the Mummy, 1909,
67

4.1
Oedipus and the Sphinx shown on a
Greek amphora, 450–440 BC. © 2003
Museum of Fine Arts, Boston, 73

4.2
Frontispiece of Paul's *Die neue
Sphinx,* 1877, 76

4.3
Oedipus and the Sphinx by Dominique Ingres, 1825, 80

4.4
Oedipus and the Sphinx by Ingres,
1864. Courtesy of the Walters Art
Gallery, Baltimore, 81

4.5
The Secret by Theodore Baur, 1898,
83

4.6
The Riddle by Michael Parkes, 1999.
Courtesy of the artist, 85

5.1
Hans Eichler's reconstruction of the
Ephesus Sphinx, 1959. Courtesy of
the Oesterriche Archaeologische Institut, Vienna, 90

5.2
Eichler's completed reconstruction.
Courtesy of the Kunsthistorisches
Museum, Vienna, 93

5.3
Illustration for "If I Could Read Your
Heart" by H. P. Jeddy, 1905, 94

5.4
Oedipus and the Sphinx by Gustave
Moreau, 1864. Metropolitan Museum
of Art, bequest of William H. Herri-
man, 1920, 97

5.5
from Conti's *Mythologiae,* 1551, 98

5.6
Sphinx and Chimera by John Singer
Sargent, 1925, 99

5.7
Engraving of the violated female
Sphinx of Giza by E. Goodall, 1829.
102

5.8
P. M. Griffith's cover for "Burning
Sands," 1922, 106

5.9
Columbia Phonograph ad, 1905, 107

5.10
"Sphinxes," by Robert Schumann,
1835, 110

6.1
The Sphinx's Kiss by Franz von Stuck,
1895, 119

6.2
Sphinx by Perino del Vaga (1500–47).
Courtesy Harvard University Art Mu-
seums, 123

6.3
Drawing of the Sphinx by Felicien
Rops, 1886, 124

6.4
A Parisien Sphinx by Alfred Stevens,
circa 1870, 131

6.5
Mona Paiva as Sphinx, circa 1920, 131

6.6
Ad for the Sphinx brothel in Paris,
1931, 133

7.1
Freud's commemorative medal, 1906,
146

7.2
Freud on Austrian banknote, 1986,
147

8.1
Cover of Steinhardt's *Schwarze
Sphinx,* 1927, 157

8.2
Sphinx on a Grand Casino token,
1994, 161

8.3
Sphinx on the wheel of fortune card
from the Oswald Wirth tarot, 1896,
165

8.4
Sphinx meets UFOs, cover of *Amazing
Stories,* 1957, 167

8.5
Amédée Vignola's final Sphinx for
Fragerolle's *Sphinx* song cycle, 1896,
169

8.6
Illustration by George Roux from
Verne's *Le Sphinx des glaces,* 1897, 170

8.7
Hatshepsut as Sphinx. Metropolitan
Museum of Art, Rogers Fund, 1931,
173

8.8
Cover of *Sphinx,* 1932, 174

8.9
Sphinx on silver coin of Chios, 400
BC. 176

8.10
Sphinx on Roman silver denarius, 46
BC, 176

8.11
Central Bank of Egypt, 100 pounds,
1997, 177

8.12
The Nile reclining on a Sphinx, circa
200 AD, 181

8.13
Sphinx on Duke cigarette card, 1888,
185

8.14
Sphinx Egypt customs tax stamp,
1893, 185

8.15
Sphinx insignia for the British Lincolnshire Regiment in Egypt, 1941,
187

8.16
Sphinx of Amenhotep III in St.
Petersburg, 189

8.17
Sphinx Head Rock, Briggs Landing,
Oregon, 1920, 193

8.18
Sphynx cat stamp, Afghanistan, 1996,
194

8.19
Sphingidae, 1903, 195

8.20
Sphinxes on chariot card from the
Oscar Wirth tarot, 1896, 196

9.1
Oedipus slays the Sphinx, Etruscan
gem, third or fourth century BC, 204

9.2
Oedipus and the Sphinx by François
Léon Sicard, 1903. Musée de Orsay,
Paris. Copyright Réunion des Musées
Nationaux / Art Resource, New York,
204

9.3
Drawing of the murdered Marika by
Mittis, 1896, 207

9.4
"A World for the Winning," cover of
The New Warriors, 1991. © 2004 Marvel Characters, Inc. Used with permission, 208

B1
Curt Liebich's tailpiece for Richard
Voss's *Sphinx,* 1913, 215

B2
Place de Châtelet, Paris, 216

B3
Oedipus on the Menu, Liebig Co.,
Antwerp, 1902, 252

B4
World War I Memorial, Kuringai
Chase, New South Wales, 286

prrrrrrr

Preface

pssssssss

Sir Francis Bacon advised nobility to approach the Sphinx as Prince Oedipus did: slowly. The Sphinx is a breathtaking mystery, a fascinating man-eater. Come close to her, she gets you. Unsought a Sphinx slips out of sight, but sought the Sphinx seems everywhere, from the zenith of the sun to the end of the world, tough old Sphinx, yawning at bluster and profundity.

Sphinxes come at the hint of an invitation, and come hungry. They inspire songs and novels, shine in silver and gold. They're as unpredictable as a deck of cards. If they don't like their company, they eat it.

An aspiring know-it-all must study Sphinxes. The first Sphinx scholar was Athanasius Kircher, sj (1602–80), a curious man with a sunny disposition. Three popes valued Kircher as a universal genius, an opinion he repaid with grandly illustrated treatises on music and magnetism, a proposal for a global language, vistas of stars and the underground, and an introduction to China. He adored the Virgin and loved languages, athletics, and machinery. In his prime he gave the Holy Roman Emperor *Oedipus Aegyptiacus* (1652–54), a four-part compendium of all that was known about Egypt, and then some. By work and miracle Kircher deciphered Egypt's hieroglyphs, triumphantly revealing their tremendous secrets. In a short reprise he published *Sphinx Mystagoga* (1676), his guide to the Sphinx.

Kircher studied in France, taught in Rome, and published in Amsterdam. He is a baroque example of the Renaissance ideal, the scholar who knows everything about everything. At an age when men begin to dote he was sniffing the Sphinx. He says so: "ludibundae Sphingis τεχνάσματα & Machinas subolfaciens," scenting the tricks and devices of the playful Sphinx. Kircher thought he outwitted the Sphinx, but in retrospect *Sphinx Mystagoga* exposes how the Sphinx played him. Sphinxes trick, they're famous for it, and Kircher fell for a false surrender.

The Sphinx appears the moment that certain victory turns to total defeat. It is a symbol of secrets and secret keeping, a symbol that carries messages from the distant past to those precious few (you and I) who can comprehend them. It makes fools of everyone else. It is the symbol of the tease: wherever a Sphinx is, a secret is. It is a nimble symbol, subtle and obsessive.

The Sphinx attracted thinkers of big thoughts like Augustus, Napoleon, and Hegel. In his 1820s aesthetics lectures, Hegel proposed the Sphinx as the symbol of the symbolic itself. What an idea, a symbol of the symbolic! How rhetorical, how Greek, was Hegel's Sphinx. The Sphinx synthesizes other symbols, private and public, sacred and recycled, the sticky charnel of history and spun sugar of fantasy. Incomparably various, the Sphinx is as diverting as an illustrated catalog, as dreadful as a casualty list.

If you want to know something short and solid about Sphinxes, any dictionary will do. If you want to see Sphinxes in their habitats, watch them hunt and bewilder, marvel at their mating rites, then come along, at whatever pace you like. For Sphinxes and Sphinx lovers this is a bedtime book, but with its cat hair, insomnia, and simooms, it is not for everyone.

1 : Phix and Horemakhet

We [Sphinxes] sit before

the pyramids for

the judgment of nations.

Goethe

1.1. Photograph of Horemakhet by A. W. Elson, 1899.

In ancient Egypt, Syria, and Greece, Sphinxes guarded gates of temples and cemeteries, perched on high columns, came in storms of wings and claws, and perfumed air like poison. Up the Nile, down the Euphrates, and all around the Mediterranean, they were thought to be supernaturally vigilant and wise. Patient, supple, strong, a Sphinx is a dream of mastery, concentrated thought annoyed by chatter. A sleepy Sphinx curls up like a cat, a question mark, a hook.

There are Sphinxes of Isis, Sphinxes for Christ, Sphinxes of heights and abysses, Sphinxes in ranks, rows, and pairs. Two Sphinxes rise above the rest.

In Egypt is the Great Sphinx of Giza, flat on its belly amid ghosts of the gods. He has a very old name, *Horemakhet,* Sun on the Horizon.[1] The Great Sphinx has also been called Harmarkhis, Son of the Sun; Harmais; Balhouba; and Abu-Hol, the Father of Terror. Its face is supposed to be the face of Pharaoh Chephren, or Kafre, from the golden age of sun worship, 4,500 years ago. Blowing sand has eroded the Sphinx, but its scars, holes, and demolished features are mainly the work of religious zeal.

In Greece is *Phix* the riddler, the singer, the strangler, staring down the brink of incoherence. Michel Serres blurts, "She is a chimera, half-lion and half-woman; half four-legged, also and half two-legged, and perhaps partly bird."[2] Apollodorus (first century BC) and Hyginus (third century AD) summarize her story. Hyginus says:

> The Sphinx, offspring of Typhon, was sent into Boetia, and was laying waste the fields of the Thebans. She proposed a contest to Creon, that if anyone interpreted the riddle which she gave, she would depart, but that she would destroy whoever failed, and under no other circumstances would she leave the country. When the King heard this, he made a proclamation throughout Greece. He promised that he would give the kingdom and his sister Jocasta in marriage to the person solving the riddle of the Sphinx. Many came out of greed for the kingdom, and were devoured by the Sphinx, but Oedipus, son of Laius, came and interpreted the riddle. The Sphinx leaped to her death.[3]

1.2. Phix and Oedipus depicted on a painted bowl from Attica, circa 470 BC, at the Vatican Museum.

Most mythographers are also brief. Giovanni Boccaccio, Thomas Bulfinch, and Edith Hamilton finish off the Sphinx in a paragraph or less. Sophocles (fifth century BC) scarcely sketched her.

Before their extinction (Goethe's Sphinxes say Hercules killed the last of them)⁴ Sphinxes ranged Anatolia, Thrace, the Peloponnese, Crete, the Cyclades, Italy, Sardinia, and Spain. Like Sphinxes of Egypt and the Levant they often appeared in couples beside gates and doorways. Sphinxes took shape as pottery, jewelry, coins, and carvings, again often in pairs.⁵ When Egypt peacefully surrendered to the army of Alexander the Great in 332 BC, the Greeks brought the riddle of Phix back where Sphinxes began, where her ancestors silently waited in old holy places.

"Of what invisible flock are those huge sphinxes the guardians," asked a French Cleopatra, "crouching like dogs on the watch, that they never close their eye-lids and forever extend their claws in readiness to seize? Why are their stormy eyes so obstinately fixed upon eternity and infinity?

What weird secret do their firmly locked lips retain within their breasts?"[6] Symbolically speaking, these are real questions.

Hegel exalted the Sphinx as "the symbol of the symbolic itself."[7] Hegel's Sphinx is the Sphinx of Sphinxes, a mix of Phix, Horemakhet, and the Sphinxes of Luxor. His Sphinx is a species of idea, a fantastic body and dazzling mind, a Sphinx with a history, an anatomy, a line of descent, and arrested evolution. By the time it reached Hegel, the symbol of symbols was deceptive. Hegel's Sphinx is the symbol of the *defeat* of the Sphinx. His Sphinx commemorates the overthrow of Egypt by Greece, the overthrow of enigma by thought, of nature by man, of mystery by clarity.[8] His Sphinx is a loser. Hegel died, then his symbol of symbols revived, returning with makeup and cigarettes, a smile with fangs behind it, sweet and epidemic charm. The Sphinx stepped out of Hegel's interpretation and vindicated his high regard: his symbol of symbols symbolizes almost anything and specializes extensively.

Sphinx? What makes Phix and Horemakhet two of a kind, he harmless and mute at Giza, and she winged and deadly?

ANTITYPES

Except for their Sphinxiness, Phix and Horemakhet are like night and day. From her mountaintop Phix puts riddles to passersby. Solitary Horemakhet silently rides the Sahara. He appeals to the eyes, she to the ears. In novels, movies, stories, and ads, Horemakhet is a prop, Phix is a character. He attracts visitors. She slits them open.

Phix is wet with homicide. Horemakhet suns on the sand. She dies repeatedly, he watches empires fall. Phix flirts with the giant at Giza. He magnifies her and she gives him something to think about. He has been a refuge and she an avenger, he a counselor and she a femme fatale. Horemakhet basks in front of three manmade mountains that rise like rotten teeth above the royal dead. Eating young men on her mountain, Phix picked a king.

Horemakhet is older than Moses; according to Hesiod, Phix is older than Zeus. Horemakhet flies on postcards everywhere, Phix appears in

Paris and New York. With a smile Horemakhet stumps geniuses; Phix is contradiction incarnate. Horemakhet survived his civilization, upstaging pharaohs and their redundant pyramids. Peremptory Phix is wild as madness.

Mighty Horemakhet, Son of the Sun, sunbaked for a thousand years before Oedipus answered the riddle of Phix of Thebes. Horemakhet caught Phix's habit and now poses riddles of his own.[9] Phix speaks through Horemakhet; he sees through her. He listens to riddle after riddle as if he could solve them, as if he cared.

MONSTER

Phix, the monster, brought out the monster in Horemakhet. "What a monstrous idea was it from which this monster sprang!" exclaimed Harriet Martineau when she saw the Great Sphinx in 1846. "I feel that a stranger either does not see the Sphinx at all, or he sees it as a nightmare." Visiting Egypt in 1893, Lord Alfred Douglas felt

> that on the sand
> Crouches a thing of stone that in some wise
> Broods on my heart; and from the darkening land
> Creeps Fear and to my soul in whisper speaks.[10]

Damaged by wars and fanatics, sand-pocked, pickaxed, and buried up to his neck, Horemakhet suffered horrible degradation. His ancient Egyptian name, Per-Hol, or place of Horus, was confused with *Hol,* the Arabic word for terror, and to this day his name remains Abu-Hol, Father of Terror.

As Abu-Hol, Horemakhet greeted visitors from distant lands. Gustave Flaubert frowned when he met Horemakhet in 1851 and did what he was taught to do: he saw the Great Sphinx as "le père de la terreur."[11] William Perry Fogg's 1875 travel guide commented, "Time and ill-usage have made sad havoc with the monstrous face, but there is a placid beauty about its features, an abstracted expression, resembling that of the large Buddhist idols of Japan and India. The conception is a grand one, and well calculated to inspire with terror the weak minds of its worshipers."[12]

1.3. Photographing the photographers at the Great Sphinx, circa 1910.

The terror tradition persists in thrillers and comic books. Again and again Horemakhet rose up as a monster controlled by magic or aliens. Villains and supervillains are often named Sphinx.[13]

There are terrorist Sphinxes, the worst of worst enemies. "A Morte" is the name of the archvillain of Henry Carew's *The Secret of the Sphinx* (1924). Master of disguises and poisons, A Morte leads his Caravan of Death into Egypt to fight the British. In the Egypt of Ken Follett's *Key to Rebecca* (1980) Sphinx is a Nazi spy. In Dan Schmidt's *The Sphinx Prophet* (1991) the Sphinx is the emblem of a cruel charismatic Egyptian and his Sphinx Soldiers, "a bad-ass collection of some of the most dangerous terrorists in the whole Middle East" armed with enough nerve gas to kill the planet.[14]

With his lion body and man-high paws, Horemakhet makes terror explicit. The lion is a symbol of agility, stealth, lightning reflexes, and overwhelming strength, all of which suit warlike kings. Pharaohs kept lions as pets and hunting companions, powerful servants of their pleasure. Ramses the Great and his beloved lion fought together. Pharaohs officially claimed the title "He who inspires great terror." Philo of Alexandria wrote that the Pharaoh was the King of Terror, whose pride was so unbound he claimed to be sovereign of animals.[15]

Lions were reputed to use their tails to sweep away their tracks, showing an intelligence and secrecy advantageous to administration. All the more admirable is a giant Sphinx whose tremendous paws left no tracks.[16] Two thousand years ago Egyptians told Pliny that Horemakhet walked in from some place where there were more like him. For a while the Great Sphinx observed worship at an altar placed between its paws and at a temple nearby.[17]

Horemakhet looks past humanity fearlessly, his heart hard as stone. He is usually described as a "dimorph," a human head upon a lion's body. Less obvious is his third part: the serpent. Centuries ago, when he was complete, a cobra (or asp) slinked upon his forehead. Horemakhet's parts — lion, human, and snake — embody the animals who rule the earth and underground, and he was intimately connected to the sky. Jean François

1.4. "When Wakes the Sphinx!" the cover of *Strange Tales,* August 1959.

1.5. "The Power of the Sphinx," the cover of *Fantastic Four,* July 1979.

Champollion, the decipherer of hieroglyphics, thought that a giant metal hawk once stood on Horemakhet's shoulders.[18]

Viewed from the side, the Great Sphinx is an extralong lion: the head is carved at a scale considerably smaller than the scale of the body (30:1 and 22:1), a large disproportion of small importance.[19] Its elongation was well disguised and long concealed. Pharaoh's builders were not lazy or artless. They could have cut down the limestone as easily as they built it up, adjusting the body and head to a uniform ratio. Why didn't they? An economic explanation: the costs and protracted schedule of chopping the body down to size would favor a small head, big body. An artistic explanation: its lion parts magnify its latent power and ferocity — upon its great body its smaller human head looks higher up and farther away. A geologic explanation: in its middle the rock cracked, compromising the sculptors' design.

Wicked scars are chiseled across the Sphinx's face. To preserve the secrets of ancient Egypt, Theosophists professed, the Great Sphinx had been brutally violated. Marie Farrington wrote, "The Egyptian sphinx was at first feminine, a fact conclusively proved by typology."[20] John Anthony West, archenemy of academic Egyptology, takes up Theosophy's opinion: Chephren's face on the Great Sphinx proves nothing else than Chephren's revision of history. Chephren ordered workmen to hack off the Sphinx's female face and make it his, reshape her hair as his headdress, erase her utterly. (Vain pharaohs and deified caesars routinely recarved the heads of Sphinxes to impose their own faces.) If Farrington is right, before Chephren wrecked it the Sphinx's eyes — a woman's eyes — looked out from deeper antiquity. Chephren made it a symbol of male monstrosity with a head too small for its body. J. F. A. Heath-Stubbs saw in the Great Sphinx "the implacable image / Of male power that smoothly worships itself."[21]

It is like a Sphinx to argue from silence and be irrefutable. It has come a long way, and it has not always been a monster.

1.6. Engraving of Horemakhet by I. L. Rüdisühli from Vögelin, *Denkmaler des Weltgeschichte,* 1870.

1.7. Postcard view of Horemakhet from the south, L. Scortzis & Co., circa 1910.

ANGEL

Lionel Casson translates a fragment of Harpocration's *Eulogies,* inscribed at the feet of the Sphinx of Giza in the second century AD:

> This Sphinx who lacks naught is a vision divine.
> If you ponder her shape you will note the sure sign
> That her form is all made like a sacred apparition:
> Above is she holy, her face of heaven's rendition,
> But a lion, king of beasts, in limbs, body and spine.[22]

A vision divine? We have it on good authority that Sphinxes flew with the angels.

Cherubim are Sphinxes. W. F. Albright, founder of the Anchor Bible, says so. The best of Sphinxologists, Heinz Demisch, notes that the identification of the Cherubim and Sphinxes is consistent in point after point, particularly with Assyria and Babylon as intermediary cultures: Sphinxes and Cherubim were thrones of God, they were associated with the sun, and they were given the tasks of guarding sacred spaces. After studying Sphinxes on three continents, André Dessenne decided that the biblical Cherubim were "probably only Sphinxes."[23]

Nahum Sarna has doubts about the shapes of Cherubim. "By the end of the Second Temple period [70 AD], reliable traditions about their nature no longer existed."[24] But creatures of the Bible are creatures of the Lord. Who can neglect them? Traditions about the shape of the Cherubim persisted. In the seventeenth century, Jacob Gaffarel cited Theodoret, Bar-Cepha, Procopius Gazaeus, Jacobus Chius, Kimchi [David Kimhi], Pagnin, Pradus, Villapandus, and Oleaster as participants in centuries of dispute about the shape of Cherubim.[25]

Archaeologists unearthed Sphinxes in Israel. The Newell collection of ancient seals includes a hematite seal on which "two seated winged sphinxes face each other with a sacred tree between them."[26] Cherubim guarded the Garden of Eden (Genesis 3:24). If Albright, Demisch, and Dessenne are right, there are Sphinxes throughout the Bible, protecting the Tree of Life and Tree of Knowledge.

1.8. *Precursors* by V. Kortabinsky,
circa 1910.

1.9. Ninth-century BC Phoenician
ivory, Sphinx stamp, Israel, 1966.

1.10. *L'énigme* by Gustave Doré, 1871.

During the Exodus the Lord commanded Moses to make two Cherubim of gold to cover the Ark of the Covenant with their outspread wings (Exodus 25:18–22 and 37:7–9). A psalm of David describes the Lord enthroned on Cherubim.[27] Cherubim are among the army of angels, the "angels of governance," in the Book of Enoch. Midrash Shemot Rabbah describes the Cherubim as "angels of destruction."[28]

Sphinx angels often dropped into modern literature. In Alfred Jarry's *César-Antechrist* (1895) Caesar meets a silent Sphinx walking between tombs. Caesar says, "You are a queen and a goddess; like the angels you have ribs fastened in front, and the substance of your brain differs from mine as little as the seed of a woman from the sperm of a man. Because you are a woman, you infinitely reflect and represent the world and know things that escape mortal eyes."[29]

Angelic Sphinxes walked the streets of Paris. Charles Baudelaire admired one, Anatole France another. Abdiel, a rebel angel who reads too much, explains, "In Paradise we have Cherubim and Kerûbs in the shape of winged bulls, but those are the clumsy inventions of an inartistic god." Mademoiselle Angèle came from Paris for a bit part in Von Hornstein's *Die Sphinx und der Sadist* (1930).[30] Gustave Doré's Sphinx consoles an angel in agony on a rock overlooking the bombardment of the Paris commune. The Sphinx and Angel are symbols grieving at the sight of the real. If the Angel is the Angel of France, it is the Archangel Michael, the angel warrior, defeated.[31]

In James Thomson's *The City of Dreadful Night* (1870, 1874) the poet seeks peace in a cathedral.

> opposite my place of rest,
> Two figures faced each other, large, austere;
> A couchant sphinx in shadow to the breast,
> An angel standing in the moonlight clear.

The poet sleeps, until awoken by a "sharp and clashing noise . . . The angel's wings had fallen."

> The sphinx unchanged looked forthright, as aware
> Of nothing in the vast abyss of air.

Again the poet sleeps, until awoken by a louder crash. He sees that the angel had become a man, and the man

> Had fallen forward, stone on stone,
> And lay there shattered, with his trunkless head
> Between the monster's large quiescent paws,
> Beneath its grand front changeless as life's laws.[32]

FUSIONS

Otto Rank declared: The Sphinx "is a female being with a male member."[33] Horemakhet and Phix merged, their genders blending in plain sight.

His Excellency Horemakhet, crouched in the sand, discreetly covers his private parts. Or she covers hers. In 1936 Thomas Mann imagined Joseph, son of Jacob, standing before the Great Sphinx and wondering what sex he'd see if the Sphinx stood up.[34] Despite the testimony of pharaohs, Egyptian and Arabic names, Pliny's publicity, and an abundance of other manly Egyptian Sphinxes scattered throughout the world's collections — despite all this, for most of history Horemakhet has been a she. The evidence that the Great Sphinx is male is great, but long ago and not so long ago the world believed the Sphinx of Giza was female.

"Ex parte Leonem & Virginem," wrote Kircher in 1676: part lion, part virgin. In his seventeenth-century tour book, Herberer von Bretten described the Sphinx of Giza as "Oben ein Jungfraw / Unden ein Löw" [a maiden above, a lion below]. In 1867 Mark Twain saw a female Sphinx at Giza, looking out "from her throne in the sands as placidly and pensively as she had looked upon its like full fifty lagging centuries ago."[35]

In the nineteenth century fierce Phix was a knockout. Her riddles agitated pleasingly, and so did she. Her apparitions from the palettes of Dominique Ingres, Gustave Moreau, Odilon Redon, Félicien Rops, Ferdnand Khnopff, Edvard Munch, and Franz von Stuck depict the Sphinx as woman and woman as Sphinx.[36]

Unhappy Eugene Auenbrugger told Princess Maria Theresia the common notion that "Frauen seien Sphinxe" [women are Sphinxes]. The princess corrected him. Sphinxes are "immer männliche . . . aber die Män-

1.11. Sphinx on the cover of *Life*, April 22, 1909.

ner geheimnissen in uns allerlei hinein, das macht ihnen Freude" [always male . . . but men impute secrets to us, that makes them happy].[37]

Muriel Rukeyser describes Oedipus, old and blind, back on the road. "He smelled a familiar smell. It was the sphinx." They chew the fat. Old Oedipus learns too late that he had answered her riddle wrong. "You answered Man," she says. "You didn't say anything about woman."

"When you say Man," Oedipus answers, "you include women too. Everyone knows that." She replies, "That's what you think."[38]

2 : Secrets

The Sphinx who devours is an enigma.
And its true key is not, **Divine, or I devour
you!** But: **Divine, because I devour you.**

Paul Valéry

In Europe Egypt was a symbol upon which the Sphinx attached as a super-symbol. Philo thought Egypt stood for childhood, a stage that must be left behind. For the *Hermetica* of Hermes Trismegistus, Egypt was the "widow of the gods," an ancient land that once held divine wisdom and lost it. To church fathers and reformers Egypt meant oppression and tempta-tion. In the sixth century Cassiodorus explained, "Egypt stands for this world, which afflicts the Christian people with various calamities, but is inspired with fear by the Lord's strength and power. Egypt denotes the af-fliction which does not release faithful souls without their being oppressed by grim toils in that dominion."[1]

The symbol of Egypt inspired the fear of the Lord and extraordinary am-bition. Napoleon's conquest of Egypt in 1798 was done in the name of emancipating Egypt from despotism. He won a major victory in the Battle of the Pyramids but did not persuade Egyptians that he was their liberator. Egypt expelled Napoleon and brought forth its own Napoleon, Muham-med Alī, whose armies annexed Arabia, Yemen, Syria, and the northern Sudan. He ruled Egypt from 1805 to 1848, the years when Europe redis-covered the Sphinx.

Muhammed Alī controlled the ports and shores of the Red Sea and taxed their traffic. He tried to dominate the slave trade. He considered dismantling the pyramids for stone to line the Nile. Negotiating between bidders, he permitted infidels to dig in Egypt's ruins. European excava-tors easily recruited hundreds of men and boys to dig for them, working under the blazing sun to avoid capture by Muhammed Alī's conscription and corvée. Such was Egypt when Horemakhet reappeared.

THE DREAM SPHINX

In 1818 Giovanni Caviglia dug down to the Sphinx's front feet and found a tall granite slab between them. It is engraved with a story. Thutmose IV (circa 1420 BC) slept one day in the shade of the Sphinx. In a dream the

Sphinx spoke to him, calling itself Harmarkhis, the sun god, his father. The Sphinx prophesied that Thutmose would be pharaoh and rule long, but complained of the sand and asked Thutmose to remove it. Thutmose awoke, seized power, and cleared the sand away from the Sphinx in gratitude for the inspiring dream. As far as we know, Thutmose IV was the first to find the Sphinx buried in the desert and to clear the sand away. After Thutmose died, the sand returned, immersing the Sphinx and the slab. The sand was removed again and it returned again, a clinging garment.[2]

The history of Horemakhet as a sculpture, site, and symbol of pharaohs and gods, buried and unburied, is told in Christiane Zivie-Coche's *Sphinx: History of a Monument*. In *A Search in Secret Egypt*, Paul Brunton sums up five thousand years: "Seven times have the ever-active sands buried the sphinx; seven times it has been freed."[3]

THE GREAT SPHINX

About 77 AD Pliny the Elder visited Horemakhet. Pliny said little and said why: "the Egyptians have passed it over in silence. The inhabitants of the region regard it as a deity. They are of the opinion that a King Harmais is buried inside it and try to make out that it was brought to the spot."[4]

Horemakhet benefited from Roman engineers and imperial patronage. Nero subsidized Sphinx worship. An inscription found near the Sphinx identifies it as the goddess Latona and distinguishes it from the Sphinx of Thebes.[5] Later caesars continued to keep the Sphinx clean. Antoninus Pius (138–161 AD) reinforced a stone retaining wall to keep out sand. More reinforcement was provided by Emperor Verus (161–169 AD), Marcus Aurelius (161–191 AD), and Septimius Severus (193–211 AD).[6] The Sphinx, already older than memory, had seen invaders from Anatolia, Nubia, Libya, Persia, and Greece; witnessed successions of civil wars and competing religions; observed statues smashed, obelisks shattered, temples desecrated. The Romans saw a crumbling Sphinx, but it was new compared to what survives, and what survives is awesome.

The Great Sphinx is 240 feet long, 66 feet high, carved whole from rock and reinforced with fitted block. The ancient Egyptian engineers quarried stone that once was as deep as the Sphinx is high. As the stone was cut and hauled to a temple or tomb, the engineers left behind a broad plateau. In its midst they carved the Sphinx.

The Great Sphinx is the world's oldest monumental carving and perhaps the world's oldest Sphinx.[7] Most Egyptologists concur that the Sphinx was carved in honor of Pharaoh Kafre (or Chephren) in Egypt's Fourth Dynasty (2613–2494 BC). Excavations south of the Sphinx revealed that it once was surrounded by an active community of officials, bakers, caretakers, and builders, and had a nearby temple built of granite and alabaster, rich and tempting materials stripped for buildings and pavements. Four colossal Sphinxes, each more than 28 feet long, guarded another temple nearby. In time they, too, were taken away. In time the desert buried the rest.[8]

For most of history the head of the Sphinx was all that could be seen. Its body lay beneath sand.

Egypt teems with Sphinxes not so great, inscribed on walls and bas-reliefs, painted on papyrus and wood, and carved in statuary large and small. In the first century AD, Plutarch observed that Egyptian priests placed Sphinxes before their shrines "to indicate that their religious teaching has in it an enigmatical sort of wisdom."[9] Much of the Sphinx's reputation rests on Plutarch's short explanation, incessantly recited. Proclus repeated it in the Academy of Athens. In 1487 Pico de Mirandola, a scholar of scholars, wrote that Sphinxes symbolize that divine things "should be enveloped in the veil of enigma and in poetic dissimulation."[10] Hartley Burr Alexander had Plutarch's words inscribed in Greek on books held by female Sphinxes in the downtown Los Angeles Public Library. With barely

2.1. "An enigmatical sort of wisdom": Sphinx (and an admirer) in Los Angeles Public Library with inscription from Plutarch.

perceptible smiles, the Los Angeles Sphinxes hold open books, their secrets in Greek.

An axiom: the Sphinx is a symbol that means it hides meaning.

Writing in Greek when Greece set fashions for Rome, Plutarch extended his authority on Sphinx symbolism through the empire. From him descend all Sphinx science and history. From Plutarch's hint — "enigmatical wisdom" — come Sphinx esoterics, poetry, music, astrology, and riddle books for young and old.

Rome treated Sphinxes as the French would: as symbols, as art, and as furniture. In Cicero's day a large Sphinx was a status symbol.[11] Athenaeus described "a hundred gold couches with feet shaped like Sphinxes" in second-century Alexandria.[12] On tombstones and sarcophagi rich Romans carved images of the honored dead seated on Sphinxes.

Rome fell, the sand returned and reburied Horemakhet. When England and France beheaded their kings Horemakhet was just a head; for centuries it was a secret that the Sphinx was a Sphinx. In his *Cosmographie de Levant* (1556) André Thevet said he saw only the head. An English traveler observing the pilgrimage to Mecca described the Sphinx of 1580 as "a great head of stone somewhat like marble, which is discovered so farre as the necke joyneth with the shoulders, being all whole, saving that it wanted a little tippe of the nose." Five years later John Sanderson saw only "a Head of stone, standing upright to the necke out of the ground." In 1601 Radzivilius saw no more than that.[13]

The burgeoning book trade of the seventeenth century added illustrations of the head, imaginary Sphinxes in imaginary Egypt. An engraving of the Sphinx in Boullaye-le-Gouz's *Voyages et observations* (1657) gives the head a coiffure and the neck an encircling scarf or collar. Kircher imagined it as a Greek ruin in *Turris Babel* (1679). Sharp's 1735 engraving crowns the Sphinx, restores its nose, and centers it amid steeple pyramids. The Sphinx of Richard Pococke's *Description of the East* (1743–45) also had a fine full nose.[14]

2.2. Engraving of Giza from Kircher's *Turris Babel*, 1679.

2.3. Engraving of Giza by Sharp, 1735.

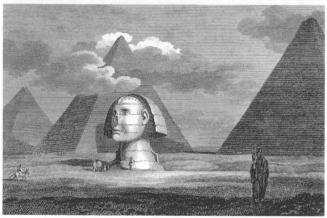

2.4. Engraving of Giza by Benard Direx in Diderot's *Encyclopedia*, 1752.

2.5. *Colossal Sphynx's Head* by T. Wallis after a drawing by W. M. Craig "from an original sketch of a gentleman lately returned from Egypt," 1804.

2.6. Engraving of the Sphinx by Page after a drawing by Vivant Denon from Cooke's *Universal Geography*, 1807.

2.7. Engraving of Horemakhet from *Description de l'Égypte*, 1822.

The great *Encyclopedia* of Diderot depicted a blank-eyed Sphinx, nose intact. W. M. Craig drew a Sphinx peeved to be noseless. Charles Norry, one of the architects participating in Napoleon's conquest of Egypt, doubted that it had a body. Napoleon's draftsmen were precise but problems with funding and foreign wars delayed publication of their drawings till 1822. Only then was Horemakhet's face depicted free of exaggeration and fancy.[15]

2.8. Engraving of Horemakhet from Cacciatore's *Nuovo atlante istorico*, 1831.

2.9. Emblem of Horemakhet, headpiece from *Sphinx: Monatsschrift für Seelen- und Geistesleben*, 1893.

2.10. Engraving of astigmatic Horemakhet from Menzel's *Die Kunstwerke vom Alterthum*, 1857.

In 1816 and 1817 it took Giovanni Caviglia two tries and a force of a hundred men to unbury the Sphinx's breast and forepaws. Caviglia found a fragment from the Sphinx's beard (now in the British Museum), the head of the uraeus from the Sphinx's brow, Thutmose IV's dream stela, and the altar between the Sphinx's paws.[16] Sand slides thwarted further excavations. Soon the Sphinx was again a head stuck in the sand, while its images wandered. Cacciatore's 1831 engraving moves the three great pyramids in front of the Sphinx. Sixty years later *Sphinx,* the Theosophy journal, put all three behind it.

Howard Vyse hired men and boys to haul sand away and drill through stone. From February 28 to March 2, 1837, and from May 22 to July 21, Vyse bored into the shoulder and tail of the Sphinx. He complained, "The boring-rods were broken owing to the carelessness of Arabs, at a depth of twenty-seven feet in the back of the Sphinx. Various attempts were made to get them out, and on the 21st of July gunpowder was used for that purpose; but being unwilling to disfigure this venerable monument, the excavation was given up, and several feet of boring-rods were left in it."[17]

In 1843 Richard Lepsius once more cleared sand down to the stele between its paws, and the sand once more rolled back. Thereafter came photography and a more exact record. In 1849 Maxime Du Camp, Flaubert's companion in Egypt, took the first photographs of the Sphinx. The Sphinx's head and shoulders look out from the hole dug by Lepsius, filling in with sand.[18] Photos did not inhibit illustrators. Menzel's 1857 survey of world monuments included an astigmatic Horemakhet staring where his nose had been.

How long does it take for the Sahara to rebury the Sphinx? About thirty years. Gaston Maspero, director of Egyptian Antiquities (1881–86 and 1899–1914), had a modern idea: he used rail carts to haul the sand away. Ernst Koerner painted the procedure: a line of men, their shoulder baskets full of sand, from the Sphinx to handcarts on a rail line that emptied into the Nile. Maspero's technology and motives were up-to-date: he foresaw the Sphinx as an economic boon, a ready-made tourist attraction. By 1886 he had cleared the foreparts and south flank of the Sphinx, but work ceased when funds dried up. The reburial began immediately. The

2.11. *Die Ausgrabung der Sphinx* by Ernst Koerner, 1880.

2.12. Horemakhet, Cairo Postcard Trust, 1895.

2.13. Stereograph of Horemakhet by H. C. White, 1901.

2.14. Detail of postcard of Horemakhet by H. H. Stratton, circa 1910.

desert covered the Sphinx's left paw in a decade, by 1900 the right paw, by 1905 sand rose to the breast, and by 1910 its face was again within reach. For millennia Horemakhet was reduced to a stool and pedestal. Travelers rested on his shoulders, natives posed on his head, and military corps rode him like an enormous camel.

Between 1925 and 1935 Emile Baraize completely excavated the Sphinx plateau to the south and east. He added concrete under the Sphinx's headdress and poured concrete in its cracks and cavities. In 1936 Selim Hassan demolished Baraize's retaining walls in order to excavate further to the left flank of the Sphinx, and by the end of the year he had excavated the sand behind the Sphinx all the way to the western wall. By 1937 he had removed about 250,000 cubic meters of sand. For the first time since Rome ruled Egypt, the Sphinx was free.[19]

Horemakhet became the Sphinx of Sphinxes.

SECRETS OF THE SPHINX

Very big Horemakhet has long been reputed to have a very big secret: an underground vault full of gold, perhaps a magic chamber or an ancient library. Vyse was looking for treasure when he drilled and blasted the Sphinx. The discovery of King Tut's treasure-filled tomb quickened ambitions for finding more: the Sphinx could not be merely a Sphinx, it had to be hiding something. "The Sphinx has not yet told us all his secrets," wrote Maspero.[20]

The size of Horemakhet has always mattered but what matters most nowadays is its antiquity. To know its age is to know when to look for its secret. Modern science competes with a stubborn wish to place the Sphinx farther in the past. The "inventory stela" (found by Mariette in 1853) declares that Khufu, who ruled before Kafre, repaired the Sphinx, but the inscription is Saite, engraved two thousand years *after* Khufu, an early example of backdating events to vindicate the present.[21]

There is not quite a consensus that the Great Sphinx was built at the same time as Kafre's pyramid and a dispute whether it depicts Kafre continues to spark and flame. In the long span of the Sphinx's history these ideas are contaminated by conspiratorial expertise, a worldly arrogance

heartily despised by the starstruck.[22] In a crowded lineage, writers have expected to find near the Sphinx an ancient book that tells of two kinds of future: the future that has happened since the book was hidden and the future still to come. Optimistic Edgar Cayce, at home in every time but his own, foresaw precisely that archaeologists will discover a buried Hall of Records that will prove the Sphinx of Giza was built in 11,016 BC by the stonecutter Araaraart.[23]

Equipped with maps, telescopes, and theodolites, other Sphinx seekers deduce that the Sphinx and pyramids have much to tell to those who know how to ask. The Reverend Walter Wynn, closely following the postulations of Davidson and Aldersmith's *The Great Pyramid* (1926), went to Egypt to see with his own eyes what locks were opened by the pyramids and Sphinx. He discovered prophecy of astonishing refinement. The Great Pyramid is "the Bible in Stone," predicting the time and place of the birth of Jesus, and in conjunction with the orientation of the Sphinx, Wynn foresaw that the world would be delivered from evil by September 16, 1936. He passes along exciting news: "The Pyramid gives the Rapture of the Saints as lying between the dates of February 19, 1931, and September 16, 1936."[24]

2.15. *Secret of the Sphinx* by Elihu Vedder, 1863.

2.16. *Secret of the Sphinx (Homage to Elihu Vedder)* by Mark Tansey, 1984.

In *The Great Sphinx Speaks to God's People* (1942) James A. Jeffers revealed that the Sphinx dates from the longest day of the year of 3996 BC, the day God created man. Jeffers's Sphinx marks the first summer solstice in the very first week of the very first year. With spiritual certainty, Jeffers declared the Sphinx was present at the Creation.[25] Jeffers is one of those blessed souls who found in the secret of the Sphinx exactly what they were looking for: original religion, confirmed by mathematical proofs and fulfilled prophecy.

Georges Barbarin's *L'énigme du Grand Sphinx* (1946) assembled a breviary of prior guesses at the secret of the Sphinx, all pointing toward a common conclusion: the Sphinx is the symbol of the coming Messiah, or better, both comings. His expert readings of the Sphinx led him to anticipate the second coming in 1969.[26]

For centuries Sphinxologists took the Great Sphinx back as far as ten thousand or twelve thousand years ago. In overlapping versions it is used as evidence of a lost civilization and of life on other worlds. The Sphinx has been attributed to an extinct red race, to ancestors from Atlantis and Lemuria, and to visitors from outer space.[27] Some say the secret of the Sphinx is top secret: extraintelligent extraterrestials use it as a landing place. At the dawn of Indo-European retrojection in the early 1800s, Horemakhet was linked to the infinite gods of India. Poet Robert Southey and linguist Sir William Jones connected the Sphinx to Narasingh, or Man-Lion, the fourth avatar of Vishnu, praised for saving the world sixteen thousand years ago.[28]

Artists of all kinds have ventured a "Secret of the Sphinx," often under the premise that its secret is worth dying for.

> The wisdom of the nations thou hast heard;
> The circling courses of the stars hast known;
> Awake! Thrill! By my feverish presence stirred,
> Open thy lips to still my human moan,
> Breathe forth one glorious and mysterious word,
> Though I should stand, in turn, transfixed, — a stone![29]

Shortly after her death in 1923 Sarah Bernhardt returned as the inspiration for Maurice Rostand's *Le secret du Sphinx*. It has a play within the play entitled *Sphinx*. Paris, the author of the inner play, informs the audience that he cannot allow *Sphinx* to be performed; it has already devoured him and could devour them as well. They insist but he departs, off to see "the real Sphinx in the real Egypt." Quick scene change and Paris is in Egypt with his brother, Marcellus. The brothers brave the threat of death and ask the Sphinx of Giza to reveal its secret. The Sphinx, in art nouveau glitter and beautifully feminine, whispers to Marcellus alone, who promptly pales and dies.[30]

It is a common inversion: the Sphinx does not ask a question but answers one—with an answer that kills. The secrets of the Sphinx are dangerous: anyone who discovers them dies.

2.17. Ida Rubenstein as the Sphinx, *La petite illustration,* May 1924.

2.18. Panel from "Priestess of the Sphinx," *Chilling Tales,* June 1971.

The secrets of the Sphinx are secure: confide secrets to it and it keeps them. Sphinx silence is absolute silence, every reason for silence: no lies, no noise, no pearls before swine, no blasphemy, no contradiction.

THE STARRY SPHINX

The stars wheeled by while the Sphinx stayed firm, looking "directly at the equinoctial point of the sun in any and every epoch, past, present, and future, forever."[31] An Iberian coin from 50 BC shows a Sphinx with a star at its mouth. Perhaps she speaks with it or sings it forth, perhaps she is about to eat it.

Rostand's Sphinx serenades the Night. "I have my questions. / She, she has her stars." She seduces the Night with a secret only she knows.[32]

Hassan describes an astrological Sphinx in "a book written by a man named Gamal-ed-Din Abu Garfa El-Idrissi during the 6th century AD, *The Light of the Science of the Heavenly Bodies in the Discovery of the Secrets of the Pyramids*.[33] Then and now the stars and Sphinx converse.

Horemakhet is an unswerving witness, a model of patience, a guide to higher things. Seen under stars he's inspirational. Rainer Maria Rilke describes the Sphinx as the stars' companion:

2.19. Helmeted Sphinx on Celto-Iberian coin, circa 50 BC.

The mornings of millennia, a people of winds, the rising and setting of countless stars, the great presence of constellations, the glow of these skies and their spaciousness were there and were there again and again, working on it, not ceasing before the deep indifference of this face, until it seemed to gaze, until it showed every sign of gazing at just these images, until it lifted itself up like the face to some inside in which all this was contained and occasion and desire and need for it all. And then, at the moment when it was full of all that confronted it, and formed by its surroundings, then its expression too had already grown out beyond them. Now it was as though the universe had a face.[34]

SECRETIONS OF THE SPHINX

Another would-be Oedipus, Dr. Louis Berman decoded the riddle of the Sphinx in the endocrine system. To know yourself, know your glands. In his *Glands Regulating Personality* (1921) Berman foresaw true freedom in "the chemistry of the soul." He diagnosed the mighty dead: Julius Caesar ("too much adrenal"), Napoleon ("it was his pituitary which first failed him"), Oscar Wilde ("thymocentric"), and Florence Nightingale ("It is most regrettable that we have no statement of the findings of a gynecological examination"). "Friedrich Nietzsche is about as good a case as there is on record of a genius blasted by migraine," beset by "an unstable pituitary" and a "supernormal ante-pituitary." Berman cites Galton's *Bible of Eugenics* and adores "the greatest naturalist of all time," Charles Darwin, who was saved by his "congenitally superior pituitary (the nidus of genius) and the overacting thyroid." From that imbalance, he declares, "Darwin changed Fate from a static sphinx into a chameleon flux."[35]

It is the fate of Fate to provoke rebellion. Once a lion at rest, the Sphinx became a chameleon, a furtive reptile in camouflage. "The abdication of Fate can therefore be confidently expected in due time," Dr. Berman predicted.[36] His fate-baiting book went through several printings, began to be popular, promising readers that if they managed their glands properly they could be as gods. Dr. Berman's gland manipulation could repair the races. He describes "the ideal Negro," he explains why Mongols have "a certain variety of idiocy," then shows his own: "Their relative deficiency in internal secretions constitutes the essence of the White Man's Burden."[37]

Long a friend of Sphinxes, Wyndham Lewis read Berman's book and drew the necessary conclusion: it had been dictated by Berman's glands. "Dr. Berman, then, speaks principally for the glands of secretion; it is they that speak in a hot and oily language to us through his lips." Body language. Lewis sought to clear the field "of any of the more troublesome lookers-on or camera-men, who would perhaps attempt to prevent us from questioning the Sphinx, on the ground that we were using words instead of other symbols. . . . Instead of being the Cause of Causes, he is the Effect of Effects."[38]

The Sphinx warns that the more you know the more you should bite your tongue.

3 : Confrontations

Craft, deep enigmas, an almost cruel precision, an implacable and half-bestial cunning, all the signs of feline watchfulness and of fierce spirituality are visible in the images of those stone deities. The skillfully proportioned blend of acuteness and coldness produces in the soul a peculiar sense of uneasiness and disquietude. And these monsters of silence and lucidity, infinitely calm, infinitely alert, rigid and seemingly endowed with imminence, or with a suppleness about to be, have the semblance of Intelligence herself, in guise of beast and animal – impenetrable – all-penetrating.

Paul Valéry

Laius, king of Thebes, believed an oracle of Apollo who foretold he would be killed by his son. At the time he had no son, and thus no one to kill him. To prevent one Laius abstained from women, angering Jocasta, his wife. He did not abstain enough. Drunk one night, Laius forgot the oracle's warning. He was stark sober when Jocasta bore him a son.

Jocasta's tears and pleas were in vain. Laius hired a man to take the baby out of the city and kill him. The man took the baby into the wilderness but was unwilling to kill him quickly or by himself. He pinned him to the ground with a nail in his foot and walked away, leaving the rest to fate. The baby's cries might bring help before the smell of blood brought animals — not likely, but, well, let heaven decide. The screaming baby was soon found and saved by a herder, who took him to another city, Corinth, where Polydeuces was king. Polydeuces and Queen Merope had no son and promptly adopted the wounded boy. They named him Oedipus and raised him as a prince.

Oedipus grew up a loved and loving son. He walked with a limp, but he stood straight and strong. He was brave, intelligent, and religious. Disturbed by rumors as he reached manhood, Oedipus sought heaven's help by consulting Apollo's oracle. The oracle frightened him as it had his father; sad but true, it said Oedipus would kill his father. True to his faith, he believed the prediction. Thinking his father was Polydeuces, whom he loved, Oedipus decided to stay away from his father forever, to defy fate with resolute duty and filial love.[1]

Meanwhile, Laius had come up with a new solution for safe sex: a beautiful boy, Chrysippus, kidnapped for his pleasure. Hera, queen of gods and protector of marriage, was horrified. She sent Phix the riddling Sphinx to Thebes to chastise the city, torment its king, and kill its young men.

Phix trampled down crops. She charged like a lion. Like an eagle hidden in the sun, she struck suddenly from the sky. She amused herself by conversing with her victims, asking a riddle, playing with her food. If anyone answered her correctly, she promised she would go away. Those who guessed wrong were prey.

King Laius had no solution for this. He gathered a retinue and sped to the oracle of Apollo for advice. At a point where three roads meet he met Oedipus, coming the other way. Laius ordered Oedipus to move aside or be run down. A second time he threatened Oedipus's feet. Oedipus, outnumbered five to one, later said Laius struck first. But Oedipus was faster and killed the king and his men. He spared only a slave, who ran for his life back to Thebes. Bloody Oedipus stood alone at the crossroads. He was in unknown country where roads were watched by wolves and robbers. Arming himself with a sword and spears, he took the road the slave had chosen. The slave ran to Thebes without stopping. Behind him Oedipus limped.

Along the way Oedipus met refugees from Thebes who told him news. King Laius had been killed by thieves and his widow, Jocasta, would marry any man who could defeat the monster Sphinx. Raised as a prince — smart, confident, and educated — and now uprooted, single, and with little to lose, Oedipus thought it over. He had killed four armed men. Kill one Sphinx to win the queen and a city? How hard could it be?

He climbed the mountain of the Sphinx, overlooking miserable Thebes. He saw scraps of leather, crushed and splintered bones, flies and dragon-flies. A stench curled between the stones in a shallow mist, below the reach of breezes. On a rock bathed in sunlight, the Sphinx smiled as if she had expected him. Her face was beautiful, her hair flowed over her shoulders down her back, she wore jewelry — and that was all she wore. Oedipus limped closer. She stood up to let him see all of her.

She was sleek and muscular. Her wings huffed the air. She scratched a shrieking rock and began to sing. She sang the riddle, the dirge of many men, but Oedipus was jubilant because he knew the answer right away. He enjoyed the song and the silence afterward and he enjoyed staring at the Sphinx. His delay gave her time to wonder. He held back, holding his answer like a knife.

So far the story is a fairy-tale testosterone cocktail. The poor and un-wanted son dreams of rich and loving parents, a king and queen no less.

The pious man accepts the word of God without question, does what must be done, and overcomes all obstacles to enter the kingdom. The bold youth fears nothing: no predicament he can't master or sneak past. The inquisitive, impatient man takes his chances and trusts his luck. The lonesome man spurned by women turns her wits against the inquisitive woman, humiliates her with a single honest word. For thousands of years and in elaborate variations a confrontation with a Sphinx puts a man, any man, in Oedipus's feet and a woman, any woman, in the body of a Sphinx. André Gide's Oedipus says that every riddle in the world has one answer: man. Not some man, but every man, and in vain. Oedipus, or any man, may be king of himself, a servant of God, a lord of fire, a nemesis of women, and still be as stupid as dice.

Fate has rules. Oedipus must kill his father before he meets the Sphinx. He must kill the Sphinx to inherit the kingdom. Phix the Sphinx is the last barrier between him and his mother.

JESUS AND THE SPHINX

In a fragment from the Nag Hammadi library in Upper Egypt Hermes Trismegistus informed his disciple Asclepius that "Egypt is the image of heaven. Moreover, it is the dwelling place of heaven and all the forces that are in heaven."[2] For the persecuted remnants of Egyptian Christianity, Egypt was holy land, a place of refuge, where Abraham and Sarah fled, where Joseph took in his brothers. The Holy Family hid from Herod by escaping to Egypt. Egypt was sanctuary.

Early Christianity appropriated symbols aggressively. Because of the unspeakable power of the sovereign word of God and because the Sphinx will attach to anything, the first Christian Sphinxes arrived shortly after the first Christians. In the third century AD the *Acts of Andrew and Matthias* circulated among the faithful. The work was reputed to have been written by Leucius Charinus, a disciple of John, author of the Gospel. Two brave early missionaries, Andrew and Matthias set out to bring salvation to cannibals.

As they walked Andrew told Matthias about a marvelous event he had seen. Jesus and the disciples went to a temple of Jews where two marble Sphinxes sat. Jesus said, "Behold the replica of heaven, for these are similar to the cherubim and seraphim of heaven." Addressing the Sphinx on the right, Jesus said, "I tell you, O model of that which is in heaven, which the hands of artists sculptured, be loosened from your place, come down, answer, disgrace the high priests, and prove to them that I am God."

"And immediately, that very hour, the sphinx leaped up from its place, acquired a human voice, and said, 'O foolish sons of Israel, the blindness of their own hearts is not enough for them, but they want to make others to be blind like themselves.'"

The priests were not persuaded by the rebuke of a Sphinx. Jesus commanded the Sphinx to go into the land of the Canaanites and summon the spirits of Abraham, Isaac, and Jacob. "When it heard these words, immediately the sphinx walked before us all, went into the land of the Canaanites. . . . the three patriarchs went with the sphinx, came to Jesus, and refuted the high priests."[3]

Andrew calls the priests gentiles, the Sphinx calls them sons of Israel. And so it was in the early church, when a gentile was anyone who was not Christian. Jews were gentiles then. An entertaining story, *The Acts of Andrew and Matthias* was too far-fetched to impress the bishops who closed the book on scripture. *The Acts* was set adrift with other apocrypha.[4]

Jesus makes Oedipus look stupid. Jesus does not kill the Sphinx or drive it mad, he calls it and commands it, twice setting it to fetch.[5]

Good Sphinx. St. John Lucas's fable *The Marble Sphinx* (1907) has another good Sphinx. In a tale populated by dryads, satyrs, a centaur, Erôs with his golden bow, and a march of dead gods, a marble Sphinx as beautiful as a goddess comes alive to wrestle Death himself, all in readiness for the coming of Jesus. The Sphinx of Madeleine L'Engle's *The Sphinx at Dawn* (1982) sleeps in the desert, has wings and a broken nose, asks riddles, remembers Oedipus, is female and famished, and converses with Jesus, Prince of the Jews. She tells him, "We are part of one another now."[6]

ALEXANDRIA

The sacred history of the West was born and hell-bent in a small triangle, with one point at Babylon, the second at Athens, and the third at Alexandria, the capital city of Christian Egypt. In its bloom Alexandria was richer than Babylon and wiser than Athens. Philo of Alexandria, born about 20 BC, studied in Alexandria when Joseph, Mary, and the infant Jesus dwelled in Egypt. Unaware of the holy refugees nearby, Philo looked around him and saw Egypt as a living symbol of the passion-loving body, the senses, and sins.[7]

A city of sinners, Alexandria attracted saints. Saint Mark—his insignia a winged lion—wrote his Gospel in Alexandria and was buried there till Venice bought his bones. For centuries Alexandria was the most important city of Christianity. The Church of Saint Mark in Alexandria supervised desert monasteries, educated bishops, and fought in the streets and pulpit for bodies and souls. It battled the stubborn gentiles of Egypt. It tamed the wild breeds of Christianity that refused to obey it. It scrapped with rival churches at Ephesus and Rome, suppressed the Gnostics, murdered Hypatia, denounced the false gospel of the Egyptians, and opposed animal worship of all kinds. It was a busy church.

Philo wrote, "the God of real being is apprehensible by no one . . . He is incapable of being seen." Yet all around Alexandria were the statues of pharaohs and caesars with inscriptions that said they were gods. It was a religious city with ferocious religions. The church and its heresies competed fist and stone with each other and with the cults of Isis, Serapis, and Tutu, a Sphinx.[8]

Saint Jerome, the patron of scholars, praised Clement of Alexandria (circa 153–circa 220 AD) as the most learned of the early Christians. Clement wrote, "It is not by nature, but by learning, that people become noble and good," asserting that "it is impossible for a man without learning to comprehend the things which are declared in the faith."[9] Faith is possible for anyone but understanding requires study. Clement drew heavily from Greek and Roman sources and respected the priority of the Egyptians,

Chaldeans, and Hebrews. Like his contemporaries Tatian and Theophilus, he disparaged and demystified Greek gods, cults, and mysteries. He reproached their immorality and their worshipers. "Zeus is dead," he declared, like the Pater Nietzsche never knew.[10]

Early Christian authors cited pagan stories in order to denounce them as snares of the devil. False gods and their followers, their rites, books, and images, made fine fires.[11] The statues of the old Egyptians were again attacked. Clement defended the religions of the Greeks, Egyptians, and Jews because they had sincerely sought truth before the truth was gospel, because their souls were turned in the right direction. Long before the event that divided time, they understood truth well enough to want it. Openhearted, open-minded Clement believed that Christianity was spacious and that there was plenty of room for Plato and Homer and all that. Clement saw plainly that the wisdom of the ages was at stake. He wrote the *Stromata,* his masterpiece, to save it.

Clement commended the Greeks of Egypt and the Greeks of Greece for preparing the soil for the sowing and harvest of God's word. The Greeks were prepared by Babylon, Persia, Syria, Scythia, Egypt, and most of all by the Hebrews. Clement believed that "truth-loving" Plato "learned from the Hebrews."[12] Truth-loving Clement accepted Adam and Hercules as historical figures, blended Pindar with Proverbs, Homer with Psalms. He was mindful that Homer and Moses were born in Egypt, as he was.

Clement wrote that Greek thought is nourishing, but not all of it: it is "like nuts," not wholly edible.[13] Stories don't have to be historical (like Adam or Hercules) to be worth keeping. For instance, Odysseus and Oedipus. Clement wrote, "For sailing past the Sirens one man has sufficient strength, and for answering the Sphinx another one, or if you please, not even one."[14] Clement doubts whether Oedipus defeated the Sphinx.[15]

The Oedipus story has details that scrupulous Christians like Clement were bound to dislike. The plot implies inalterable fate, and Clement believed in free will. Its incest was unmentionable. But this is not just a question of Oedipus, there is also Odysseus.[16] Clement's comparison, like a nut in its shell, bears digging out. What is compressed in it?

— Odysseus and Oedipus need no explanation. The Sirens' song and riddle scene are so well known, they go without saying.

— The less said, the better. The Sirens sing men to doom. The Sphinx asks lethal questions.

— After Odysseus passed the Sirens and Oedipus passed the Sphinx, no one else need try. They solved the problem.

Put Clement's comparison back in its shell and it rattles like a maraca. Clement again, but longer:

> Not only a simple mode of life, but also a style of speech devoid of super-fluity and nicety must be cultivated by him who has adopted the true life, if we are to abandon luxury as treacherous and profligate, as the ancient Lacedaemonians adjured ointment and purple, deeming and calling them rightly treacherous garments and treacherous unguents; since neither is that mode of preparing food right where there is more of seasoning than of nutriment; nor is that style of speech elegant which can please rather than benefit the hearers. Pythagoras exhorts us to consider the Muses more pleasant than the Sirens, teaching us to cultivate wisdom apart from pleasure, and exposing the other mode of attracting the soul as deceptive. For sailing past the Sirens one man has sufficient strength, and for answering the Sphinx another one, or if you please, not even one.

In context, the comparison of Oedipus and Odysseus is offered as an exhibit of densely packed brevity.

— Odysseus, tied to the mast, maddened with desire for the Sirens, crying, pleading, begging to be set free, is an example of strength. In the case of Oedipus, strength doesn't matter.

— Oedipus and Odysseus are unique. Both are needed. Clement cites a source: "Our struggle, according to Gorgias Leontinus, requires two virtues — boldness and wisdom, — boldness to undergo danger and wisdom to understand the enigma."

— Clement hears the unsaid said by induction and metaphor. "There are times when silence is better."

— Odysseus left the Sirens behind. The Sphinx is still there.

Clement adopts the reserve of the Sphinxes of Egypt. The *Stromata* advises, "Some things my treatise will hint; on some it will linger; some it will merely mention. It will try to speak imperceptibly, to exhibit secretly, and to demonstrate silently." Like Hellenic philosophy, his book contains the truth "covered over and hidden, as the edible part of the nut in its shell." Clement obeys the admonition of Jesus not to cast pearls before swine. Clement concludes, "It is requisite therefore, to hide in a mystery the wisdom spoken, which the Son of God taught."[17]

The truth of the *Stromata* is esoteric, saved for the few: "For there is a contest, and the prelude to the contest; and there are some mysteries before other mysteries."[18] Clement is an early advocate of occult Christianity, where gates to the truth are marked clearly by Sphinxes. "Very useful, then, is the mode of symbolic interpretation for many purposes; and it is helpful to the right theology, and to piety, and to the display of intelligence, and the practice of brevity, and the exhibition of wisdom." Clement clumped this all into Sphinxes, agreeing with Plutarch: "The Egyptians places Sphinxes before their temples, to signify that the doctrine respecting God is enigmatical and obscure." He adds, "Perhaps also that we both ought to love and fear the Divine Being."[19]

To Clement the Sphinx is abstract and grand. "The Sphinx is not the comprehension of the universe, and the revolution of the world, according to the poet Aratus; but perhaps it is the spiritual tone which pervades and holds together the universe." He goes on: "It is better to regard it as the ether, which holds together and presses all things."[20] The Sphinx is invisible gravity, cosmic glue. Odd parts somehow stuck together.

Sphinxes guard the Holy Family in poetry, paintings, and postcards. Luc Olivier Merson's *Le repos en Egypte* (1879) depicts Madonna and Infant sheltered between the forelegs of a Sphinx. Joseph lies apart, almost out of the picture, while a smiling male Sphinx, gazing into heaven, reflects the holy light of mother and son. In *La Vierge,* the tenth tableau of Fragerolle's *Le Sphinx,* Amédée Vignola paints a radiant Virgin and Child huddled on Horemakhet's paw; again Joseph keeps a respectful distance.[21] Oscar Wilde's *Sphinx* (1894) mentions the Virgin and Child asleep in the

3.1. *Le repos en Égypte* by Luc Olivier Merson, 1879.

Sphinx's shade; Joseph the father is nowhere. No Joseph, either, in Agnes Repplier's "Le repos en Egypte." In her poem the Sphinx of Merson's painting reminisces:

> Within mine arms she slumbered, and alone
> Lay stretched o'er-wearied. On my breast of stone
> Rested the Crucified.

The scene is the centerpiece of Susan E. Wallace's *The Repose in Egypt* (1888), a travelogue of Egypt, informed by the Bible and Shakespeare, anecdotal history and oriental tales, complete with the Holy Family, the courtesan Rhodope, Cleopatra, and Napoleon. Wallace describes the sleepers on the Sphinx as viewed by two "sons of the Sahara," attracted by a "pale light, in tone and tint like the ivory-white of moonbeams."[22] They flee, afraid of the sight.

3.2. *La Vierge* by Amédée
Vignola from Fragerolle's
Sphinx, 1896.

"Behold me," says the Sphinx to Theosophist Édouard Schuré, "I am the Nature-Sphinx. Angel, eagle, lion and bull, I have the august visage of a god and the body of a winged and roaring beast. . . . *I am, I see, I know*— from everlasting. For I am one of the eternal Archetypes that exist in the Light Unmanifest." Schuré synopsizes from the crowded heights of angels: "The Chaldeans, Egyptians and Hebrews symbolised the Cherubim under the forms of the Bull, the Lion, the Eagle and the Angel (or the Man). These were the four sacred animals of the Ark of Moses, of the four Evangelists, and of the Apocalypse of St. John. The Egyptian sphinx summarizes them in a single form which is a symbol, marvelously adapted from visible and invisible nature, of the whole course of evolution, human and divine."[23]

Hegel's Sphinx and Schuré's Sphinx are both Egyptian, both half human. But Hegel's Sphinx is half beast and Schure's half divine. Hegel's Sphinx was defeated; Schuré's Sphinx still speaks somehow. Schuré's Sphinx says, "it is forbidden to me to speak otherwise than by my presence," and then speaks wonders. Schuré claims that the secret of the Sphinx was revealed by Christianity. The Sphinx "symbolizes the whole evolution of the human soul, its descent into matter and its return to spirit. Thanks to the Christ, the veil of the sanctuary is torn, the enigma of the Sphinx is solved."[24]

FACING THE SPHINX

Behind the veil, a face; behind the face, contemplation. Touring Egypt in the 1840s, the German countess Ida Hahn-Hahn mused, "Mental composure, power of thought, and sybilline contemplation, have probably never found a more magnificent representation than the countenance of the sphinx."[25] It depends on where you are and how you look at it.

FACE 1: SPHINX IN FRONT OF KHUFU'S PYRAMID

Horemakhet looks at home with a pyramid behind him, lines framing curves. Up close the Sphinx seems as large as or larger than the great pyramid of Khufu.

3.3. Egypt stamp, 10 para, 1867.

3.4. Mali stamp, 1971.

3.5. Horemakhet on token from Luxor Casino, Las Vegas, 2000.

3.6. Crown Prince Wilhelm of Prussia and Crown Princess Cecilie at the Sphinx, 1911.

FACE 2: SPHINX WITH KAFRA'S PYRAMID

On Egyptian stamps for years and years, the Sphinx (nose restored for government work) and his pyramids made every piece of Egyptian mail an invitation to a voyage. The stamps were popular and widely collected; forgeries promptly appeared.

As Maspero predicted, the unburied Sphinx enhanced tourism. A favorite photographic pose put Kafre's pyramid behind Horemakhet and Horemakhet behind visitors.

3.7. Horemakhet, Egypt stamp, 2 1/2 piastres, 1872.

3.8. Horemakhet, Egypt stamp, 10 piastres, 1888.

3.9. Photograph of Horemakhet by the Zangakis, circa 1880.

3.10. Well-to-do tourist at Giza, circa 1900.

FACE 3: SPHINX HEAD WITH PEOPLE

You can't get as close to Horemakhet as old-timers did. For centuries people clambered up the Sphinx to whisper in his ears or stand on his head like passengers. Thousands of feet trampling up and down wore down the Sphinx. When his body was buried his head was easily climbed; at times he was overrun. Nowadays, heavily damaged Horemakhet needs the steady care of masons to clad him in new stone. He needs armed guards to protect him from souvenir hunters.

Horemakhet's head is his best part. Even after his body was uncovered photographers preferred views that showed only a head in the sand. As a big head in the desert, Horemakhet was a symbol of decapitation. Freud identified decapitation as a symbol of castration.[26] Sphinx encodes decapitation, decapitation encodes castration: an instance of the Sphinx as a symbol of symbols.

In *Moby Dick,* mad Ahab addresses the decapitated head of a whale as if it were a Sphinx. Ahab stands on his peg leg like Oedipus, imagining he has killed a Sphinx. In the end a whale kills Ahab, repeating the Oedipal tragedy, as avenging nature destroys the would-be master.[27]

On tombs rich Etruscans carved Sphinxes with human heads between their feet, the heads chiseled to resemble the deceased. The Romans adopted the style and spread it throughout the empire.[28]

Facing page: 3.11. Photograph of Horemakhet by Félix Bonfils, 1878.

3.12. Horemakhet on a Keystone stereoview, 1899. This is the second version of Keystone's stereoview #9781 and is probably the most popular Sphinx stereoview of all time. It was included in at least seven different Keystone series.

3.13. Detail of Keystone stereoview.

3.14. Roman funerary Sphinx with head between paws, first century AD.

FACE 4: SPHINX FROM BELOW

Most depictions of Phix pose her higher than Oedipus. Her posture, position, and wings display her heavenly descent. When the Parthenon was new it sheltered a monumental statue of Athena, goddess of wisdom, divine virgin warrior, towering above Athens. On Athena's helmet lay a Sphinx, higher than Athena herself.[29]

Horemakhet's overhanging head emphasizes his size. Roman architects built what the people desired, the Colosseum of Rome, and a grand staircase in Giza, opposite the face of the Sphinx. The staircase rose thirty steps to a large landing, thirteen more steps to another—points of view built for maximum admiration.

Horemakhet's majesty is best appreciated forty feet beneath his chin. His pose seen from below appeared on Egyptian coins minted on alloys between 1953 and 1958 and on silver and gold in 1993.

What does the Sphinx see? Nothing, really, but it makes you wonder what it would be like to see like a Sphinx, if a Sphinx could see. Mark Twain described the Great Sphinx "looking over and beyond everything of the present, and far into the past. It was gazing out over the ocean of Time—over lines of century-waves which, further and further receding, closed nearer and nearer together, and blended at last into one unbroken tide, away toward the horizon of remote antiquity."[30]

3.15. Sphinx on Athena's helmet, detail from 1,000-drachma banknote, Bank of Greece, 1939.

3.16. Horemakhet, Cairo Postcard Trust, #207, circa 1905.

3.17. Egypt, 20-piastre coin, 1957.

FACE 5: SPHINX, EYE-TO-EYE

Depictions of the riddle scene often show Oedipus and the Sphinx conversing with their eyes. Binoculars and panoramic lenses allow the modern visitor to gaze at Horemakhet minutely.

Victor Hugo, a whale of a Sphinxophile, followed Jean Valjean through the dark damp length of *Les misérables* to face the Sphinx. "We must be accustomed to fatality and its encounter, to dare to raise our eyes when certain questions appear to us in their horrible nakedness. Good and evil are behind this severe interrogation point. 'What are you going to do?' demands the sphynx."[31]

Miguel de Unamuno placed the Sphinx firmly in front of him as a spiritual exercise, a way to look at harsh reason and the sickening mystery of death. He writes, "The remedy is to consider it without flinching, to fasten our gaze upon the gaze of the Sphinx, for it is thus that its evil spell is broken."[32]

3.18. *Complaint* by Rozenfeld, circa 1910.

3.19. Postcard of prayer before Horemakhet, Lehnert & Landrock, circa 1918. This photo was obviously posed. The praying figure faces north, away from Mecca.

DEFACING THE SPHINX

For thousands of years wayfarers saw Horemakhet buried up to his neck. Some wrote comments, a few scratched initials on him. El-Makrizi (780 AD), reports that Saim-ed-Dahr, a Sufi iconoclast, disfigured the Sphinx.[33]

An English traveler remarked that the Sphinx of 1580 "wanted a little tippe of the nose." How had his nose been broken? Johann Michael Wansleben reported in his *Travels in the Orient* that "its nose has been broken by a Moor. . . . This same maniac who mutilated the Sphinx did the same to the lions decorating one of the bridges of Cairo." Abdel-Latif said the Sheik Mohammed struck the Sphinx "in the belief it would be agreeable to God."[34]

In the era of Enlightenment Mamelukes aimed their cannon at Horemakhet's broken nose and made a crater of it. Napoleon is often blamed because his soldiers shot at it, too. No doubt they did: it is a tempting target for riflemen. Just as the great Buddhas of Afghanistan were destroyed by the Taliban, the Sphinx is a conspicuous target, as easy to shoot as a cat in a cage. It is a casualty of many wars.

Napoleon's purpose in Egypt was republican and patriotic. With flags and drums, cavalry and artillery, Napoleon led the army of France to liberate an ancient land from a cruel and careless despot. Napoleon conquered the land of the Sphinx in a few weeks. He held onto it a few years, 1798 to 1805, which cost him dearly. His navy was blown to the bottom of Alexandria harbor, his army dissolved in dysentery. Napoleon retreated to practice warfare in Europe, closer to allies and a food supply. But for a short while Napoleon felt like Caesar, conqueror of Egypt. With victory close behind him and defeat unforeseeably ahead, he faced the Sphinx like a man the Sphinx ought to notice. He had an Oedipal moment, thinking he had won. Emil Ludwig guessed his thoughts: "Alexander stood here. Caesar stood here."[35]

In 1886 Jean-Léon Gérôme painted a moment in history, Napoleon face-to-face with the Sphinx. The image was immensely popular and often reprinted, sometimes with the caption "Oedipus."[36] The Napoleon and the Sphinx duet is Oedipus and the Sphinx updated. Napoleon stares at the Sphinx, so must we. What are the right questions? Is the invading general

3.20. *Napoleon and the Sphinx* by Jean-Léon Gérôme, photogravure by Goupil & Co., 1886.

accused by the grave immense? Does the face of the Sphinx express disdain or approval? After Gérôme, Napoleon at the Sphinx became a favorite subject, a classic confrontation of fame and ruin.

Among the swarm of things it stands for as it lies there, the Great Sphinx is a memento mori of dead conquerors, worn out religions, vandalism, war, ignorance, and greed. In 1857 Herman Melville saw the Sphinx at Giza. He recalled it in *Clarel,* his epic of yearning:

> Unmoved by all the claims our times avow,
> The ancient Sphinx still keeps the porch of shade;
> And comes Despair, whom not her calm may cow,
> And coldly on that adamantine brow
> Scrawls undeterred his bitter pasquinade.
> But Faith (who from the scrawl indignant turns)
> With blood warm oozing from her wounded trust,
>   Inscribes even on her shards of broken urns
> The sign o' the cross—the spirit above the dust![37]

Melville's Sphinx is a site of quarreling inscriptions, a scarred symbol strewn with litter. Mark Twain watched a souvenir hunter chipping away at Horemakhet's jaw. James Russell Lowell rebuked the fame-seeker who "in the desert's awful frame, / Notches his cockney initials on the Sphinx."[38] At the turn of the twentieth century, American tourists threw soda water bottles at Horemakhet: ha-ha, splashed glass, Sphinx "high jinx."[39]

3.21. Masthead of *The Sphinx: An Independent Magazine for Magicians,* 1932.

3.22. *Les deux Sfinxs* by W. Kossak, Wydawnicto Salonu postcard, 1918.

3.23. Russian postcard of Napoleon and the Sphinx, 1907.

THE AMERICAN SPHINX

American presidents form a parade of Sphinxes. George Washington's wigged head looks like Horemakhet in his headdress. Joseph J. Ellis's biography of Thomas Jefferson, *American Sphinx* (1997), describes Jefferson as a hero of contradictions. Jefferson Davis is the Sphinx of the South.

A jolly puzzle of power, Theodore Roosevelt is the president of president Sphinxes. Shortly before he left office in 1908, *Life* magazine put his face on the Sphinx, big Roosevelt guffawing at little Napoleon. Popular Roosevelt could have been president indefinitely, but the job was no longer fun and he decided not to run for reelection. Out of office, he stayed in the public eye: it was international news when he and his son Kermit went on a year-long safari. Instead of shooting his father as a good Oedipus would, Kermit took turns with Teddy mowing down Africa's animals.[40] Roosevelt's hunting trip eventually took him to Egypt where, of course, he met the Sphinx. An English cartoonist depicted him raring to shoot it.

3.24. Teddy Roosevelt as the Sphinx stares down Napoleon, *Life*, February 27, 1908.

3.25. "Big Game to the Last": a *Punch* cartoonist takes aim at Roosevelt, March 23, 1910.

3.26. Carol Vox, *The Sphinx and the Mummy*, illustration by H. Boylston Dummer, 1909.

T HE Sphinx was a solemn old pile
And was never before known to smile,
Till a wireless tip
Brought the news of the trip,
And that Teddy would tarry a while.

Then she said to a sober old mummy,
"Cheer up! It's no time to be glummy."
We've just got to smile
In the happiest style,
If with Teddy we want to get chummy.

Gone is the romance of communing with the Sphinx in solitary moonlight. Visitors bump against each other, a constant stream, preventing anything like a private interview. But this remains part of the Sphinx attraction, that it strikes each visitor personally, affronting fantasies of genius and might. No matter who approaches, regardless of attitude or station, the Sphinx impartially probes the heart.

4 : Riddles

There sits the Sphinx at the road-side, and
from age to age, as each prophet comes by,
he tries his fortune at reading her riddle.
Ralph Waldo Emerson

In Greek the riddle of the Sphinx looks stately and severe:

Τί ἐστιν ὃ μίαν ἔχον φωνὴν τετράπουν καὶ δίπουν καὶ τρίπουν γίνεται

"What has one voice and yet becomes four-footed and two-footed and three-footed?"[1]

Who's afraid of it now, this old thing? Who ever feared it? Joseph Conrad, Karl Kerényi, and John Symonds described the riddle as "childish." Walter Benjamin called it *einfältig*—foolish, simple. D. H. Lawrence added, "To us it is rather silly." Thomas De Quincey judged the riddle "deplorably below the grandeur of the occasion."[2]

Quick retellings of the riddle keep the Sphinx safely in the past, her riddle solved and her danger gone. The riddle is kid's play. Rhondi Vilott's *Secret of the Sphinx* (1985), time travel for children, sends a boy back to the Sphinx. Since he heard the riddle as a kid he answers it easily.[3]

The Oedipus tragedies of Sophocles, Seneca, Anguillara, Corneille, Voltaire, Centofanti, and Foscolo do not recite the riddle. Why would they? Everyone knows it. Seneca saw the dramatic potential in the riddle scene, but narrates rather than reenacts it: Oedipus recalls the bone-strewn road, the Sphinx with bloody jaws gnashing, her wings poised to strike, her claws raking rock.[4] In such a situation wouldn't any riddle terrify?

Maurice Blanchot takes the Sphinx and her riddle in dead earnest. Her question is "frivolous and frightening; it is distracting, attractive and mortal. . . . The most profound question is such that does not allow one to understand it; one can only repeat it."[5] It is a riddle of a riddle. Lowell Edmunds remarks that it "seems to bear no necessary relation to any detail of the legend. . . . It is not clear why it must be this riddle and not some other."[6]

Look at the riddle in bright light, as Oedipus did: it is a trick, its foolishness confuses and glazes. The riddle scene is a trauma site, a frightening magnification of the trivial, a nightmare test. Cocteau's Sphinx allowed one man to go back alive, as an idiot. If you stop to think about it, the riddle attacks like a pick at the back of the skull.[7]

W. E. B. Du Bois saw the murderous riddle in the abolitionist rebel gunman John Brown. "Shall we hesitate and waver before his clear white logic, now helping, now fearing to help, now believing, now doubting? Yes, this we must do so long as the doubt and hesitation are genuine; but we must not lie. If we are human, we must thus hesitate until we know we are right. How shall we know it? That is the Riddle of the Sphinx."[8]

Robert Collier opened his seven-volume *Life Magnet* (1928) with a "present-day Riddle of the Sphinx": "How can I earn more money?"[9] His earnest answer: faith in Jesus.

OEDIPUS AS A PROBLEM

The riddle of the Sphinx plays with its feet: *pous, dipous, tripous.* To answer the riddle correctly, Oedipus considered a *pous* (foot) as other things: a baby's crawling hands and knees are four feet in the morning and a crutch is a foot at dusk. Early Greek versions of the riddle consistently count four, two, and three feet. As the riddle moved through languages, its anatomy changed. The step between Greek *pous* and Latin *pes* only flattened a vowel; in the learned Latin of a thousand years, *pes* also meant leg. *Pas* (foot) is preferred in France. German Sphinxes say both *Fuß* (foot) and *Bein* (leg); English Sphinx riddles are answered by legs and feet.[10] Foot or leg doesn't matter, does it?

Oedipus's feet were body parts he could not take for granted. The strange name "Oedipus" might mean "swollen foot." His name draws attention to his feet and brings him nine steps closer to the Sphinx. If a baby's hands can be a riddle's feet, then a man's feet can be legs. The Sphinx understands misunderstanding. She's the queen of code.

The riddle's feet are locks; morning, noon, and night are keys. In the morning the riddle is as cloudy as an eagle in an egg.[11] At noon two feet and full light plainly pair; at this point, with a third left unsaid, an especially bright person like Oedipus could guess the riddle already, and guess what comes next. At evening when feet are sore and legs ache, the answer is painfully obvious.

At what time of day was the riddle asked? According to painters and filmmaker Paolo Pasolini, Oedipus meets the Sphinx in bright sunlight. Sphinx and Oedipus, high noon.

OEDIPI

The riddle scene is visited by several types of Oedipus.

1. A champion like Hercules who, fearless, astute, and unique, dared to answer the riddle in the face of the Sphinx. This is Oedipus's high opinion of himself in Sophocles' *Oedipus Rex* and its successors.

2. An adept, a sensitive set of spiritual antennae, a visionary, dreamer of prophecies. According to Pausanias, Oedipus learned the answer to the riddle in a dream.[12]

3. A gambler who staked his future on a once-in-a-lifetime opportunity.

4. A retentive student with a riddle repertoire.

4.1. Oedipus and the Sphinx by the Achilles Painter, Greek amphora, 450–440 BC.

5. A lucky guy. The lucky man passes for a genius, says Euripides.[13] Oedipus was lucky on a number of counts: no one guessed right before he did; he won a queen and kingdom for a minute's work; he wore a rosy reputation before his past caught up with him.

6. A statistic. Unless the Sphinx ate Thebans faster than they ripened, her riddle would eventually be answered. Given a steady supply of Thebans, an Oedipus is inevitable.

7. A cheat who never risked a thing, because the Muses gave him the answer in advance. Apollodorus reports that Oedipus knew the riddle and answer before the Sphinx asked it.[14]

8. An ingenuous man who trusted the Sphinx to be fair.

9. A man with weapons, who did not depend upon the answer alone nor trust the Sphinx to be fair. The answer would give him an advantage in the moment of the Sphinx's surprise — then sword or javelin.

What to think of Oedipus? If he was told the answer in advance he did not think. If he deduced the answer he's a hero of intellect. If he dreamed it he's passively prophetic. If he worked his answer out by examining the mistakes of the Sphinx's victims, he makes sense of their mistakes, finds what they sought, and moves from guesses to science.

BRAIN TEASER

Charles Sanders Peirce (1839–1914) proposed other answers to the famous riddle. His first answer was "a guess," certainly correct since "a guess" answers any riddle. He later thought the answer was the order of the world: first chance, then law, then habit. Put in the three-legged spot, habit holds up Oedipus like a crutch.[15] Peirce planned to make a third guess in *A Guess at the Riddle*. He predicted the book would be "one of the births of time." It was his habit to start books and not finish them; habit left *A Guess* unmade.[16]

THE ANSWER "MAN"

D. H. Lawrence declared that "the sphinx-riddle of man is as terrifying today as it was before Oedipus, and more so. For now it is the riddle of the dead-alive man, which it never was before."[17]

Oedipus answered the riddle with *anthropon* in noble Corinthian Greek — man the species, rather than man the gender. It is common knowledge that "man" answers a riddle with a riddle. Gide's Oedipus advises: "And although to each one of us, my children, the Sphinx may put a different question, you must persuade yourselves that the answer is always the same. Yes, there is only this one same answer to those many and various questions; and that this one answer is: Man; and that this one man, for each and all of us, is: Oneself."[18] Like many other Oedipi, Gide's learns too late that the answer "man" is narrow-minded, maniac, selfish, and wrong.

The injunction of Apollo's oracle at Delphi is to "Know thyself," a riddle whose solution is "that you are a man." Oedipus answered the Sphinx's riddle with orthodox Apollonian doctrine.[19]

Charles Dickens wrote: "When I became enough of a man to find myself an embodied conundrum, I bored myself to the last degree by trying to figure out what I meant."[20]

If you can't figure out the answer from the front, turn to the back.

SPHINX THINK

Sphinx riddles rode the book boom of the seventeenth century. Johannes Heidfeld's collection of pious, artful, and amusing riddles, *Sphinx Philosophica* (1600), reproduced in expanded editions.[21] Improve life and profit from leisure with the most popular book of its kind in seventeenth-century England, *Sphinx and Oedipus: A help to discourse; or, More merriment mixt with serious matters: Consisting of witty, philosophical, grammaticall, physicall, astronomicall questions and answers. Together with The Country-man's Counsellor, and his yearly oracle, and prognostication,* with health tips and a small cookbook. Begun with the Sphinx's riddle, it ran through fourteen editions by 1654, each with a slightly different title. William Bagwell's *Sphynx Thebanus, with His Oedipus; or, Ingenious Riddles with Their Observations, Explications, and Morals* (1664) recommended itself as "Excellently suiting the Fancies of Old or Young, and exceeding useful to advance a Chearful Society, and to continue and preserve Mirth." These Sphinx books answered questions about history, geography, religion, and manners; they Sphinxily promised stimulation and wisdom.[22]

Stacks of riddle books name the Sphinx as author or title.[23] As a riddle book a Sphinx is a stimulant, an intimate companion loaded with secrets. Ana-gramme Blismon's *Sphinxiana* (1855) retells the riddle scene, then defines and demonstrates two types of riddle in verse: charades and logogriphs. A charade asks, what am I? A logogriph hides a word and defies you to find it.

4.2. Frontispiece of Paul's
Die neue Sphinx, 1877.

Sphinx riddle books bristle with difficulty. The Sphinx's *Everybody's Book of Riddles and Conundrums* (circa 1890) poses riddles in Latin, French, and English rhyme. Charlotte Jordan's *Sphinx-Lore* (1897) asks riddles about the Bible, classical mythology, English and American literature (especially Dickens), American military history, food, flowers, and celebrated women.

Sphinx riddle books are more or less like Sphinxes. They combine odd parts, they prize wit, they possess vast and esoteric knowledge. By Hegel's day Sphinxes had long since specialized: Zucktschwerdt's *Sphinx und Clio* (1812) and *Sphinx und Harmonia* (1813) challenge knowledge of history and music respectively. Between 1906 and 1932 *Sphinx-Œdipe* posed puzzles in mathematics. Child's play? For the thrill of it, stake your life on a random mathematical problem from Wolff's *Die lächelnde Sphinx* (1937), Berloquin's *Le jardin du sphinx* (1981), or Gardner's *Riddles of the Sphinx* (1987). Sphinxes dare you.

The Sphinx's riddle rhymes in many English versions. Robert Bird's *Booke of Merrie Riddles* (1631), for instance.

What is it that in the morning,
Upon foure legges doth goe:
And about noone it standeth fast,
Upon two and no moe:
In the evening againe it hath,
No lesser than three in store:
Which tell me Ser art thou not he,
Whom I doe take thee for?[24]

Le Sphinx, aux Œdipes présens et à venir (1803), *Frolics of the Sphinx* (1812), the pseudonymous *Sphinx Incruenta* (1835), Niemeyer's *Historisch-geographische Sphinx* (1853), Paul's *Die neue Sphinx* (1877), Wells's *At the Sign of the Sphinx* (1896), and Briggs's *The Sphinx Garrulous* (1929) are rhymed riddle books.[25]

The corona for rhymed riddles shines on Antonio Malatesti, author of *La Sfinge* (1683): 263 sonnets, 57 octaves, and 66 quatrains, each a riddle, many of them with riddles within riddles, "paradoxes of the heart, of truth." To pass his Sphinx a reader must know the cities of Italy, raise animals, play cards, and recognize what's stuffed into sausages. Malatesti's Sphinx asks riddles about fire, the sun and moon, and about himself, a riddle as self-portrait. He promises his patrons extended life.

> Amasi, king of Canopus, erected
> A Sphinx of beautiful marble,
> A somber, proud tomb
> To enclose his cold corpse.
> Even more eternal resounds
> Your SPHINX, frail paper and black poems,
> O Sphinx, without erecting a magnificent temple,
> But takes you from the sepulcher and keeps you alive.[26]

Malatesti conferred longevity to different dedicatees with different editions. (Sphinxes are made of ink, black as the bitumen that covers mummies.) *La Sfinge* poses riddles in the shapes of lauds, laments, jokes, rebukes, and strange stories.

Malatesti answers his riddles in sections called "L'Oedipo." If readers are stumped or want to confirm a guess, Oedipo lets them in on the secrets. One poem is about banned books, another was composed by a group of friends, and another describes poverty in cities and countryside. Malatesti's all-knowing Oedipo travels and reads widely, enjoys a good dinner, and appreciates varieties of wine.

RIDDLES OF THE SPHINX

Most accounts of Phix cite a single riddle with a single answer, but others say she had more. From the evidence of folklore, Lowell Edmunds speculated that "in a version of the ancient legend now lost, the Sphinx posed not one but three riddles."[27] Statius says the Sphinx asked *ambages:* riddles, plural. Francis Bacon allowed she had "two kinds; some concerning the nature of things, others touching the nature of Man."[28] The Sphinx in Eugène Ionesco's *L'homme aux valises* (1975) pesters the First Man with crossword puzzle clues. The Sphinxes of Novalis, Hugo, Péladan, and Schmied can produce a riddle for any occasion.

Thomas De Quincey expected multiple answers. "All great prophecies, all great mysteries, are likely to involve double, triple, or even quadruple interpretations; each rising in dignity, each cryptically involving another." Within the first riddle is a second or third. De Quincey was sure Oedipus missed them. "Already in itself it is an ennobling and an idealizing of the riddle that it is made a double riddle: that it contains an exoteric sense obvious to all the world, but also an esoteric sense — now suggested conjecturally after thousands of years — *possibly* unknown to the Sphinx, and *certainly* unknown to Oedipus; that this second riddle is hid within the first; that the one riddle is the secret commentary upon the other; and that the earliest is the hieroglyphic of the last." De Quincey concludes, "the full and *final* answer to the Sphinx's riddle lay in the word OEDIPUS." [29] Oedipus answered the riddle by showing up; he was the answer, a living example, a man.

At De Quincey's riddle scene, Oedipus, proud and regal, was blind already. He stabbed his eyes to spite them. If he could not see truth with his eyes, why did he need them? If truth is horrible, why look at it?

De Quincey found more riddles: herself, her purpose, her fame, her fragility. "The Sphinx herself is a mystery. Whence came her monstrous nature, that so often renewed its remembrance amongst men of distant lands in Egyptian or Ethiopian marble? Whence came her wrath against Thebes? This wrath, how durst it tower so high as to measure itself against the enmity of a nation? This wrath, how came it to sink so low as to collapse at the echo of a word from a friendless stranger?" [30]

Eventually Oedipus is "a Sphinx himself." [31]

THREE SPHINXES

To do justice to the three-part riddle, Dominique Ingres painted three versions of the riddle scene as he saw it at three different times of his life. The first (1808) presents the Sphinx with her forepaws gripping rock; in the background, Thebes is covered with dark clouds and a crimson light that could be sunset or flames. In the second version (completed 1825) the Sphinx stands up, her left forepaw raised in surprise. Her tail is in

4.3. *Oedipus and the Sphinx* by Dominique Ingres, 1825, photogravure by Goupil
& Co. It was the Goupil engraving of this painting that Freud showed a patient at
a moment of triumph. Before photographic printing, the Goupil engravings of the
Sphinxes of Ingres and Gérôme (see 3.20) were better known than the paintings.

4.4. *Oedipus and the Sphinx* by Ingres, 1864.

view, pointing toward Oedipus. In the final version (1864) the changes are profound. The figures are reversed, with Oedipus on the left and the Sphinx on the right. Oedipus has a sword, only its hilt visible, as if thrust through his back to prefigure his fate. His eyes are level with the nipples of her jutting breasts, and in addition to breasts she has teats. Her monstrosity is increased, and her reaction intensified: reading the painting left to right, her expression is the finale. The Sphinx looks away from the man in horror.

Reflecting on the riddle, Ingres reset it. In his second and third versions of the scene, the Sphinx stands on three feet, her head in the shadow, passing into the evening of her life. Oedipus stands barefooted on one leg or two; if spears can be legs, three or four. Ingres's third Oedipus no longer points to himself and to her, but to himself and to the skull and bones below him. The long triangle made by his hands and her legs point to the foot of a corpse, a clue.

The three paintings answer the riddle as Ingres aged, presenting the riddle scene as an emerging artist, an experienced man, and an elderly master saw it: he was twenty-eight when he painted the first version, forty-six when he completed the second, and eighty-five when he finished the third. In the first he looked forward to the future; in the third he looked back. On the third Ingres inscribed his name, scratched his age and the date of the painting on a foreground rock, like a burial stone.

The second version added a frightened man, perhaps the Theban whose turn had come to answer the Sphinx but who had the good luck to arrive after Oedipus. He appears ready to turn and run, but his face remains fixed on the riddle scene, gawking with wonder at the Sphinx's surprise. The other man provides what Oedipus needs to confirm his victory: a witness. In the third version, Ingres paints two witnesses, too far away to discern their faces, and placed at an angle that makes it hard to tell how much they can see. The second witness crawls up the mountain on all fours.

The 1864 version criticizes its elders (fortune's gift to all successors): Ingres's third Sphinx is caught a moment later, her reaction more aroused. His first two Sphinxes are still as the rocks. The third Sphinx is frantic.

Ingres's three riddle scenes are riddles. In the first and second versions

4.5. *The Secret* by Theodore Baur at the Chicago Columbian Exposition, 1898.

Oedipus points to himself with his right hand and to the Sphinx with his left, his forefinger raised as if to tickle her. She is shocked. His right hand answers Riddle One by pointing to a man. Riddle Two: why does he point to her?

The riddle scene invites depiction. Oedipus and the Sphinx met on bowls, jugs, and pitchers of classical Greece, with Oedipus at ease. When the riddle scene was revived by modern artists, a young woman often took Oedipus's place, spoke in the Sphinx's ear, and was in no danger. Since most artists prefer that their art be admired, the woman is likely to be lovely and scantily clad or nude. Naturally, the Sphinx is nude, too. The riddle is a pretext for a pinup, and prone to replacement by a whispered secret, kept by the silence of painting or print.

In his sequence of Sphinx paintings, Michael Parkes portrays female Sphinxes, often with nudes posed in accord with current ideals of height, age, and curvature.[32] "The Riddle" has a beautiful young woman, but she is richly dressed and subordinate to the scene. Accompanied by un-ruffled swans, she stands below an intent Sphinx, or someone dressed like a Sphinx. In the tradition of Ingres, "The Riddle" asks questions: who is she? why has she climbed there? why does she hold an egg? why swans, and why two of them? Does she ask a riddle or answer one?

The singular answer "man" is puny and dissatisfying, a prejudice, a rag. Marie Delcourt saw what mattered: not the riddle, but the riddler, the Sphinx, her rules, her way of thinking, her right and wrong. The Sphinx decides. If a man imitates Oedipus and answers Man, he must understand Man as she does, or he dies.[33]

STUPID OEDIPUS

Xena, the trademarked warrior princess, made a legend out of Lucy Law-less in black leather. In the first episode of the television series a cart-driver from Thebes recounts the legend of Oedipus: "World's biggest fool," he says.

Xena's fans followed her to Hades and Valhalla. She teaches Aphro-dite, outwits Ares (often), camps out with Amazons, and meets one amaz-ing woman after another: Calypso, Circe, Penelope, and the Sphinx, who "asks riddles of travelers and eats everyone who doesn't give the right answer — which is just about everyone." Her laugh is like "stones falling downhill." The Sphinx is angry that Oedipus spreads lies about her, say-ing she killed herself in a fury when he guessed her riddle. Xena assures her that his lies will be exposed.[34]

From birth Oedipus was a victim of geography. Men of Thebes and their region, Boetia, were famous throughout Greece for their stupidity. Homer called Boetians "thick-headed."[35] The Sphinx's easy riddle ridicules their simplicity. Why couldn't they answer it? Anyone else could. Avital Ronell finds the Oedipus myth alive in the dumbbells who think "What you don't know won't hurt you."[36]

4.6. *The Riddle* by Michael Parkes, 1999.

Analyst and infestation, Oedipus was a fool to brag about defeating the Sphinx. In Euripides's *Phoenician Women,* his daughter Antigone interrupts Oedipus at the start of the story. She's heard it too often. "You are bringing up again the reproach of the Sphinx. Talk no more of past success."[37] Sad Oedipus, out of touch with his daughter. Who would want to be Oedipus? Not Oedipus.

Johann Joachim Becher's *Oedipus Chymicus; oder, Chymischer Rätseldeuter* (1680) [Oedipus the Chemist; or, Solutions to the Riddles of Chemistry] advertised that if Becher, the Oedipus of *Chymicus,* were given silver, he could turn tin to gold.[38] Emperor Leopold I, always in need of cash, took Becher into his retinue. Becher explained that alchemy, like prayer, requires that the patron be pure of heart and favored by God. Success was sought not only for silver and gold — taxes and the sale of public offices were more dependable — but for proof of the emperor's piety. Fool's gold.

No pain or expense was spared to publish Athanasius Kircher's majestic *Oedipus Aegyptiacus* (1652–54). Sponsored by Cardinal Francisco Barberino and the Society of Jesus, it was lavishly dedicated to Ferdinand III (1608–57), emperor of the Holy Roman Empire, as a tribute to his magnificence and patronage. It was written in Latin, it contained the wisdom of Egypt, and it answered an ancient riddle. Twenty-seven eulogies precede Kircher's book. They praise the emperor, the author, and the book itself, in venerable languages: Greek, Chaldean, Arabic, Hebrew, Armenian, Ethiopian, Persian, Samaritan, Chinese, Brahman, and ancient Egyptian. The eulogies celebrate a triumph: Kircher had deciphered hieroglyphs.

Kircher made a job of it. His *Oedipus* is a bulging folio testament to the contributions of Jesuits to the Holy Empire and its glory. The English eulogy, composed by Jacob A. Gibbes, honored Kircher's triumph by claiming:

> For their Sphinx
> W'have found an OEDIPUS, doth solve the links
> Of chayn'd riddles, obscure symbols.

Kircher compared inscriptions from obelisks, amulets, statues, and tablets from Europe, Africa, India, China, and America. He studied the comparative religions of Chaldea, Persia, Greece, and India, and penetrated the mysteries of Zoroaster, the Orphics, the Kabbalists, Platonists, and Pythagoreans. In the course of two thousand pages Kircher exhibits his hard-won mastery of the elements of seventeenth-century Egyptology, its geography, astronomy, history, and religion. His patrons could afford high-quality engravings. He piles up his details like pyramids, pointing to a higher view.

His interpretations are ingenious, utterly mistaken, and raise questions about who was fooling whom. If Kircher really believed he had deciphered the hieroglyphs, if he genuinely committed himself to the learning of languages and symbolic systems, why did he not detect that the languages in some eulogies were bogus? Planted among the florid praises are booby traps and time bombs, imitation Sanskrit and an Egyptian no one spoke, exposing like flares a highly educated fantasy. Kircher dedicated *Oedipus Aegyptiacus* to the emperor as the delicious fruits of study and strain. Offered as an eternal compliment to God and the emperor, the book instead turned Kircher into "the whipping boy of Egyptology."[39] Kircher repeated the fatal Oedipal mistake: he assumed he had defeated the Sphinx, then made matters worse by declaring he'd defeated two. The climax of the book features Kircher's interpretations of hieroglyphs inscribed on two Sphinxes.[40]

If he had understood the Sphinx, Kircher would never have compared himself to Oedipus. His book prosecutes him. Despite his toil and languages he was stumbling in the dark. The Brahman eulogy was a fake, the Chaldean eulogy was a dreamwork, and the hieroglyphic preface hinted what his thousands of pages now shout: he failed. Sphinxes kept their secret.

A new Oedipus, a new victim. Kircher had made great discoveries about Egypt. He recognized Coptic as a means for interpreting older languages of Egypt. He understood that the Sphinx was no ordinary sign: it was a symbol, an "Idearum Idea," an idea of ideas. From Aven Vaschia, an Arab of Egypt, Kircher learned that the Sphinx's "summa significationis," the sum of its signs, was the Sun over the Nile.[41] Kircher had made a kind of sense of hieroglyphics, but he hadn't understood how to understand them. His Sphinx masterpiece is encyclopedic, intelligent, and sincere. Nevertheless, when he announced he had solved the riddle of the Sphinx he was wrong, and it is that mistake for which he is dimly remembered.[42] A man who would accept the name Oedipus, more so a man who would claim it, invites the fate of Oedipus.

Lame Lord Byron admitted, "I'm not Oedipus, and life's a Sphinx."[43] He went to Greece expecting to become its hero-king. Instead he died of fever in a stranger's bed.

The path to the Sphinx's rock passes through rooms walled with books and down the steps of an opera aisle. There are blazing Sphinxes who blind you and nocturnal Sphinxes waiting till you sleep.

5 : Body

The sculptor brought forth in a cloud of bright dust

A Sphinx who, under his hands, like a summoned ghost,

Awoke from an age-old granite sleep.

Léonce de Joncières

In Ephesus, where Saint John began his church and the Virgin Mary breathed her last, a statue of the Sphinx once bent over her prey. She resembled a Sphinx on the throne of Zeus carved by Phidias and may be a replica of it, a Sphinx about 2,500 years old. Wars came and shattered her; her pieces sank in the earth. In different archeological digs in the 1890s pieces were found and further separated by museums in London and Vienna. In 1937 Fritz Eichler began to reconstruct the Sphinx; the task took twenty years. By 1957 he had fit fifty-seven pieces from Vienna and fourteen from the British Museum, a small proportion of the sculpture, but enough to enable him to conceive it intact. His Sphinx has her man on the ground and has begun to tear him open. She is in no hurry.[1]

Stone Sphinxes commemorate the strength and beauty of women. The woman pharaoh Hatshepsut had her head carved on lion-size Sphinxes.[2] The face (forever young) of Gladys Deacon, the Duchess of Marlborough, was carved on a Sphinx at Blenheim Palace. The duchess tried to mold her own face with paraffin injections and ruined it. Deacon's friend Princess Marthe Bibesco wrote a romance, *The Sphinx of Bagatelle,* set when Louis XVI sat on the throne "but Marie Antoinette reigned over France." The heroine of the history is Louise de Polastron, whose beautiful face is immortalized on two Sphinxes of Bagatelle, a palace built to music. Her love is "the love of a virgin, so entire, so delicate, so timid."[3]

Aside from cats, dreams, and hallucinations, Sphinx statues are as close to real live Sphinxes as a person can get. For thousands of years Sphinx sculptors released from granite and marble beautiful Sphinxes with beckoning eyes and tempting skin. Sphinx statues are as beautiful as Venus and more gripping.[4]

In the preface to the third edition of his *Buch der Lieder,* Heine's persona adores a statue of a Sphinx:

5.1. Hans Eichler's reconstruction
of the Ephesus Sphinx, 1959.

Before the gate there lay a Sphinx —
Terror and lust cross bred!
In body and claws a lion's form,
A woman in breast and head.

The poet kisses the statue and the statue responds.

O rapturous torment and exquisite pain!
Anguish and bliss evermore!
While the kiss of her mouth was thrilling joy,
Her lion claws ripped and tore.

A nightingale witnesses the lovemaking and asks:

O lovely Sphinx!
O love, explain to me:
Why do you blend the pain of death
With every ecstasy?[5]

Heine's Sphinx is no Galatea to his Pygmalion, a work of art that returns the artist's love; instead it is stone brought to life to kill him. Pliny reported that a statue of Venus was stained by man's lust.[6] Sphinx the defender avenges violated statuary.

Beautiful Sphinxes have been sculpted for centuries and attacked and shattered for centuries. If Eichler is right, the Ephesian Sphinx was breathtaking.[7]

Eichler's reconstructed Sphinx made a Sphinx and victim from rubble. Making a Sphinx is an art as old as Horemakhet and it prepares for another art: making things out of Sphinxes. How to make a Sphinx?

The Sphinx of Wilhelmine Fould's *Le Sphinx aux perles* (1884) is a statue with ivory teeth, eyes of gold, a string of pearls glistening against her black body. The statue fascinates Odysse, broke, blasé, and recently married. The eyes of the Sphinx look alive. They enchant him. Odysse soon sees (he thinks) the Sphinx in the flesh and chases her. But she is the hunter and catches Odysse, then leads him weeping back to matrimony.

Sphinx fiction is toothed with love triangles: one man, two women, one of whom must die; one woman, two men, rivals for her. At one corner of

5.2. Eichler's completed reconstruction, 1959.

the triangle is a beautiful woman, "the most beautiful ever seen," often a cripple, a widow, an orphan, an addict, an artist, an angel, or some combination of these.[8] At another corner, another woman in another combination of the same. It is not always clear which is the Sphinx. Both, perhaps, two women in one.

The Sphinx's body shimmers in synthesis, a symbol of symbols endlessly transforming. She keeps up with the times. From pharaohs' tombs to Paris streets, Sphinxes slip in and out of fashion. Each part of a Sphinx has its own symbolic range — eyes, ears, nose, lips, wings, claws, voice, affections, hungers, and moods — and each changes.

THE FELINE SPHINX

Cats eat birds, but here is a Sphinx, a bird-cat, a wonder, a freak. The movements of the Sphinx: patient immobility, pounce, swerve, leap, swat, swipe, and bite. An ordinary magic Sphinx can pass, cut, and vanish.[9]

The vague divide between man and beast scarcely troubles the harmony in Phix, divine Phix. Her body is clean and pliant, her mouth is carnivore. Without cats a Sphinx makes no sense. Without cats the Sphinx wouldn't loll so long, jump so high, or have so many lives. Cats watch what they want, go where they will, climb high, dream deeply, and see through the night. They hide, they hunt, they play with their food. For a thousand years or longer Egypt worshiped cats. The Sphinx of Giza holds its head proudly like a cat, alert, erect, ready for anything. There are lion Sphinxes, cheetah Sphinxes, tiger and panther Sphinxes, and Sphinxes asleep on your lap.[10]

Felinity complicates the Sphinx through and through. Cats hiss, shed, and spray. There are cats so shrewd and shy they will not let you see them and cats that will stare you down. Cats command people to feed them and get out of the way. A cat caress thrills supersensitivity. Loving cats nuzzle and lean. They lift their tails like antennae and show off their cleanly licked behinds. Cats' lips twist with muscle. Cats moan for sex. For a Sphinx, love is monstrous.

A cat is built to kill, but not cruelly. Leyhausen and Tonkin say, "The cat strikes its victim in the back and shoulder with whichever forepaw is

5.3. Illustration for "If I Could Read
Your Heart" by H. P. Jeddy, 1905.

nearer it and bites immediately in front of that point." A cat kills short-necked animals with a stab; it kills larger animals by severing the cervical spinal cord, "killing them almost instantly."

Except when it plays.

"Even when the cat attacks its prey from an elevated position — a tree, boulder, etc. — it never springs directly from above onto the prey animal, whose soft and yielding body with its unpredictable movements would in any case make a rather poor landing place. Instead it always lands on the ground short of its prey and attacks it from there."[11] Lions, cheetahs, and tigers kill by grasping the prey's throat, choking it or breaking its neck. "It really does look like strangulation."[12] After the kill a cat lays down its prey, walks around it, will sometimes seem to dance and jump over it, in part to release pent-up energy, in part to be sure the prey is dead. Then the cat takes it elsewhere to eat.

The voluptuous Sphinx of Moreau, tail curled and straddling Oedipus, updated a posture seen on Greek vases and bowls: the Sphinx upon a man, predatory sex face-to-face. The Sphinx in Moreau's painting has three paws visible, all upon Oedipus. Her claws are withdrawn, or Oedipus would suffer long gashes on his chest and thighs. If she pulled at his skin he would fall on top of her. The painting is a predicament of balance. How long can she remain there, with nothing to support her but her wings?

Oedipus holds a spear in his left hand; his right hand is out of sight. He makes no effort to push her away. His unseen hand might hold the Sphinx's lower left leg to keep her from falling. Her body, stretched so tight her tail torques, asks Oedipus the enigma: does he know how to hold a cat?

SPHINXOGNOMY

The Testament of Solomon (fourth century), one of the oldest Christian books on demonology, warns that demons can be σφιγγοπρόσωπα [sphinx-faced].[13] They are subtle demons since the face of a Sphinx has no Sphinx feature, no distinguishing mark — in every way it is a human

5.4. *Oedipus and the Sphinx* by Gustave Moreau, 1864.

face. To recognize the face of a Sphinx as the face of a Sphinx, it must be attached to its body. A head is a head, a head of a Sphinx is scary.

The bloodthirsty Sphinx has been seen in bad company, a monster among monsters. Bartholomaeus (circa 1140) compares the Sphinx's riddle on the mountain to Satan's mountaintop temptation. In Tasso's *Gerusalemme liberata* (1575) Sphinxes spew from hell amid thousands of Gorgons, centaurs, and Chimeras, answering Satan's call. Mandeville's *Fable of the Bees* (1714) puts Sphinxes in the company of basilisks, flying dragons, and bulls that spit fire. In Shelley's *Prometheus Unbound* (1820) Mercury calls forth the Sphinx with Geryon, Gorgon, and Chimera.[14]

Myth and its arts often place Sphinxes near griffins and Chimeras: Chimeras share her lion body; griffins share her wings. The grand *Mythologiae* of Natale Conti (1551) depicts a Sphinx chatting with a Chimera. Tooke's *Pantheon* (1713) and Bulfinch's *Age of Fable* (1855) set them side by side. The last in the dying line of the des Esseintes family installed a Sphinx of black marble in the family château and put opposite it a polychrome terra-cotta Chimera. In the silence of the night the Sphinx and Chimera converse.[15] The last work John Singer Sargent supervised was his mural for the Boston Museum of Fine Arts, with a whole and handsome Sphinx admiring a flying naked female Chimera swooping like an angel.

5.5. The Sphinx and Chimera swap stories in Conti's *Mythologiae*, 1551.

5.6. *Sphinx and Chimera* by John Singer Sargent, 1925, a rotunda mural in the Boston Museum of Fine Arts.

Jean-Joseph Goux compares the Chimera's and the Sphinx's tripartite anatomies. He finds in each the three functions Georges Dumézil identified as the progressive trials of the hero: religion, war, and sexuality = wings, claws, and woman, in ascending order of difficulty. Goux presumes that heroes must be male, a presumption that Phix rips to pieces.[16]

Phix's monstrosity is one of her fascinations. She is built to fight; her teeth are aligned like saw blades, her claws are a long as butchers' knives. Like her big cousin in Giza, Phix is often described as a two-part hybrid, perhaps half cat, perhaps something less precise. Diodorus of Sicily called her a "dimorph beast"; Kircher, the universal expert, also judged her a dimorph. Thomas De Quincey described the Sphinx as "a mysterious monster . . . half woman and half brute." Oscar Wilde's "half woman and half animal" is customary.[17] Such custom has a decision to make: how divide her? What is woman, what is animal? Look at Phix as long as you like, her body is only the beginning of her mystery, but what a beginning! Her riddles confuse speech, her behavior is macabre, and her family comes from the wrong side of creation.

Phix's heredity is divine. According to Hesiod, her parents were Echidna and Orthus, mom and dad monsters; her brother was the Nemean lion, "a plague to mankind," slain by Hercules. Apollodorus agrees that her mother was Echidna but awards paternity to Typhon.[18] Typhon is a storm god. Orthus is a monster dog. Hesiod reports that the lineage of the Sphinx is incestuous, Oedipal before Oedipus: the mother of her father was Echidna, thus Echidna is the mother and grandmother of Phix. (In the Oedipus family Antigone and Ismene bear the same kinship to Jocasta.) Phix is three parts Echidna, one part Papa. Echidna is half nymph

> With a fair face and eyes glancing,
> but the other half is a monstrous snake,
> Terrible, enormous,
> and squirming and voracious,
> There in the earth's secret places.

Echidna never ages, never dies.[19]

In the *Frogs* Aristophanes refers to Phix as a "dusamerian kuna," an unlucky bitch.[20] Phix has been often described as half dog, in a pedigree as old as Sophocles. Sphinx dogs, Sphinx cats. Dogs bound for joy, cats snuggle. Cats purr, dogs wag; dogs snarl, cats hiss. Dogs are devoted, cats are passionate. Dog Sphinxes have their day.[21] Sophocles calls the Sphinx a ῥαψῳδὸς κύων, a "rhapsodic dog." Visiting Horemakhet in 1839, the comte de Marcellus compared the Sphinx to a "faithful greyhound, crouching on the habitations of the dead."[22] Henry Howard Brownell found the Sphinx of Giza

> Still couched in silence brave,
> Like some fierce hound long watching
> Above her master's grave.[23]

Men split Phix into thirds, or quarters, or fifths. Apollodorus described Phix with "the face of a woman, the breast and feet and tail of a lion, and the wings of a bird." The *Idylls* of the riddler Ausonius of Bordeaux (early fourth century AD) declare her "triformis": eagle, lion, and virgin. Conti relays descriptions handed down to the Renaissance: the face and breasts of a woman, the feet and tail of a lion, and wings (from Lasus Hermioneus) and the head and hands of a girl, the body of a dog, the voice of a man, the tail of a dragon, the talons of a lion, the wings of a bird (from Clearchus, a pupil of Aristotle).[24]

The Sphinx god Tutu walks the Staatliche Museen zu Berlin with four paws, two arms, a lion's body, a crocodile on his chest, wings on his back, and on his human head a headdress from which eight other animals of the Nile look out. The tip of Tutu's tail is the head of a snake. In his *Fall of Princes* (circa 1438) John Lydgate rolls Phix into a talking serpent: "a serpent" Sphinx, says Robert Bird (1631). Oscar Wilde's Sphinx has a tail "like a monstrous Asp." O. Henry's Sphinx is last seen as "a formless dark bulk, crowned by a mass of coiled, sleek hair and showing but a small space of snowy forehead above her clinging boa."[25]

In 1928 Walter Wynn described a hermaphrodite Horemakhet with "the head of a Woman, the Face of a Man, the Body of a Lion."[26] An 1829 engraving depicts the Great Sphinx as a woman attacked by a gang. An attacking Sphinx becomes a Sphinx attacked.

Phix is a strong Sphinx able to have her way. In their *Oedipus* (1679),
John Dryden and Nathaniel Lee list her depredations:

> The Monster *Sphynx* laid your rich Country waste,
> Your Vineyards spoil'd, your labouring Oxen slew;
> Your selves for fear mew'd up within your Walls.
> She, taller than your Gates, o'er-look'd your Town,
> But when she rais'd her Bulk to sail above you,
> She drove the Air arround her like a Whirlwind,
> And shaded all beneath; till stooping down,
> She clap'd her leathern wing against your Tow'rs,
> And thrust out her long neck, ev'n to your doors.[27]

Phix is a tornado.

The textbook Phix is a man-eater, an invading wilderness, enemy of cities. The Phix of the centuries is much else: a naked proctor, an international anthology, a variorum, a set of proof tests, a pastiche of pastiches.

HEAD OF THE SPHINX

Horemakhet's huge head is his finest part. The angle of vision from his paws to his eyes exaggerates the perspective and emphasizes his fourteen-foot face. Théophile Gautier imagined his hearing: "One admires its snub-nosed face and the large beaming smile upon its thick lips as an eternal irony of the fragility of human things; its ears, on which fell the crinkling of sacred mummy wrappings, have heard the collapse of so many dynasties like the fall of a grain of sand!"[28]

His hearing would be greater still if it were the hearing of a lion. The head and body of a Sphinx blend like blood. Is the body in the service of the sovereign head, is the head a sentry for the ferocious body? In Horemakhet man and beast meet at the focal point. His face is human: his eyes could be lion's eyes.

James Russell Lowell supposed the Sphinx's eyes to speak:

> Arise! be earnest and be strong!
> The Sphinx's eyes shall suddenly grow clear,
>   And speak as plain to thee ere long,
> As the dear maiden's who holds thee most dear.[29]

If this be true then though thou wert a maiden thyself the Sphinx will hold thee as a maiden does, tightly I suppose. If a maiden holds like a Sphinx, she holds with claws. Her eyes are Sphinx eyes, serious, mysterious, wide.

5.7. Engraving of the violated female Sphinx of Giza by E. Goodall after a drawing by W. M. Craig from Myers, *System of Modern Geography*, 1829.

FACE OF THE SPHINX

The gallery of faces of the Sphinx seldom resembles the face of Horemakhet.[30] More often than not, a Sphinx has a nose. Horemakhet's nose is an enormous wound, a symbol of arrogance, ignorance, and zeal. Shot by soldiers, hammered, picked, and pried by iconoclasts, hacked by tourists, it is cut by two crevasses deliberately made. The zealots who chiseled the nose off also attacked the Sphinx's eyes and lips. Its ruined face has been compared to the decay of a leper, but its disease walks on two feet.[31]

Cebes of Thebes, a student of Aristotle, is the eldest authority for explaining the symbolism of the Sphinx's face and body parts.[32] For Cebes the Sphinx symbolized three sources of human ignorance (three is the Sphinx's favorite number): levity, pride, and lust. Later writers add a virgin face.[33] The levity of a Sphinx's wings is plain enough, and the tie between lions and pride has a regal lineage. But how does a face appear virgin, and why does a virgin face represent lust? Could a virgin face be false? The learned men of the Renaissance accepted the Sphinx as a symbol of a special kind of face, ignorance in a specific combination. For all her parts, she is incomplete. She cannot reveal her meaning alone: she only reveals her Sphinxiness when she meets a man. The Sphinx is not a simple symbol of herself, her levity, her pride, her lust; she is a symbol of his. The ignorance of ignorance is masculine, liable to men's weaknesses: delusions of wit, playing with risks, prodigality, gullibility. The Sphinx needs Oedipus as a cat needs a mouse.

SMILE OF THE SPHINX

Percy Withers supposed that the smile of the Sphinx was a "smile of derision."[34] The Sphinx smiles with closed lips, concealing its teeth. It smiles at questions mortal and immortal, at views universal and unique, at conscious and unconscious motives; it smiles at epiphanies and at petty quarrels because it smiles at everything. In *The Smile of the Sphinx* (1911) Marguerite Bouvet describes Sphinx smiles as masks. "The Sphinx-smile is used by all people of the world. In the world the smile is various and manifold. We make use of it to clothe our diverse feelings: our affections, when not requited; our hatred and contempt of those who come periodically into our lives to smile and smirk, while nurturing a poisonous canker in their hearts; that of envy, jealousy, malice and all uncharitableness."[35]

The Sphinx smiles at pain. Monica, the protagonist of Ethel Knight Kelly's *Why the Sphinx Smiles* (1925), marries a man who is wise and loving but old and impotent. In the Valley of the Sphinx her sexuality awakens. With the approval of her husband she makes love to handsome young Victor and bears him a son he does not want. War and anguish pass beneath the smile of the Sphinx. It summons those who wonder and those sick of wonder who seek its indifference.

VOICE OF THE SPHINX

Pharaoh commanded his priests to compete against Moses and Aaron in making signs and wonders. Aaron struck the Nile with his staff—all the water of Egypt in cups, bowls, and wells, in cisterns and pools, and the holy Nile itself, all turned to blood. Aaron struck the Nile again and the blood became water. Ennana, chief priest of the pharaoh, struck the Nile with his staff. To the amazement of all, from the depths of the river came hard words of an ancient language, from the time of Menes, the first king of Egypt, "a language of the Sphinx, in syllables of granite," a language so old no one understood it.[36]

"You are afraid of me, because I talk like a Sphynx," Rochester says to Jane Eyre, hopefully. Not to talk at all is also to talk like a Sphinx. Sphinxes are made of silence. "It is the quiet of the will which one sees here. This Sphinx is still because she will be still. So has she been still for all these thousand years."[37]

Still still. Poets, seers, and product promoters speak for the Sphinx in many languages. Talking Sphinxes bantered with Schuré and Enel. In Péladan's *La terre du Sphinx* (1900), the Sphinx confides, flatters, tells a tale of the Tarot, takes questions, gives answers, rambles and rails. It complains that humanity is no longer religious: "Immoral and fatal economics dominates everything."[38]

"The Egyptian Sphinx will be familiar to every one of you," wrote Annie Besant, stepmother of Theosophy. "I am to try if it be possible to sketch for you something of what that Sphinx has to say."[39] What it says sounds exactly like Besant: Theosophy's Christianity expressed through the veil of the Vedas.

Maurice Rostand's Sphinx takes to the stage and informs us that "the universe is round, like a zero." In *A Search in Secret Egypt* (1936) Paul Brunton asks Horemakhet for directions and gets them. Archibald MacLeish ventriloquized seven questions through the Sphinx. A Sphinx tells Enel she's the Mother of all.[40]

Sphinx talk dresses in alexandrines, stops in the middle of sentences, dissolves in air. Alexander Kinglake solemnly warned, "You dare not mock at the Sphynx." Still, people dare. Sphinx-mockers scoff that a cat that big needs the Sahara for a sandbox. The Sphinx of Paul Eldridge's *And the Sphinx Spoke* (1921) is a Thpinx: "Slowly, hoarsely, in a tremulous voice, the Sphinx uttered the wisdom of the Centuries that passed to the Centuries that will follow: 'The . . . thand . . . ith . . . dry!' "[41] Puns on the sounds of Sphinx and sphincter have John Milton's Latin for precedent.[42] The Sphinx can be jolly. Horemakhet sang a jingle for Pepsi and grinned with delight to hear phonograph records.

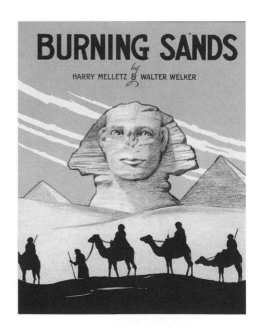

5.8. P. M. Griffith's cover for Melletz and
Welker's "Burning Sands," a foxtrot, 1922.

5.9. The Sphinx sells phonographs for
Columbia, 1905.

Call it heredity: Sphinxes are musical. Sophocles said Phix is *sklêras aoidou* and *poikilôidos,* a "cruel singer" and "riddle-singing."[43] The Muses are friends of the Sphinx. All nine Muses attended the funeral of Achilles and all nine gathered to give Phix the riddle she posed to Oedipus. Sphinxes join Muses on Roman sarcophagi.[44]

Shakespeare's one and only Sphinx has a touch of Apollo. In *Love's Labor's Lost* a lord tells his king that women's eyes contain "the books, the academes." Love is "Subtle as Sphinx; as sweet and musical / As bright Apollo's lute, strung with his hair. / And when Love speaks, the voice of all the gods / Make heaven drowsy with the harmony." An amphora in the British Museum portrays Apollo standing between two Sphinxes. Apollo strums a cithara, perhaps not at his best, since the Sphinxes turn their heads away.[45]

Charles Segal's "Music of the Sphinx" took a look at an old Greek fragment and read the antitype. Greeks thought Sphinx music was awful. Euripides "describes the riddles as a horrible shrieking whistle." In *The Phoenician Women,* the chorus agrees that her riddles are *amousotataisi* [most unmusic].[46] Like a Siren.

Like the Sirens, Phix lures men to her, has unusual music, and murders erotically. What do we know of her music? The men who heard her are dead now, dead as Oedipus. For thousands of years unriddlers, unable to record audio, concentrated on the words the Sphinx sang instead of her singing. How clear were her tones, how smooth her melisma, how high and low her range, how fast her tempo, and how sly her style, were anyone's guess, but there had to be sound. The Sphinx didn't draw Oedipus a rebus. Her riddle runs on feet — rhythm's feet, kitten up and down the keys.[47] Not just what she said, but how she said or sang it, mix with her visible mysteries. The body of the Sphinx is dangerous. Her voice is dangerous.

Hear now the performing Sphinx.

Henry Purcell (1659–95) did not complete his *Oedipus* opera. Felix Mendelssohn (1809–47) composed incidental music for Sophocles' *Oedipus Tyrannus,* but it vanished.[48] Edgard Varése (1883–1965) worked for years on an Oedipus opera based on Von Hofmannstahl's play; it was never completed and is lost.

Caught in Massenet's *Manon* (1884) the Comte Des Grieux sings: "Manon, Manon, astonishing Sphinx, veritable siren! Your heart is triply feminine!"[49] Why triply? Three women in one: a Sphinx, a Siren, Manon. The riddling man-killing Sphinx reincarnates as Weber's Turandot (1809), and Busoni's (1917), and Puccini's (1926).[50]

A winter Sphinx warms her throat with fur and opera. In *The Red Sphinx* (1907) the Sphinx is Leonore Redway, an American in Paris determined to prove to herself and all the world that she can triumph in the capital of culture. Her voice captures the attention of Fidus, a poet with failing health and a successful cabaret, the Seven Capital Sins. Fidus carves wood Sphinxes. He asks her to sing his new poem, "The Red Sphinx," a dialogue between the Poet and Sphinx. Leonore consents. His song and her voice conquer Paris. "The Red Sphinx" arouses the critics, agitates the newspapers that uphold church and state, stirs up radical students and socialist journals, and enjoys a great vogue. Leonore Redway glows in her fame and enflames a painter whose body revolts when he tries to paint her as the Sphinx. Love, more love, and unrequited love lead like a Sphinx to death by strangling.

"Love can make us monsters," Leonore says.[51]

Before he rewrote Germany's origins, reformed radical Richard Wagner contemplated the Oedipus legend. In 1851 he summarized his view of the riddle scene:

> How full of meaning it is, then, that precisely this Oedipus had solved the riddle of the *Sphinx!* In advance he uttered both his vindication and his own condemnal, when he called the kernel of this riddle *Man.* From the half-bestial body of the Sphinx, there fronted him at first the human individual in its subjection to Nature: when the half-brute had dashed itself from its dreary mountain-stronghold into the shattering abyss below, the shrewd unriddler of its riddle turned back to the haunts of men; to let them fathom, from his own undoing, the whole, the Social Man.[52]

He found no music in him for this plan, but kept a key part: he conceived Kundry, temptress of Parsifal, as a Sphinx.[53]

Composers took up the Oedipus story with great interest and usually began at the point where Sophocles' *Oedipus Tyrannus* begins, with the Sphinx already vanquished. In Ruggiero Leoncavallo's *Edipo Re* (1920), Igor Stravinsky's *Oedipus Rex* (1927; libretto by Jean Cocteau), and Carl Orff's *Oedipus der Tyrann* (1959), the Sphinx is heard of but not heard. No auditions.

The three small Sphinxes of part 9 of Robert Schumann's *Carnaval,* Opus 9, encode a love note. Using an antique form of musical notation and the German names for notes, the Sphinxes spell an abbreviation of Schumann's name—s c h a—and an anagram, the name of the town where his beloved lived—a s c h. Following Clara Schumann's practice, most performers pass over the Sphinxes in silence, unplayed.[54]

Sphinx music stays in style. William A. Pond composed a "Sphinx Galop" (1877). Francis Popy's "Sphinx?" (1906), a waltz for piano, was popular for a generation. Cyril Scott's "Sphinx" for solo piano (1908) races. Leon Carroll published "Sphinx Rag" with Sphinx Publishing Co. (1912). Henry C. Castleman set the last two stanzas of Wilde's "The Sphinx" in *Two Songs* (1913). Robert King and Harry Warren published a lighthearted "Sphinx" (1926) that "just sits and thinks and thinks and thinks and thinks." Kurt Schwabach and Michael Jary wrote a samba, "Allerdings sprach die Sphinx" (1949). Henri Sauguet composed and orchestrated the music for Boris Kochno's ballet, *Œdipe et le Sphinx* (1952). Ornette Coleman recorded his saxophone "Sphinx" in 1958, naming it "Sphinx" because "it sounded right." Alec Costandinos recorded a *Sphinx* lp with "Judas" on side 1 and "Simon Peter" on side 2 (1977). Amanda Lear's "Sphinx" (1978) wishes to be "the silent Sphinx eternally" because "the Sphinx can never cry."[55] In "Sphinx" (1982) Harry Thumman sings synthetically, "Rising up into the sky / reference is getting high." Out of the Velvet Underground, Nico sang a lonesome pentatonic "Sphinx" (1985). The "Sphinx" of Syd Straw's ballad (1989) drinks too much, sees shrinks, and is sentenced to insatiable lust. Black Sabbath put "Sphinx (The Guardian)" (1986) in a suit of heavy metal, "the sound of fallen angels." The Christian hard rock band Time Machine responded with "Sphynx (The Witness)" (1998). The Brand New Heavies released a funk "Sphynx" in 1991. Sphinx, a rock quartet, stalked Sweden and Chicago in the 1990s. Sphinxes ornament the cover of Iron Maiden's *Powerslave* (1995). New Age Oedipi, keyboardist Yanni and harpist Andreas Vollenweider, wrote "Sphinx" songs (1989 and 1991); Yanni's Sphinx sounds like a helicopter.

Silence, please.

If a sexy feline Sphinx shows up in a steamy scene, it is usually female. Her libido is emphasized over and over, but her lure is not just physical. The Phixes of Sophocles, Seneca, and Voltaire attract men because Sphinxes know more than they do. Sphinx intelligence seduces.

5.10. "Sphinxes" by Robert Schumann from *Carnaval*, 1835.

6 : Eros

She turned and faced him. She was tall and gracious, and when she looked at him that way he knew how much he wanted her. Her eyes were glowing green, and her lips were glossy in the fluorescent light of the kitchen. Her big breasts softly stretched the front of her safari jacket, and her long legs were tightly outlined in brown leather boots. And all the time there was that faint lingering scent about her, that musky scent that aroused him more than he could ever remember being aroused before.

Graham Masterton

Anton Chekhov, *The Seagull* (1895):

Medvedénko: Do you know the famous riddle? What goes on four feet in the morning, on two feet at noon, on three feet in the evening—

Sórin: (*Laughs*) Sure! And flat on his back at night![1]

THE ROMANTIC SPHINX

Novalis's *Heinrich von Ofterdingen* (1802) concludes with a tale told by Klingsohr the master poet. He says that Fable, the foster sister of Eros, searched for Eros down a secret stairway. At the bottom was a doorway, guarded by a sleepy Sphinx. The Sphinx asked Fable a series of questions:

"Do you know me?"

Fable said, "Not yet."

"Where is Love?"

"In the imagination," Fable answered. The Sphinx let her pass.

Fable was brave and untiring in her search for Eros. She found Ginnistan, her mother, ravished by Eros. Ginnistan looked exactly like Eros's mother, voluptuous and irresistible. Eros made love to the mother of Fable in sweet delusion, mistaking her mother for his.

Fable watched Eros fly back and fall asleep in the lap of her mother. Unhappy Fable returned to her home and found it in ruins. Fable again descended to the doorway and Sphinx, who asked:

"Who knows the world?"

"He who knows himself," Fable answered.

"What is the eternal mystery?"

"Love," Fable said and stepped past the satisfied Sphinx, who curled up to nap.[2]

TABOO LOVE

Why was Phix sent on her cruel mission to Thebes? Euripides explains: to punish the city for the lust of King Laius, the world's first pederast. Apollo the Sun warned Laius that he had bad seed and should not father children, so Laius kidnapped Chrysippus, a lovely boy, and loved him like a bride. Hera, queen of heaven and defender of marriage, ordered Phix to terrify Thebes to punish Laius.[3] Some say he was punished because he was a thief, a kidnapper, some say because he loved a boy.

Phix obeyed and killed and killed. A Sphinx slaying men at the command of the queen of heaven fans the friction between sexes into flame. Despite Apollo, King Laius has a son — Oedipus the unwanted, who grows up to kill his father and marry his father's widow.

Oedipus defeated the Sphinx but was not yet out of danger. His new wife had a powerful brother, Creon, who ruled in the period between King Laius and King Oedipus. Brotherly Creon offered his sister as booty to the man who beat the Sphinx. Creon believes Jocasta is a price worth paying for a Sphinx exterminator. Jocasta believes she must sacrifice herself to save Thebes. She agrees to marry the man, no matter how ugly or beastly, who kills the Sphinx. Creon protects Jocasta from foolish and cowardly suitors and from already married men. Her love is reserved for that special bloody someone; she cannot be won by wit, gifts, rank, flattery, or sexual attraction. Jocasta and Creon introduce the Sphinx to a new set of problems: love between brother and sister. Random contact, fickle fertility, and the fate of common parents entangle Orestes and Electra, Antigone and Polynices, Eros and Fable, sibling Sphinxes.

Emile Zola's novel *La curée* (1872) encloses nature in glass. Renée Saccard had a black marble Sphinx in her Paris hothouse, a very hot hothouse. One night she enticed her brother there. "Renée on her knees, leaning over him, with fixed eyes and an animal attitude that alarmed him. Her hair down, her shoulders bare, she leant upon her wrists, with her spine stretched out, like a great cat with phosphorescent eyes. The young man, lying on his back, perceived above the shoulders of this adorable, amorous beast that gazed upon him the marble sphinx, whose thighs gleamed in the moonlight. Renée had the attitude and the smile of the monster with the woman's head, and, in her loosened petticoats, looked like the white sister of this black divinity." Zola compounds the opulence of the love scene by duplicating its details: Renée and the Sphinx mirror each other. Renée "was all swollen with voluptuousness, and the clear outline of her shoulders and loins stood out with feline distinctness. . . . She gloated over Maxime, this prey extended beneath her, abandoning itself, which she possessed entirely."[4] Renée and Maxime left with something new between them, a secret. The Sphinx in the hothouse meanwhile mixed boredom, luxury, lust, Africa, felinity, femininity, rapture, capture, and sin in a single black body.

SPHINX SEX

Some Sphinxes love amicably, like the Sphinx in Richard le Gallienne's *Little Dinners with the Sphinx* (1907) and the Sphinx in John Crowley's *Aegypt* (1987). Bob Dylan's love song to Sara calls her a Sphinx. Some Sphinxes love with charity and patience and transcendent virtue. They confront riddles like pain that is good for you. Some die for love. In Cocteau's *La machine infernale* (1934) the Sphinx falls in love with stupid and selfish Oedipus. In tune with French tradition, Cocteau's lovesick Sphinx says that love is the riddle. She cannot solve it and she cannot get over it.

Turgenev's *Fathers and Sons* (1862) quickly condemns Pavel Petrovich to a Sphinx story; Pavel emerges as a profoundly unhappy bachelor. He falls in love with a princess and gives her a ring.

"What's that," she asked, "a sphinx?"

"Yes," he answered, "and that sphinx is you."

They have a romp before she tires of him and flees. He follows, and she evades him for a decade. When the weary princess dies on the brink of insanity she returns the ring to him, the Sphinx cut by a cross.

The Sphinx has sex frequently. F. Scott Fitzgerald's Marjorie, the "sphinx of sphinxes," gives seduction lessons. The Oedipus and Sphinx of Henry Bauchau were two lonesome strangers at Thebes:

She was beautiful, black and white with her mysterious
     smile. How we yearned
That after the first veil, there would be another, always
     another, forever another.
There is nothing more beautiful than the enigma, that great
     loving enigma, which constantly renews itself.

Bauchau's Oedipus liked what he saw.

My salt-eyes beheld this girl of the forests, clothed
     by the wild-flower.
The strong lines of her body, her powerful animal curves
     Discernible beneath her dress,
Igniting the passionate desire to adore, to rip and
     tear off her fur.[5]

Dreamy reminiscent rapist, seduced by lines and curves!
     Richard Howard's "The Encounter" (1967) satisfies the Sphinx's question by turning the man into a love tool:

your hands slide up her parted thighs as if
on pulleys, her knees perform, and suddenly
          she is down, and only one thing
     stands now, ready as your senseless senses
let you know that she is ready too. Impaled
          abruptly on the prong of flesh
     she writhes, yet you do not move, it is her
moving that sends the answer deeper in.[6]

Phix! Her body is a provocation, her half-and-half nature an enticement.
Like a centerfold creased in thirds she seduces lonely men. Oscar Wilde's
exotic Sphinx invades the intimacy of masturbation.

And the priests cursed you with shrill psalms
as in your claws you seized their snake
And crept away with it to slake
your passion by the shuddering palms.

Wilde's Sphinx has a list of lovers as long as the Nile.[7]

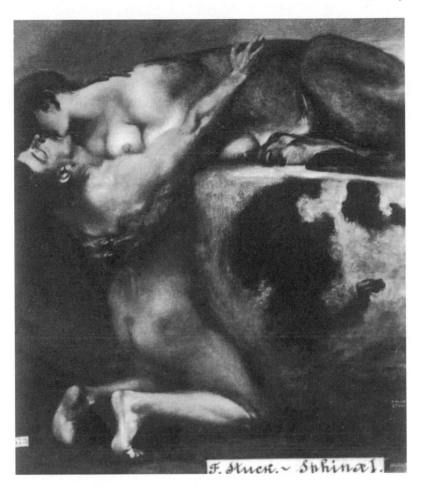

6.1. *The Sphinx's Kiss* by Franz von Stuck, 1895.

D. H. Lawrence wrote frankly about Sphinx sex. For him, the Sphinx is a man thing, a heartfelt male fantasy, "sirens and sphinxes and the other Greek fabulous female things . . . had not been created by fancy, but out of bitter necessity of the man's human heart to express itself." Lawrence reproached women for being "sphinxes of self-consciousness." When a lovely young lady asks him, "But why do I feel so strangely about you?" he did as Thebans did, "I took to my heels and ran."[8] Sphinxes run like lions.

Graham Masterton's fantasy *Sphinx* (1978) goes all the way. On his wedding night dull Gene watches his bride undress, his anticipation turning to horror when he sees a naked Sphinx: six breasts and thick hair down her thighs. She mates with a lion while Gene watches.

Esther M. Friesner upped the ante in her Atlantic City tale, *Sphynxes Wild* (1989). The Sphinx of Thebes and the Sphinx of Egypt meet face-to-face and fight. She subdues his roar with lust. At last "the male thrashed, held fast, and the Answer burst from him."[9] A moment later he dies. Like a Sphinx, Lady Luck is a killer.

CLEOPATRA SPHINX

Sextus Aurelius Victor's *De Viris Illustribus* (circa 360 AD) reported that Cleopatra indulged her lovers for a single night, then killed them in the morning. Théophile Gautier's tale, *One of Cleopatra's Nights* (1858), depicts Cleopatra perpetually surrounded by Sphinxes, whom she ponders and hates. Luxuriant, royal, she is amused by an adoring young man, whom she kisses, then poisons.[10] Alexander Pushkin (1799–1837) wrote "Egyptian Nights," a story within a story wherein three men give up their lives for one night of love with Cleopatra. Pushkin died in a duel before he finished the tale.

L'âme du Sphinx (1906) throbs in an Egypt of sex and cats. Léonce de Joncières describes Cleopatra's bored Ethiopian guard, whose thoughts wander back home, to great forests and crystal lakes, beautiful tattooed women and dangerous snakes.[11] Joncières approaches his Sphinx like a man in thrall. For Joncières the African woman is especially seductive:

—O my dear! O my idol!
Tomorrow, no less than yesterday and today,

I will be unable to read your soul.
And I will search in vain:
You will guard the enigma, o woman,
Charming and exasperating Sphinx.[12]

Agnès Varda's film *Cléo de 5 à 7* (1961) describes its heroine as "Cleo-patra! Egypt! The Sphinx . . . the asp . . . the tigress." Each comparison is a compliment to the hard-to-win woman.

Cleopatra, the ultimate seductress, is surrounded by Sphinxes.[13]

SPHINX APPEAL

Claelia, princess of Rome, hired an assassin to kill the man who had re-fused her love. She sat where he had left her, masked, with her arms straight out before her, the nails of her hand nipping the table. "So sat the fabled sphynx: so sits a tigress."[14]

In 1862 Villiers de L'Isle-Adam published the first sections of *Isis,* an ambitious work he never completed. It introduces Princess Tullia Fabri-ana, "a beautiful Promethean virgin" who, like the virgins of Sparta and Thebes, has courage, beauty, and strength. In her twenty-first year, alone and melancholic, she decides to retreat within her labyrinthine palace and abandon herself to the sublime attractions of Thought. One night she closes her books and murmurs:

> Sphinx! . . . O you most ancient of the gods! I know that your kingdom resembles the arid steppes and that one must walk a long time in the desert in order to approach you. Ardent abstraction does not know how to frighten me; I will try you. The priests in the temples of Egypt placed before your image the veiled statue of Isis, the symbol of Creation; on the pedestal, they inscribed these words, "I am what is, what has been, what will be: no one has lifted the veil that covers me." [Plutarch again.] Be-neath the transparent veil, whose sparkling colors dazzle the eyes, only the initiated were able to fathom the form of the stone enigma. At inter-vals, they overlaid it with more concealing pleats and mysterious plies to

make it more and more impossible for the vision of men to profane it. But centuries have passed over the veil fallen into dust; I will leap across the sacred threshold and dare to look upon the problem without flinching.[15]

Fabriana begins days and nights of meditation in pursuit of belief, love, and forgetfulness. She passes through dreams, delirium, anguish, ecstasy, despair, fevers, splendors, hallucinations, the entire "cortège of thought," and emerges seven years later as if returning from a voyage. She arrives with inestimable secrets and great power. She has learned how to dominate with a hidden strength, how to exploit obscurity and inattention, how to answer questions briefly and ambiguously. She believes she will decide who will be king of the world.

Henry James's "Beast in the Jungle" (1903) is a Sphinx story. May Bartram "was the picture of a serene, exquisite, but impenetrable sphinx, whose head, or indeed all whose person, might have been powdered with silver. She was a sphinx." John Marcher's failure to recognize May as his personal Sphinx costs him his life, lost in waiting.[16]

Love is a ring; it comes back. Late in life the famous philanderer Victor Hugo supposed that if the Sphinx lifted one paw the one-word answer to the riddle of creation could be read: *Amour.* "I know a kiss that never ends," says the Sphinx of Maurice Rostand. Princess Marthe Bibesco chimed that the Sphinx "long kept her secret, but now it has been stolen from her. There can be but one answer to the riddle of life — *it is love.*"[17] The Sphinx is a favorite site for lovers' rendezvous.[18]

Jean-Joseph Goux locates the riddle scene in a line of ancient initiation ceremonies.[19] The test of Oedipus was a test for kingship, but more than that, it was a test for marriage. Before winning his queen Oedipus must understand the mysterious language of women. In *The Diary of a Seducer* (1843) Kierkegaard congratulates modern suitors that there are "no sphinxes that have to be conquered first." Kierkegaard himself wooed, engaged, and broke the engagement, trembling and fearful of love.[20] In N. H. Chamberlain's puritan *Sphinx in Aubrey Parish* (1889) the Sphinx is the sign of the sacrament of marriage, it "is always a life opening out into a mystery unsearchable and to the wise, at least, demands another life to interpret and fulfill the present."[21]

To aid the urbane Oedipus, Balzac wrote a guide. "For you, witty man, the Sphinx deploys its coquetries, it stretches its wings, its folds; it shows you its lion paws, its woman's throat, its equine hips, its intelligence . . . it smiles, it wriggles, it murmurs; it has the expression of a joyful child, a grave matron; above all, it mocks." It speaks of itself lovingly. It says:

I am in love with love.
—I love news.
—I love a thick mane.
—I love a secret.
—I love to reveal one.[22]

The heroine of Barbara Cartland's *Moonlight on the Sphinx* (1984) does not fear Sphinxes. There was a full moon over Giza, "and as the light grew stronger and stronger Octavia could see very clearly the body of the lion, symbol of Kingship, with a woman's head." Here in the heart of romance is the Sphinx, a symbol of the woman king. Octavia "felt as if the Sphinx had a message for her and she only had to listen while her vibrations reached out to meet the vibrations of the strange, beautiful enigma which had stood there for so many thousands of years." Octavia's dangerous adventures conclude at the villa of well-armed Kane Gordon amid passion-

6.2. *Sphinx* by Perino del Vaga (1500–47).

ate kissing. She recalls the first time he kissed her, near the Great Sphinx. Breathless she says: "I did not . . . know that love was like . . . moonlight and . . . fire."

"It is all that and so much more."

"Perhaps . . . that is the real . . . meaning of . . . the Sphinx."

"But of course it is, the mystery, the enigma, and the eternity of love which we all have to find for ourselves."[23]

The Sphinx takes your breath away, one way or another.

6.3. Drawing of the Sphinx by Felicien Rops from Péladan's *La décadence latine*, 1886.

THE SUPREME SPHINX

Émile Zola's twenty-novel portrayal of France's nineteenth century, *Les Rougon-Macquart* (1871–93), was written according to Zola's notions of nature and science. In open competition to it, Joséphin Péladan's twenty-one-volume *La décadence latine: Éthiopée* proposed to depict the decline of all Europe at the end of the nineteenth century and to do so from the higher perspective of spirituality.[24] A fire-breathing Sphinx (drawn by Félicien Rops) recurs as an emblem in the books, bearing the motto *Vives unguibus et morsu* [You will live by claws and biting].[25]

The first volume of his ambitious enterprise, *La vice suprême* (1884), wasted no time introducing a Sphinx. She appears on the first page, alone at night. She is Princess Léonora d'Este and her bestiality is emphasized immediately. She "enjoys the happiness of beasts," she "savors the ecstasy of the brute, she is as happy as an animal," but has escaped the "sexuality of drunken animals." She has always been extraordinary. She learned Greek, Latin, Italian, French, German, and English as a child, as well as heraldry, mathematics, the names of flowers and stars. She could draw, play piano, and as she grew, she grew more beautiful.

She marries because she must, but her husband, Duke Malatesta, is so enflamed by her beauty on their wedding night that his lust forgets all tenderness. He hurts her, he ignores her pain, he destroys her hopes for physical love. The next day she begins her vengeance, tormenting him with voluptuous inaccessibility. When a journalist deprives her of her victim by killing Malatesta in a duel, she arranges for the journalist to be slain. After murder, she reads.

> Her thought turned the pages of the Book of the Sphinx, which rustled like a feeble echo of numerous and muted kisses, and where bookmarks slipped; dried flowers less alive than the lovers who exchanged them; faded letters, survivors of loves born dead, preserving on their vellum the perfume and caress of corsages.
>
> In a lost and distant place a poets' choir sings the hymn of eternal love. Human ears strain for those chorales that seem the same as angels.[26]

Wanting love and despising men who love her, she tantalizes and denies them, one by one. At wit's end, the duc de Quercy declares she is "a monster" and asks her what she would do if she were as miserable as he. She suggests suicide.

When the comte de Kerdanes asks her why she tempts but never satisfies, she answers, "My dear Count, when one is not Oedipus, one does not interrogate the Sphinx."[27]

ETERNAL LOVE

H. Rider Haggard's breezy best seller *She* (1887) pumps the Eternal Feminine through the pen of a scholar, L. Horace Holly, an ugly old misogynist. The She of *She* is unaging Ayesha, She-Who-Must-Be-Obeyed, who dies for seven years before returning reincarnated and immortal again in Haggard's sequel, *Ayesha* (serialized 1904–5). She is now Hesea, priestess of Isis, Mother of All.

Ayesha's temple in the mountains is carved in the shape of an ankh, the Egyptian symbol of life. The temple vault rises higher than any European dome, its sanctuary is lit by twisting columns of fire. An elliptical altar stands at its end, forming the eye of the ankh, and on the altar stands a silver statue of a mother and child, so beautiful it makes a moment eternal. "Hours, years, ages, aeons seemed to flow over us as we stood there before glittering silver curtains that hid the front of the black altar beneath the mystery of the sphinxlike face of the glorious image which was its guardian, clothed with the frozen smile of eternal love and pity."[28]

Through the centuries Ayesha loves Leo, a lion of a man. In his latest body he shoots a lioness, knifes a leopard, and throws a small cat in a fire. Leo is young, handsome, athletic, and has curly golden hair. On his twenty-fifth birthday his foster father, the ugly scholar Holly, presents a surprise: an ancient chest banded with iron. Inside the chest is a magnificent silver casket, its "four legs were formed of Sphinxes, and the dome-shaped cover was also surmounted by a Sphinx." Inside the casket they find an ostracon on which lines are written in many languages and "at the foot of the writing, painted in the same dull red, was the faint outline of a somewhat rude drawing of the head and shoulders of a Sphinx wearing two feathers, symbols of majesty."[29] The red writing convinces Leo that he must travel to Africa, to seek out a certain woman and kill her. An enormous stone on the African shore shaped like the head of a Sphinx will show him where to hunt.

He finds She, Ayesha, who in the course of two novels is loving and ferocious, at home high on a mountain or down in a catacomb. She is loyal to a fault, beautiful, intelligent, bored, miserable, furious, jealous, a Valkyrie calling down winds and bolts of lightning, evanescent, enshrouded, naked as Eve, as moody and ambiguous a woman as ever wore purple prose. She loves Leo above all else, more than her own life, and promises him, "Like that old Sphinx of Egypt shalt thou sit aloft from age to age, and ever shall they cry to thee to solve the riddle of thy greatness that doth not pass away, and ever shalt thou mock them with thy silence!"[30]

She kills him with a kiss.

Reincarnation repeats itself in Marie Corelli's *Ziska: The Problem of a Wicked Soul* (1897). Charmazel was murdered by her lover Araxes when the Sphinx and pyramids were young. She returns to modern Cairo as Princess Ziska. Standing between Sphinxes she greets her guests with her feet strewn with roses and lilies. Her marvelous beauty strikes them spellbound. In due time she lures Armand Gervase, a celebrated French painter, into an underground trap; surprised Gervase discovers he is Araxes reborn. Beneath a pyramid she kills him by taking his breath away.[31]

It is folly to seek a Sphinx and hard to shake one. The tormented poet in Giuseppe Lanciarini's *Sphinx* (1898) asks the Sphinx about love and death. She replies:

> The woman in your heart
> Concentrates the sphinxes.
> He who loves her cannot enter there.
> He who harms her dies.[32]

In Abel Hermant's *Deux Sphinx* (1896) Henri Chalon, a French painter, falls in love with Marika; admiring her he felt the same cold fear he felt before the Sphinx, a fear "of the infinite and of a mystery greater than solitude." Es-siddeeh, the hero of Robert Nichols's *The Smile of the Sphinx* (1920), dies imploring Horemakhet, "O Sphinx, O Life of the Enchantress . . . my true and only love, take if thou wilt my heart and the seal upon it, for thine am I only, thee only would I aid, thee only do I love, thee only would I worship."[33]

SPHINX OF THE SEINE

En route to her own rendezvous with the Oedipus complex, Simone de Beauvoir encounters the Sphinx everywhere: "Man is delighted by this very complexity of woman: a wonderful servant who is capable of dazzling him — and not too expensive. Is she angel or demon? The uncertainty makes her a Sphinx. We may note here that one of the most celebrated brothels of Paris operated under this aegis, the sign of the sphinx. In the grand epoch of femininity, at the time of corsets, Paul Bourget, Henri Bataille, and the French cancan, the theme of the Sphinx was all the rage in plays, poetry, and songs: 'Who are you, whence come you, strange Sphinx?' "[34] And whither? Paris.

In *Mad Love* (1937) radiant André Breton wrote: "The fiancées were shining in the windows lit with a single indiscreet branch, and their voices, alternating with those of the young men below, ardent for them, mingled in the perfumes unloosed in the May night in a restless murmur, vertiginous as the signal, over the silk of the deserts, of the Sphinx approaching."[35]

Breton began *Nadja* (1928) with the obvious Oedipal question, "Who am I?" To find out he repeatedly identifies his beloved Nadja with the Sphinx. On one of their walks they pass the Sphinx-Hôtel on Boulevard Magenta where she first stayed in Paris. Breton believes "I know that in every sense of the word, she takes me for a god, she thinks of me as the sun. I also remember . . . having appeared black and cold to her, like a man struck by lightning, lying at the feet of the Sphinx." Eventually he asks her a question that "sums up all the rest": "Who are you?"

Nadja is a merciful Sphinx. She "spared us, one after the other." She is a Sphinx who does not know she is one. Not knowing who she is, she cannot tell him. "For me it was for all eternity that this succession of terrible or charming enigmas was to come to an end at your feet. . . . you have turned me from enigmas forever."[36]

COURTESAN

Sphinx love comes with Sphinx dangers and diseases. For protection, Sphinx condoms were mass produced in Los Angeles and New York City.[37]

Old Sphinxes practiced the oldest profession. About 228 AD, the Egyptian Greek Athenaeus wrote, "You may call every harlot a Theban Sphinx; they babble not in simple language, but in riddles, of how they like to love and kiss and come together."[38]

The attraction of the Sphinx to notorious women is sharply illustrated by the example of Rhodopis. In the *Histories* of Herodotus she is a renowned prostitute, made so rich by her trade that local folk said she financed the second pyramid. The stories that Murtada ibn al-Afif (1154–1237) found in the old histories of Egypt embellished her afterlife. "They say that the Spirit of the Meridinal Pyramid never appears out of it but in the form of a naked Woman and she has not even her privy parts covered, beautiful as to all other parts, and whereof the behaviour is such, as when she would provoke anyone to love and make him distracted she laughs on him, and presently he approaches her, and she draws him to her, and besots him with love, so that he immediately goes mad and wanders like a Vagabond."[39] Rhodopis subsequently moved from pyramid to pyramid and from pyramid to Sphinx. In 1601 Radzivilius said the head of the Great Sphinx portrayed a famous courtesan, Nitocris or Rhodopis, "buried in the Third Pyramid, and it is her spirit which allegedly haunts the Sphinx."[40]

In 1610 came George Sandys, who claimed to be an honest witness, correcting mistakes of Pliny and providing details previously unreported. The Egyptian Sphinx, he wrote, was in "the forme of an Aethiopian woman . . . an Harlot, having an amiable and alluring face; but withall the tyrannie, and rapacitie of a Lion: exercised over the poore heart-broken, and voluntarily perishing Lover."[41]

In his *Mundus Symbolicus* (1669) Filippo Picinelli describes the Sphinx's monstrous body, emphasizes her femininity, and connects her to chapter 7 of Proverbs, where the son is warned about the harlot, her bed dressed with fine linen of Egypt. A man who follows her goes "as an ox goeth to the slaughter." He cites Saint Ambrose: "Irretivit eum multis sermonibus, & blanditie laborium pertraxit illum" [with her much fair speech she caused him to yield, with the flattering of her lips she forced him. . . . She has cast down many wounded; yea, many strong men have been slain by her].[42]

With a patron's expertise Victor Hugo wrote, "Prostitution is an Isis whose last veil no one has ever lifted. There is a Sphinx in this gloomy odalisque of the awful sultan Everybody. All half-open her dress; no one opens her enigma. It is the All-Naked masked. Horrible specter."[43] Hugo's friend Alfred Stevens painted a Paris Sphinx who examines the viewer while the viewer looks at her features, her hair, her clothes, the fur around her neck.

In *Nightwalker* (1926), Louis Aragon described Paris nights. "Where humans pursue their most promiscuous activities, the inanimate will sometimes reflect their deep-seated motives: our cities are thus populated with unfathomed sphinxes who will not halt the passing dreamer to ask him questions of life and death if he doesn't train on them his wandering inner eye. But should this sage spy them, then, interrogating these faceless monsters, he will discover in them the replica of his own abysses." Later, in the "Alhambra of harlots," Aragon concludes his walk "at the base of these founts, these moral confusions bearing the claw-marks of the lion," where "transfigured like the Virgin, radium-fingered Error reappears, my singing mistress, my pathetic shadow. . . . In this whirlpool where the conscious mind feels like a mere level of the abyss, what has become of the wretched certitude which once seemed so important? I am but a moment in some eternal fall. One's footing lost, it can never be regained."[44] From the Sphinx to the abyss is a short step.

Mona Paiva, best remembered for posing nude on the Acropolis, launched her career in Paris as a dancer for the Comédie-Française. Anaïs Nin remarked in her *Diary* that Henry Miller found a photo of Paiva, "a courtesan of a hundred years ago," on a Paris quay and fell in love with her. When "the demands of the flesh had become too vehement," Miller went to the Sphinx.[45]

In 1930 at 31 Boulevard Edgar de Quinet, next to the Montparnesse cemetery, Marthe Lemestre built the Sphinx, an "American bar," to sell

6.4. *A Parisien Sphinx* by
Alfred Stevens, circa 1870.

6.5. Mona Paiva as Sphinx,
circa 1920.

sex and Champagne. She was greeted as Madame Sphinx, who knew her business, boldly advertised, accommodated private rendezvous, and organized orgies. The Sphinx bar glittered with stars—Marlene Dietrich, Clark Gable, Gary Cooper, Cary Grant; Max Jacob, Jean Cocteau, Colette, and Blaise Cendrars stopped by. It had a secret passageway to the catacombs for clients to sneak in or out.

Madame Sphinx said the Sphinx took its name from the discreet Masonic motto, "See all, hear all, and say nothing." It beat the heat and the competition with Egyptian design and air-conditioning. The Sphinx "livened up the Montparnasse area, which had been dead for years." Merry bands of medical students "would bring heads of cadavers or shinbones to the Sphinx, and pull cut-off hands out of their pockets." It was copied in Algiers, Cairo, and Dakar. Michel Leiris loved a black angel at the Sphinx of Dakar.[46] A young singer told Madame Sphinx "the more men I have in my bed at any one time, the better I sing the next day."[47]

In *The Sphinx in the City* (1991), Elizabeth Wilson adopts a Sphinx persona to prowl London and other great cities. She sees ugly monuments to masculinity: tall, rectilinear corporate towers built up to keep women down and out. City after city ruined by men's mad buildings. Wilson's Sphinx stalks cities, attacks men, and confounds them. It is her nature to snarl at idiots, hating them. "It almost seems as though to be a woman— an individual, not part of a family or kin group—in the city, is to become a prostitute—a public woman."[48] So says a Sphinx.

FATAL LOVE

Murder and mystery novels are natural terrain for Sphinxes. John Dickson Carr's *The Sleeping Sphinx* (1947) involves his portly detective, Dr. Fell, with a desktop Sphinx. Dr. Fell, "the sport of fates and devilry," investigates whether a woman's death was natural, a suicide, or murder. Stirred into the plot are a game between murderers, lies that tell truth, an extraordinary act of chance, "sexual hysteria," and a pair of secret love affairs. Dr. Fell first finds poison, then finds the poisoner in a fortune-teller's shop. On a desk is an inscribed plaque: "Here is a sleeping Sphinx. She is

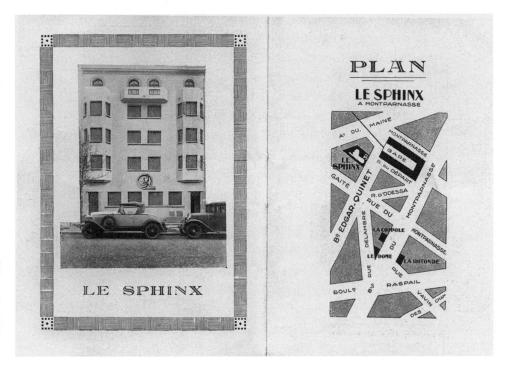

6.6. Ad for the Sphinx brothel in Paris, 1931.

dreaming of the *Parabrahm,* of the universe and the destiny of man. She is part human, as representing the higher principle, and part beast, as representing the lower. She also symbolizes the two selves: the outer self which all the world may see, and the inner self which may be known to few." "The two selves," Dr. Fell thunders, "is the true application."[49] In the midst of a pursuit of a killer, he interprets a symbol like a clue.

Strangely, the sleeping Sphinx also sleeps on Dr. Fell's ring. It overrules the plaque's explanation. The ring, he explains, "was cut for Prince Metternich of Austria. . . . there isn't another like it in existence. . . . It was designed, during the days of Metternich's Black Cabinet, so that the impression of the seal couldn't be copied or forged or replaced once it had been stamped on a soft surface." The plaque on the fortune-teller's desk interprets his ring anew. Before, his sleeping Sphinx was a sign of state secrecy. Now, her invocation of *Parabhram* calls out to "the highest wisdom," "beyond being," "supreme spirit."[50] Even asleep, the Sphinx strides through corridors of power.

The dreaming desktop Sphinx just lay there, as Sphinxes do, then suddenly broke open a murder investigation. What could be clearer? There is a Sphinx: therefore, the woman was killed by her lover.

7 : Mind

On the royal road to Thebes

I had my luck, I met a lovely monster,

And the story's this: I made the monster me.

Stanley Kunitz

The Sphinx couchant is an emblem of dreams. Apollodorus reports that Oedipus learned the answer to the Sphinx's riddle in a premonitory dream. The Sphinx of Giza, wrote Arthur Silva White, "is a dream in stone."[1]

DOCTOR SPHINX

Sigmund Freud (1856–1939) was Freud's most studied case. He published his "fundamental work," *Die Traumdeutung* (*The Interpretation of Dreams*), in the winter between 1899 and 1900. The book disclosed the deep meanings of dreams: who would not want its keys? The dreams he interprets are often his own. His interpretations introduce his personal history and medical problems in a sequence of unhappy episodes, previously repressed but now composed, published, and revised. Peter Gay, one of Freud's most perceptive biographers, writes of the dream book, "It is an autobiography at once candid and canny, as tantalizing in what it omits as in what it discloses."[2]

It discloses a woman killer. To explain one of his dreams, Freud narrates the facts of the case called "Irma's Injection":

> I had on one occasion produced a severe toxic shock state in a woman patient by repeatedly prescribing what was at that time regarded as a harmless remedy (sulphonal). . . . My patient—who succumbed [*erlag*] to the poison—had the same name as my eldest daughter. It had never occurred to me before, but it struck me now almost like an act of retribution on the part of destiny. It was as though the replacement of one person by another was to be continued in another sense: this Mathilde for that Mathilde [Freud's daughter was ill at the time], an eye for an eye, a tooth for a tooth.[3]

Freud introduces the inscrutable unconscious, a creature within a creature, a secret self that happens to be expert in sulphonal and sacrifice. Freud admits he poisoned a woman named Mathilde, but he exculpates himself three times:

1. He consulted another doctor who agreed with the prescription.

2. The drug was not known to be harmful at the time.

3. He "almost" felt the retribution of destiny [*Schicksalsvergeltung*] in prescribing the drug, killing one Mathilde (his patient) for another Mathilde (his eldest daughter).

This is a riddle: if Freud believed at the time that sulphonal was harmless, how could his unconscious know how to poison Mathilde? Was his unconscious a pharmacist ahead of its time? By crediting his unconscious with Mathilde's death, Freud — or a part of him — accepts responsibility for the death, now no accident, but deeply calculated murder. He is Oedipus, the judge who condemned himself.

As Freud spills one secret, he hides others. Is the poor poisoned woman a victim of his wishes or a victim of his fantasy, a delusion of guilt? Is this a confession or alibi? Freud is more Oedipal than he knows; he'd be the first to admit it.[4]

THE DREAM WORK

Freud's research on dream interpretation was extremely thorough, drawing on scholarship from around the world. His book would be the dream book of dream books: vast, deep, and universal.

He risked and rested his reputation on *Die Traumdeutung*. Dreams told the truth that could not be told. Freud informs his readers that he worked hard on the dream book all his life, even when he suffered horrible pains from "a boil the size of an apple" at the base of his scrotum.[5] *Die Traumdeutung* was the longest work of his long career. A second edition of *Die Traumdeutung* appeared in 1908, addressed to the readers of the first. Freud made additions, deletions, and changes in the second edition, and again in the third, and the fourth, until eight editions bulged with new prefaces, replaced examples, appendices, and altered parts. In later editions Freud divided his bibliography in two: works written before 1900 and works written afterward. Freud's teachers appear in the first; his students thereafter. *Die Traumdeutung* divided two centuries like a mountain range, its snowy peaks poking the sky, its abysses too deep for sunlight.

The Oedipus complex was still in its infancy when Freud tucked it into *Die Traumdeutung.* Between 1896 and 1897 Freud found, described, and named it. The elation of the discovery quickly fled. Freud stood where Oedipus had stood, between the chasm and rocks at the Sphinx's feet.

A greater discovery followed, by one account the "greatest" of his discoveries: the Oedipus complex was not rare or unusual, it was universal.[6] You have it, Hegel's sons had it, Freud and Moses had it. Freud famously wrote, "The Greek legend seizes upon a compulsion which everyone recognizes because he senses its existence within himself."[7] The universality of the Oedipus complex made Freud's work urgent everywhere, a dream come terribly true.

Freud took his Oedipus from Sophocles, the Oedipus who learns to his surprise that he killed his father and fathered four children with his mother. The Oedipus complex connects two taboos: a son's lust for mother and his urge for parricide, a complex that is natural, inescapable, and worldwide. It does its work in the dark — in dreams and in the cravings of the invisible tyrant, the unconscious.

Little by little the Oedipal story came out. Neither infant Oedipus with his swollen foot, nor fetal Oedipus doomed at birth, nor Oedipus the prince of a boy, made much of an impression on the Oedipus myth. The myth is for adults only: who but they can comprehend Oedipus the young man and Oedipus the old? Oedipus by himself cannot be Oedipus, and not all at once.

Oedipus needs the Sphinx. Without the Sphinx Oedipus would be an ordinary prince who killed his father the king. To be Oedipus, the Oedipus of legend, prince of Corinth and king of Thebes, to be the hero Oedipus, Oedipus must climb to the Sphinx. No Sphinx, no Oedipus. No way around it.

Here she is, eye to eye: the Sphinx and her split personality, her cat eyes like canyons.

Freud scarcely mentions the Sphinx in *The Interpretation of Dreams.*[8] Writing to Carl Jung, April 14 1907, Freud went further: "the original Oedipus was himself a case of obsessional neurosis — the riddle of the Sphinx."[9] He had Oedipus figured out: "Oedipus . . . means swollen foot, i.e., erected penis."[10] He had the riddle figured out: "The riddle of the Sphinx—that is, the question of where babies come from."[11] And where did Freud's Sphinx come from? The reproduction of a reproduction: one of Freud's earliest biographers recounted: "At one time, when Freud had brought an analysis to a successful conclusion, he used to show the patient an engraving after a painting by Ingres, 'Oedipus solves the riddle of the Sphinx.' "[12]

Sir James Frazer and Carl Jung described familial myths and common fertility ceremonies all around the world. They saw phalluses spring up from Fiji to Vienna. Myths are incredibly true, myths unite the masses, they are beliefs beyond belief and remnants of the archaic memory of ancestral nomads and their aching feet. Myths are older than history; they abound with prohibitions; they terrorize; they praise secret powers, hide in shadows, and in certain cases kill and maim. Myths are old as pain. Laistner and Róheim place the riddle scene at the origin of mythology.[13]

Freud to Jung, September 1, 1911: "The Oedipus complex is at the root of religious feeling." He explained, "Religion would thus be the obsessional neurosis of humanity; like the obsessional neuroses of children, it arose out of the Oedipus complex, out of the relation to the father."[14]

TRANSFERENCE

Freud was called Oedipus, victor over the Sphinx. Years passed and he was called a Sphinx.[15] Involution, metamorphosis, promotion.

Oedipus's father also had an Oedipus complex, and his father before him. Oedipus's complex hadn't been discovered when Oedipus suffered from it, but it was whirring like an engine in his encounter with the Sphinx. He went to the Sphinx's riddle willingly and never got past it. Instead, it got into him, became an obsession. It was destined from the moment he was born, and grew with him as he grew.

Freud knew Oedipus well enough to be wary of following in his footsteps, but he could not stop himself.

SPHINXUALITY

Life hangs lighter than a feather of the Sphinx. Her riddle comes with teeth the size of chisels, claws that cut like knives, penetrating eyes, and muscles rippling over her ribcage. Behold the Sphinx, the Slayer.

Psychoanalyst Theodor Reik researched the Sphinx more than Freud did. Reik's 1920 essay, "Oedipus und die Sphinx," summarizes the conclusions of nineteenth-century German scholars and Reik's European contemporaries. He recognized that there are many kinds of Sphinx other than the Sphinx of the Oedipus tale. Men have the Oedipus complex in common; the Sphinx complicates and evades. "No complete reconstruction of the original version is practicable."[16]

Reik accepts Carl Robert's phases of the Sphinx:

1. Originally there was no Sphinx in the Oedipus story. Parricide and incest were there, but Phix wasn't.

2. Phix appeared later, a man-eating monster whom Oedipus killed, as Hercules killed the Nemean lion, her brother. (Like Oedipus, Hercules was born in Thebes.) Thanks to the Sphinx, Oedipus's reputation improved.

3. Instead of a contest of strength, speed, and weaponry the scene became nakedly intellectual: Phix told a riddle and the stage is set for Sophocles. The riddle is a relatively recent addition to ancient underlying layers of the myth: the death of the Sphinx, the incest, the murder of Oedipus's father, the abandoned child.

The renovation of the Sphinx from Egypt to Greece is singular. In Egypt Sphinxes could be male or female; in the Roman Empire Sphinxes were carved with caesars' faces on them; in Egypt and Rome Sphinxes were totemic, solar, and powerful. But in Greece, with rare exceptions, Sphinxes were female and mortuary. A thoroughly feminized Sphinx entered the Oedipus myth and stayed there through the centuries. The Greek Sphinx with her breasts and song is the Sphinx of modern stories. Reik asks why.

Why did Sphinxes cease to be two sexes and become only one? "The synthesis of the Sphinx, with her male and female components, would thus reflect an unconscious hostility to the father god, an impulse of repudiation which directs the heterosexual libidinal tendencies against the religion based on homosexual associations. We should compare this ag-

gressive trend with a repression which set in during the period of late antiquity, and a modified judgment of homosexual practices. We still see
the last remains in the derision of homosexuality in Greek and Roman
satyrists."[17]

As years went by the founders of psychoanalysis placed the Sphinx and
her riddle farther back in prehistory and placed the riddle scene farther
back in the life cycle. Freud put the Sphinx at the first stirrings of the
libido. Later Melanie Klein wrote that the Sphinx appears in infancy when
the mother ceases to breastfeed. For Otto Rank the Sphinx stood at the
trauma of birth.[18]

MOTHER OF TERROR

As Abu-Hol Horemakhet is the "Father of Terror." Jung has another
idea: "The Sphinx is a semi-theriomorphic representation of the mother-
imago, or rather of the Terrible Mother." Claude Lévi-Strauss calls her
"the phallic mother," kin to the Hopi "Mother of the Animals," who rapes
young hunters.[19] Jung concluded that "the riddle was, in fact, the trap
which the Sphinx laid for the unwary wanderer. Overestimating his intellect in a typically masculine way, Oedipus walked right into it, and all
unknowingly committed the crime of incest. The riddle of the Sphinx was
herself—the terrible mother-imago, which Oedipus would not take as a
warning."[20]

F. C. S. Schiller's *Riddles of the Sphinx* (1891) places the Sphinx at the
birth canal, crushing brains: "there is a physical limit to the size of the
head of an infant which can be born. It would follow from this that since
there is almost certainly a relation between intellect and the size of the
brain, the bulk of our geniuses even now perish in their birth."[21]

Rank also placed the Sphinx at parturition.

> The Oedipus saga is certainly a duplicate of the Sphinx episode, which
> means psychologically that it is the repetition of the primal trauma at the
> sexual stage (Oedipus complex), whereas the Sphinx represents the pri-
> mal trauma itself. . . . The Sphinx, conforming to its character as stran-
> gler, represents not only in its latent content the wish to return into the
> mother, as the danger of being swallowed, but it also represents in its

manifest form parturition itself and the struggle against it, in that the upper human body grows out of the animal-like (maternal) lower body without finally being able to free itself from it. This is the riddle of the Sphinx.[22]

In *The Universal Design of the Oedipus Complex* (1950) Francis Mott sees the Sphinx from the perspective of the newborn: "The Sphinx represents the female configuration which is at first associated with the mother's womb. . . . The Sphinx is the uterine female lover who at birth becomes the devouring gut."[23] The Sphinx is a mother, the mother of every child.

In a 1499 illustration for Dante's *Purgatory,* a mother Sphinx suckles her child. The Sphinx of Rose Terry Cooke was a Mother of Terror who bore Nero, Calvin, Elizabeth I, Cromwell, soldiers, thugs, persecutors. It was the Sphinx's good fortune to be unaware of the evil her children did. "Happy Sphinx, to be left even of that dull existence! Blessedly unconscious of that granted desire! . . . the mysterious symbol of a secret yearning and a vain desire!"[24]

Rank thinks the Sphinx does double duty: as "homosexual fixation" and as mother. "In our sense, then, the Sphinx would only be a doubling of the mother. According to [Bernhard] Schmidt [in *Griechische Märchen, Sagen, und Volkslieder,* 1877], a modern Greek riddle portrays Jocasta and the Sphinx as one person; Schmidt considers this version to be more original, since in all similar versions it is the wooed queen herself who asks the riddle." "The Sphinx and the mother originally coincided."[25]

SPHINX AS SISTER

The Sphinx's classical pedigree was everywhere a scandal of incest. The old Greek Sphinx was a child born of Orthus's incest with Echidna, his mother.[26] Pausanias recounts a version of the Sphinx story in which she, like Oedipus, is a child of Laius, who killed her brothers one by one until Oedipus arrived to claim the throne of Thebes.[27]

Psychoanalysts perceived in the Oedipus story both an expression of the incest taboo and a suppression of it, a tale of a truth so frightening that it had to be covered with stacks of distraction and detail. Even now.

In *Man and His Symbols,* his coffee-table proof of collective conscious-

phinx

ness, Carl Jung reproduced Ingres's "Oedipus and the Sphinx" with a brief explanatory caption identifying Phix as a "negative anima" that led to male stress on intellectualism. Elsewhere Jung described the motherly Sphinx as "lovely and attractive," but her lower body, "the horrible animal half" made her monstrous; all in all she was a sharp warning against incest, the very crime that Oedipus was about to commit. "The riddle of the Sphinx was *herself*," but Oedipus did not decipher it.[28]

In 1914 Freud rebuked Jung and his symbols. Freud mocked Jung's version of Freud: "the Oedipus complex has a merely 'symbolic' meaning: the mother in it means the unattainable, which must be renounced in the interests of civilization; the father who is killed in the Oedipus myth is the 'inner' father."[29] Jung analyzed a patient's latest fantasy. Freud dug at the roots.

OEDIPUS AS SPHINX

A few psychoanalysts looked past the riddle and Oedipus to consider Phix's psyche and physique. One was Marie Delcourt, whose work underlies the Sphinx of Claude Lévi-Strauss. Delcourt recognizes the Sphinx's connections to the earth and her sexual aggressivity. In her analysis of the sedimented significance of the Sphinx legend, she suggests that the ancient monster raped boys. Delcourt notes that amid the five mythemes bundled in the Oedipus story—killing the old king, climbing the mountain, solving the riddle, defeating the monster, and marrying the royal bride—the Sphinx has the central role. It is the Sphinx who confers the chance to obtain power. "She alone is presented as having assured the ascension of the hero."[30]

The first audiences of Sophocles and Seneca considered incest a secondary crime. Oedipus had done worse: killed his father, his father the king, becoming at once a prototype of parricide, assassin, and fool of fate. His crimes, accidental and unintended, were still crimes, very great ones. What of his encounter with the Sphinx? Was it, too, an accidental crime?

SITUATIONS

Any Freudian knows what to make of a tall column. At the temples to Apollo in Aegina, Delphi, and throughout the Hellenistic world, Sphinxes sat upon columns. One sits on a column overlooking the restaurant of the Metropolitan Museum of Art.[31] It grins like a cat after dinner.

To commemorate Freud's fiftieth birthday in 1906 friends gave him a medallion with his profile on one side, Oedipus and the Sphinx on the other. The inscription read:

ΟΣ ΤΑ KLEIN
ΑΙΝΙΜΑΤ 'ΗΙΔΕΙ
ΚΑΙ ΚΡΑΤΙΣΤΟΣ 'ΗΝ ΑΝΗΡ
[Who knew the famous riddle and was a mighty man].[32]

There is slip of the alphabet in the first line: a Latin "L" appears instead of a Greek lambda in *KLEIN*, transforming the Greek word *κλειν*, "famous," into the German *klein* [little], and accidentally advertising Melanie Klein, whose work on aggression surpassed Freud's own.

In 1908 Freud famously identified money (*Geld*) with feces.[33] In 1986 Freud's face appeared on the Austrian fifty-schilling banknote.[34] A Sphinx in profile stares past him. Her line of sight cuts across his throat.

7.1. Freud's commemorative medal, 1906.

7.2. Freud on Austrian banknote, 1986.

INNER SPHINX

In the admonitory avalanche that concludes *Walden* Thoreau advises, "If you would learn to speak all tongues and conform to the customs of all nations, if you would travel farther than all travellers, be naturalized in all climes, and cause the Sphinx to dash her head against a stone, even obey the precept of the old philosopher, and Explore thyself." Thoreau's years in the woods deepened his restlessness and his travels on rivers and roads brought him back to the inscription of the Delphic Oracle, the same oracle Oedipus consulted.[35]

Rollo May expatiated: "The man (Oedipus) who guesses the Sphinx' riddle is he who takes the Sphinx back to its rightful place within himself. . . . who understands that he has within himself both good and evil, who understands the Sphinx within."[36]

This, too, has its antitype. Like Oedipus, darling Narcissus was a descendent of Cadmus, the dragon-slayer. Narcissus's mother, Liriopë, asked the seer Tiresias if her baby would live long. "Only," he said, "if he shall fail to know himself."[37]

The blind librarian of labyrinths Jorge Luis Borges saw the Sphinx in the mirror:

Fourfooted at dawn, erect in the day
and with three feet wandering through the vain
compass of the evening, thus appeared
the eternal Sphinx to her changeable brother,
the man, and with the evening a man came
who deciphered terrified in the mirror
of the monstrous image, the reflection
of his descent and his destiny.
We are Oedipus and of an eternal
large and triple beast we are, all
that we will be and that we have been.

Borges looks but not too long.

It would annihilate us to see the enormous
form of our being; mercifully
God gave us succession and forgetfulness.[38]

Borges is no Apollonian to thank God that we cannot see what we are, to think we can turn away from whatever we see in ourselves that frightens us, and to suppose we can forget about it. Borges indulges a little wishful thinking. The inner Oedipus will wish otherwise and look for the inner Sphinx. Sphinxes guard the narrow abyss that divides narcissism and introspection, naughty infatuated ego on one side, science and sun worship on the other. To see the Sphinx in a looking glass, a diary, or photo album, and to see yourself in the Sphinx, or the Sphinx in you, surprises self-admiration with a shock. Oedipus is the hero of climb and cling: to look at himself he dares to looks back. Oedipus limped up to that sharp-as-glass precipice; ready to risk everything, he accepted the riddle. Young when he met the Sphinx, Oedipus saw the tragedy of the meeting much later, in middle age, when at last he discovered his own history; only then did he know who he was when he saw himself, and he could not bear the sight. The horror of self-scrutiny, the realization of a fatal mistake reached by stretching too far, looking too far over the edge, is very like the start of a fall—breathless, sudden, irreversible.

Unamuno's play *La Esfinge* (The Sphinx) plays a game of find the Sphinx: no Sphinx appears in the cast, no one mentions a Sphinx. The Sphinx is the play itself, its hero, or its most studied scene, when Ángel, a rebel, talks to a mirror. "Poor thing! You wanted to pulsate with everything: to heave with the entire universe; to receive and restore your eternal energy, which comes from infinite worlds and returns to them. And with so much desire to pour yourself out, you throttle me . . . , yes . . . , you throttle me!"[39] *La Esfinge* combines familiar Sphinx themes: frustrated revolt, the horror of self-discovery, an angel, death by choking.

Benjamin Disraeli, "the Primrose Sphinx," advised, "One should never think of death. One should think of life. That is real piety." In his *Tragic Sense of Life,* Unamuno disagreed. He looked at the Sphinx on the eve of the First World War and saw death eye to eye: "Consider our mortal destiny without flinching. . . . fasten our gaze upon the gaze of the Sphinx."[40]

A mirror suffices.

Calling up the riddle scene, Roy Fuller remarks that Oedipus "Went on to symbolize mankind's disgrace," and men still encounter the Sphinx and her handiwork.

> Down corridors of night an awful thing
> Brushes against us softly like a wing.
> Our hands that reach across the bed for her
> We love meet unexpected, frightening fur.
> And looking in the glass we find at last
> The claw-made lacerations of the past.[41]

THE SPHINX TYPE

Wilfred Bion, a student of Melanie Klein (thus a student of Freud's student) observed that a psychoanalyst posing questions took on the fearful posture of the Sphinx, and in group therapy the group itself seemed a Sphinx, "the enigmatic brooding, and questioning Sphinx from whom disaster emanates," to each of its members. Carole Sturdy, pursuing Bion's study of group psychology, described a Sphinx type, who mysteriously assumes the role of authority. They are "far too dangerous" to question.

They would respond ferociously and could frighten and even destroy groups they join.[42]

A common cause of Sphinx deaths at the turn of the twentieth century was neurasthenia, a vague all-purpose diagnosis for weak nerves, hypersensitivity, susceptibility to addictions, and split personality. Trouble between the mind and body infuses Sphinx fiction. Beoni the Sphinx becomes a great surgeon, but dies of shock when repressed memories overtake him. Research on frustrated sex drives Dr. Crippen to his cruelties in *Die Sphinx und der Sadist.*[43]

The Sphinx Agnes Jersome is an angelic charity worker, "the physical perfection of a beautiful woman," and also Lais, a lascivious Parisian courtesan. As she expires from the strain of her double life she pleads with her beloved to campaign for eugenics, to prevent people like her from having children, to prevent people like her from being born. As Agnes, a sacrificial lamb, she dies to kill Lais, the alter ego she cannot control.[44]

The suicidal heroine of David Lindsay's supernatural *Sphinx* (1923) is Lore, a composer, whose works include a piano piece entitled "Sphinx." Lore's man-troubles draw in Nicholas, inventor of a dream-recording machine, who believes dreams forecast the future. Nicholas worries about his machine because it might work. If it does, it might reveal what would better remain unknown: dreams "make us act, and we may misinterpret them. That's what I understand by the riddles of the Sphinx."[45]

Ambiguous as dreams and deceptive as introspection, flouting analysis and defying art, Sphinxes lurk, patient, cunning, and cutthroat.

8 : Symbol of Symbols

> There is no such thing as an insignificant symbol. By giving meaning to the sign I do not transcend the symbol but complete it.
>
> **Wittgenstein**

That Hegel selected the Sphinx as his symbol of symbols settled nothing. The symbol of symbols has competition. There are symbols of symbols in music, chemistry, poetry, and physics. In search of divine knowledge, Aristotle stopped to wonder about numbers and geometry—powerful invisible rulers, hidden within nature and shining on it. Zero is a potent symbol of symbols, creating something from nothing, capable of infinite replication.

In *Riddles of the Sphinx* (1891) F. C. S. Schiller asserted that "the Crucifixion is the greatest and divinest of all symbols," a symbol that left the Sphinx behind.[1] But Hegel was Christian, too, and knew much more about symbols.[2] Moses knew that to choose a symbol of symbols for worship is idolatry. To think that the highest of symbols must be the symbol of symbols mistakes a peak for a mountain; the height of arrogance is a fraction of a fraction of what a symbol of symbols symbolizes.

The symbol of symbols is a symbol of catalogs: strings of things to want and wish for. Sphinx symbolism starts with its body parts, swells with their assembly, extends to events and situations, traditions, dissensions, and frays.[3] Socrates says, "I think that sort of thing is the work of people who care nothing for truth, but only for the shape of their mouths; so they keep adding to the original words until finally no human being can understand what in the world the word means. So the *Sphinx,* for instance, is called *Sphinx,* instead of *Phix,* and there are many other examples." Hermogenes replies, "Yes, that is true, Socrates."[4]

The Sphinx won Hegel's favor for historical reasons: he saw history struggling forward in the body of the Sphinx. Wagner echoed him: "the human visage of the Sphinx is in the act of striving outward from the animal body."[5] Hegel and Wagner thought a Sphinx strives to separate, to cease to be a Sphinx. Instead, it strove to be more and more a Sphinx, till there was little it was not.

THE X OF X

The "symbol of symbols" is a specimen of a species, the "*x* of *x*." The figure reposes in lofty places:

   — "*manaso mano . . . vāco ha vācam*" [mind of mind . . . speech of speech] — *Kena Upanishad* 1.2

   — "*Elohey Elohim*" [God of Gods] — Deuteronomy 10:17

   — "*Tahāfut al-Tahāfut*" [Incoherence of Incoherence] — Averroës

   — "*Zeichen der Zeichen*" [sign of signs] — Hegel again, here translating Aristotle.[6]

The Pentateuch, Psalms, and John Milton's Jesus assert a "Heaven of Heavens." "Reason," Goethe testified, "is the art of arts." The Sphinx, said Edgar Cayce, is the "Mystery of Mysteries."[7]

   The master rhetoricians of Group μ explore "classes of classes," "deviations of deviations," and the "signification of signification."[8] The trope runs like a needle through European philosophy: Nietzsche's "danger of dangers," Husserl's "principle of principles," Levinas's "temptation of temptation."[9] Jacques Derrida confronts the problems of "of" better than any other writer I've read.[10] Placed between a pair of *x*'s, an "of" is a multipurpose preposition. The holy of holies has Sphinxes.

   That soft and tiny "of" stands between its *x*'s like the pivot of a tilting scale: though each *x* looks like the other, one rises, one falls, because of "of." "Of" dissolves the identity of *x*, no matter what *x* is. The book of books surpasses all others. The god of gods commands all of all. An "*x* of *x*" puts "of" between crosses and under guard. Symbols of symbols annex other symbols and remake them, sometimes chewing them up, licking them clean, and spitting them out. Of lion, of eagle, of angel, of sun, on and on the ofs and *x*'s of the Sphinx increase.

   Often "of" asserts rank: "Lord of lords" and "King of kings" are titles of pharaohs. According to the *Mishna*, the Holy One is "The King of kings of kings."[11] The *Song of Songs* of Solomon sang in a land of Sphinxes.

   Of course "of" signifies possession: the servant of the servant.

   Or it signifies sequence: a son of a son, a promise of a promise, a prophet of a prophet.

"Of" can be *antanaklastic:* writing of writing, the lesson of the lesson.[12]

It can organize the cosmos in circles of circles, cycles of cycles, galaxies of galaxies.

It renders judgment: the myth of myth,[13] the best of the best.

It is quintessent: truth of truth, heart of hearts.

An "*x* of *x*" can be two of these, or three, or an ensemble, tumbling like kittens. The "death of death" can be (1) the death of no return; or (2) the last death; or (3) the worst death; or (4) a bright Sunday morning hope for immortality; and thus (5) another contradiction; (6) spilled ink; and (7) a short story. Unamuno met a man who said that if he discovered he had little time to live he'd spend it writing a book. "Vanity of vanities!" Unamuno exclaimed in a quotation of a quotation.[14]

The "*x* of *x*" can make sense out of nothing. Franz Kafka felt that he was "the pawn of a pawn, a piece which doesn't even exist, which isn't even in the game."[15]

Symbol of symbols, Sphinx of Sphinxes: in either case the "of" is as promiscuous as a Sphinx, something of a Sphinx itself: Sphinx sphinx Sphinx. Sphinx phonetics mixes silence and hisses. Sphinx grammar keeps tenses in suspense and loves the interrogative.

The Sphinx's aggregated symbols make it fabulously versatile. The Sphinx in Carl Hauptmann's *Uralte Sphinx* — his Sphinx primeval — transforms as he speaks. In 1915 Hauptmann told the Freie Studentenschaft of Berlin that World War I, just begun, was a Sphinx, an alluring man-killer, multiplied. Hauptmann gives a standard description: "The Theban Sphinx had the allure of a virgin with a woman's tender breasts and a woman's loving heart. But at the same time she was a terrible beast of prey. In the same body intractable enmity and human love inseparably entwine."[16]

Soon Hauptmann abruptly admits, "The Sphinx is myself!"[17] an identification also claimed by De Quincey, Emerson, Unamuno, and Borges. The Sphinx that was World War I is briefly Herr Hauptmann, a writer at wit's end. Hauptmann's Sphinx then changes again, as if Hauptmann forgets himself:

No other symbol made by human imagination has embodied so completely and clearly the deepest source of all human evil, as the symbol of the Sphinx.

Through all the ages of humanity man looms menacingly. The age-old riddle-creature with the woman's loving heart and the hard paws and cruel talons of a raptor. From the mouth of the world's everlasting nightmare, the first and fundamental question comes, a question that eats at our hearts again, more vehemently than ever, and chokes us: Where have you come from? Where are you going? What do you mean?[18]

This is familiar territory, but not for long. Hauptmann then tells the students that the "old image of the Sphinx, Life, rapes us inside and out."[19] Raped not by a Sphinx, but by the image of one. The Sphinx alters whenever Hauptmann touches it: war, himself, a rapist, a beast that eats his heart, a source of all evil, and Life. Sphinx sphinx Sphinx.

Hauptmann, describing his Sphinx in a babble of panic, is a victim of circumstances. What but tales and nonsense could he say to young men when old men want war? Besides, his multipurpose Sphinx is a recognizable descendent of other Sphinxes.

When a symbol can mean so many things, does it begin to be meaningless? Certainly not: a symbol of symbols is immense, it is not more and more nothing. The Sphinx is the symbol of symbols in several assemblies. It is itself a lion, eagle, and woman. A Sphinx head and Sphinx body, bonded like schizophrenia, symbolize inseparable distinctions, like teacher and student, order and chaos, killer and victim. Hauptmann's Sphinx is all his own, as Hugo's is his and Cleopatra's is hers, and all of theirs are the Sphinx's, too. Add to the Sphinx its explanations and revivals, its capacity to collect and convey other symbols, its riddles and riddle scenes, and its arts, and still there's more. The Sphinx exceeds its sum of symbols; it is a speedy vehicle from one to another. Hauptmann's Sphinx leaps all over the place, as fit Sphinxes do. It is more than a load of meanings and more than all the answers in the world: it stands beside questions that have no answer yet. A Sphinx contracts and expands with memory and attention span. Nothing else limits what a symbol of symbols can symbolize. It ciphers A to Z.

AFRICA

Horemakhet's African outlook, features, and posture rest firmly on a continent that defies mere history. His face is an African face. George Sandys supposed that the Sphinx of Giza was in the form of "an Aethiopian woman." In 1850 Flaubert wrote that Horemakhet's protruding ears made its head look "comme un nègre." An American traveler observed in 1875 that the Sphinx has "the thick lips and high cheek bones of the Nubian, which was the type of beauty to the ancient Egyptians."[20] Sheldon Peck, an orthodontist, looked at the Sphinx's jaws and detected bimaxillary prognathism, a condition "more frequently found in people of African ancestry than in those from Asian or Indo-European stock."[21]

"Africa, Africa," muses W. A. Prestre, as if it were listening. "The claws of a lion, the talons of an eagle, the coils of a boa are less cruel than you. The question of the executioner is more compassionate than your enigma of the Sphinx."[22] Steinhardt's *Schwarze Sphinx* (1927) is all about Africa.[23]

W. E. B. Du Bois asks the "Soul of White Folk" a plain question: "Is the world wide enough for two colors, for many little shinings of the sun?" He answers in a poem, "The Riddle of the Sphinx," which begins with an African woman:

8.1. Cover of Steinhardt's
Schwarze Sphinx, 1927.

Dark daughter of the lotus leaves that watch the Southern Sea!
Wan spirit of a prisoned soul a-panting to be free!
The muttered music of thy streams, the whisper of the deep,
Have kissed each other in God's name and kissed a world to sleep.

The slumber must end, broken by the cries of enslaved women. To wake the world's soul Du Bois lists the crimes of "The white world's vermin and filth," scum, spoilers, drunkards, breeders of bastards, shameless, greedy, lustful liars.

I hate them, Oh!
I hate them well,
I hate them, Christ!
As I hate hell!
If I were God,
I'd sound their knell
This day!
Who raised the fools to their glory,
But black men of Egypt and Ind?

After hatred comes prophecy:

they that raised the boasters
Shall drag them down again, —
Down with the theft of their thieving
And murder and mocking of men;
Down with their barter of women
And laying and lying of creeds;
Down with their cheating of childhood
And drunken orgies of war.[24]

Six years later Comte Renaud de Briey published *Le Sphinx noir: Essai sur les problèmes de colonisation africaine.* The comte arrived in Africa on January 19, 1917, then traveled into the Congo, seeing World War I from "a new world, a sphinx who has mysteries and perhaps would devour those who cannot decipher them." Briey saw problems: white colonists lived like oriental potentates, they built wonderful tramways but would not let the indigenous blacks use them, they used government to impose racial segregation. He visited colonies of Belgium, France, England, and Germany, finding everywhere insatiable Europeans with widely varying systems of administration.

Briey gives grisly examples of colonial exploitation, but with a foregone purpose: to improve, not remove, colonial administration of the Sphinx. His answer? Imitate the British: train and educate the native populations so that competent natives who care about their land and people do the administrative work, rather than rely on inept and dishonest European bullies, sloths, and dullards. Blacks were as intelligent as whites, but lacked character, he wrote. European education would fix that. Briey emphasized that it was possible that an entire district could be run *"without a single white agent,"* but also with rigorous discipline, frequent inspections, and with prominent portraits of the royal family displayed everywhere. Briey informs France that the changes must be made soon, before the Congo succumbs to Anglo-Saxon missionaries or German arms.[25]

Du Bois wrote:

> One cannot, to be sure, demand of whole nations exceptional moral foresight and heroism; but a certain hard common-sense in facing the complicated phenomena of political life must be expected in every progressive people. In some respects we as a nation seem to lack this; we have the somewhat inchoate idea that we are not destined to be harassed with great social questions, and that even if we are, and fail to answer them, the fault is with the question and not with us. Consequently we often congratulate ourselves more on getting rid of a problem than on solving it. Such an attitude is dangerous; we have and shall have, as other peoples have had, critical, momentous, and pressing questions to answer. The riddle of the Sphinx may be postponed, it may be evasively answered now; sometime it must be fully answered.[26]

On October 16, 1995, Louis Farrakhan, minister of the Nation of Islam, led a Million Man March in Washington DC. From the Capitol steps he described the Sphinx of Giza as a symbol of racial violence. "White supremacy caused Napoleon to blow the nose off the Sphinx because it reminded him too much of the black man's majesty."[27]

ANGUISH

Miguel de Unamuno's *Tragic Sense of Life* (1913) asked: "If we all die utterly, wherefore does everything exist? Wherefore? It is the Wherefore of the Sphinx; it is the Wherefore that corrodes the marrow of the soul; it is the begetter of that anguish which gives us the love of hope." [28]

ANXIETY

Otto Rank believed "the feelings of anxiety produced in the process of repression are placed in the figure of the Sphinx." He agrees with Ludwig Laistner that her riddles "have their source in anxiety-filled nightmares of interrogation." [29]

ATHEISM

Madame Teste complained that her husband was impenetrable. "I don't believe anyone can be as adamant as he is. He breaks your spirit with a word, and I feel like a flawed vase rejected by the potter. He is stern as an angel. . . . He does not know his own strength." She tells her priest that Monsieur Teste is a mystic without God.

"Brilliant nonsense," says the priest, "Godless mystic! . . . Why not a Hippogryph, a Centaur!"

She responds, "Why not a Sphinx?" [30]

BOREDOM

The Sphinx is the symbol of the spectator, often a bored one. Gautier imagined "the sadness of a Sphinx weary of eternally gazing upon the desert, and unable to detach herself from the granite pedestal upon which she has sharpened her claws for twenty centuries." In Flaubert's *L'éducation sentimentale* (1869) a consumptive woman dressed as a Sphinx spits her own blood and says, "If it wasn't this, it would be something else. Life isn't much fun." [31]

CAPITALISM

"The revolt of the workers and the spontaneous organization of human solidarity through the free but involuntary and inevitable [!] federation of all working-class groups into the Council of Action! This, then, is the answer to the enigma which the Capitalist Sphinx forces us to-day to solve, threatening to devour us if we do not solve it"—Michael Bakunin, 1867.[32]

CHANCE

In 1932 the Caille Company produced the "Silent Sphinx," a slot machine. In the 1990s Sphinx tokens were in use in casinos throughout the United States—Deadwood, Laughlin, Reno—and are still in play at the Luxor in Las Vegas. A great Sphinx lies atop the Luxor's underground parking lot.

8.2. The Sphinx as one of the Seven Wonders of the World on a Grand Casino 2-dollar token, 1994.

CONSOLATION

American George Shepard Burleigh (1821–1903) invited his readers to embrace the Sphinx:

> Read thy life's Riddle, what thou art.
> The great tide wafts thee with eternal flow
> And young-eyed Beauty like the boundless air
> Shall fold thee sweetly till thy last sun sinks,
> And fresh Life still shall be thy ever-smiling Sphinx.[33]

CONTRARIES

Few symbols rival the Sphinx for crisscrossedness. It laps up contradictions. In his *Ziffern der Sphinx* [Ciphers of the Sphinx], Reverend Alois Gügler proceeds through the *Gegensatz des Gegensatz,* the opposite of the opposite. Speaking for a society enamored of symbols, Freemason Albert Pike wrote, "To reconcile the moral law, human responsibility, free-will, with the absolute power of God; and the existence of evil with His absolute wisdom, and goodness, and mercy,—these are the great enigmas of the Sphynx." Pike described an insignia in the Kabala that portrayed two Sphinxes "pulling contrary ways" and a Mithraic "armed Sphinx [that] represents the law of the Mystery, which keeps watch at the door of initiation, to repulse the Profane."[34]

Freemasonry preserves the distinction between a Sphinx as a supersymbol and Horemakhet as a special case. A motto of the Freemasons—"Audi, Vidi, Tace" [Listen, See, Be Silent]—could be a Sphinx's own.

CURSE

Sometime around 1628 Descartes wrote most of his *Rules for the Direction of the Mind,* a book of charming symmetry: he planned thirty-six rules in three volumes, twelve rules in each. Rule 13 dismissed the riddle of the Sphinx as "a problem of words," hardly worth a philosopher's time.[35] Before the rules were completed he died.

DOGMA

The Sphinx is the emblem of stubborn thinking. "All the great single-word answers to the world's riddle, such as God, the One, Reason, Law, Spirit, Matter, Nature, Polarity, the Dialectic Process, the Idea, the Self, the Over-soul, draw the admiration that men have lavished upon them from this oracular rôle. By amateurs in philosophy and professionals alike, the universe is presented as a queer sort of petrified sphinx whose appeal to men consists in a monotonous challenge to his divining powers. *The* Truth! What a perfect idol of the rationalistic mind!" — William James, 1907.[36]

DOUBT

In a scrap entitled "Doute" [Doubt], Victor Hugo apportioned parts: "Immense wings are given to the eagle; sharp eyes to the lynx; / To Man, the formidable face-off with the Sphinx." Like wings and keen eyes, doubt is a gift of nature; it is ours alone, and full of trouble. In his dreams Éduoard Schuré saw an Egyptian sleeping. "Truth appeared to him in the form of a sphinx. The sphinx said to him, 'I am Doubt!' And the winged beast, with its head of an impassive woman and its lion's paw, carried him away to tear him apart in the burning desert sand."[37]

EGYPT

Horemakhet emblazons stamps, coins, plates, posters, postcards, stationery, and stock certificates as the symbol of Egypt. On occasion, he is Egypt's spokesman. In the 1920s, Ahmad Shawqi, the poet of Egyptian nationalism, asked the Sphinx for guidance and consolation. Horemakhet replied: "I have preserved for you something that will strengthen you, for nothing preserves sweetness like stone. . . . The morning of hope wipes out the darkness of despair, now is the long-awaited daybreak."[38]

EMPTINESS

The prodigious Egyptologist William Flinders Petrie deduced that the rock of the Sphinx had been a "tomb made here before the Sphinx was carved."[39] The symbol of symbols: an empty tomb.

ETERNITY

Cold, austere, and sublime, the Sphinx has it both ways: unceasing rapture and comatose repetition. Christ speaks:

> Eternity stands always fronting God;
> A stern, colossal image, with blind eyes,
> And grand, dim lips that murmur evermore
> God, — God, — God!

Questions forever unanswered in everlasting vacancy. The Sphinx speaks:

> Beyond the limits of space,
> What is there, but space again?
> Look well upon my face!
> Dost thou ask, "Shall my prayers be in vain?"[40]

EVOLUTION

Hegel's Sphinx is a picture of frustration: "Out of the dull strength and power of the animal the human spirit tries to push itself forward, without coming to a perfect portrayal of its own freedom and animated shape, because it must still remain confused and associated with what is other than itself."[41] First the Sphinx had to push free from the sand, then from itself.

FAME

By craft and inquiry, men and women have become Sphinxes of famous cities. Talleyrand was the Sphinx of Paris, Bismarck the Sphinx of Berlin, Freud the Sphinx of Vienna, Vermeer the Sphinx of Delft. Arthur

Rimbaud is the "sphinx of modern literature."[42] Camille Claudel, Louise de Polastron, Madame Blavatsky, Gladys Deacon, Henrik Ibsen, Greta Garbo, Emperors Napoleon and Napoleon III, Franklin Delano Roosevelt, Gamel Abdel Nasser, and Farah Fawcett have been ensphinxed.[43]

FORTUNE

Sphinxes appear atop the wheel of fortune card on tarots designed by François Chosson (1672), Pierre Madenié (1709), François Heri (1718), Jean-Pierre Payen (1735), and many others, including Oswald Wirth's popular decks of 1889 and 1927. Card X of the Falconnier tarot (1896) is labeled "Sphinx."[44]

8.3. The Sphinx presides over the wheel of fortune card from the Oswald Wirth tarot, 1896.

FUTURE

In the dark Horemakhet watches the east, anticipating sunrise. At dusk the sun sets across his back, safely behind his protection till it rises again. "Of the giant stone figures still left upon this ravaged earth, none other gazes out of the deep past through the troubled present into the uncertain future. Nor does any other human creation so evoke the sense of superhuman powers involved in forecasting or prophecy"—David Loye, 1983."[45]

Science fiction often leaps to the future with Sphinxes. According to H. G. Wells's *The Time Machine* (1895) the predominant structure of London in 802,701 AD will be a great white hollow Sphinx. A mere five hundred years from now, the seeker in Arthur C. Clarke's *Seeker of the Sphinx* (1951) sees a Sphinx who seems to alter space into time: "There whispered the soughing of the winds of eternity as they sweep into the past."[46]

Science-fiction Sphinxes ask the riddle far into the future and past.[47] In *The Martian Sphinx* (1965) Keith Woodcott envisioned a twenty-first-century earth dominated by Asians and Africans, whose astronauts find a Sphinx on Mars. Only a lowly "Cork," a remnant white American, can solve its riddle: he knew from the history of our century that racial arrogance is the kiss of death.

Joshua Kampa, the hero of Michael Bishop's *No Enemy but Time* (1982), is a black American Air Force officer selected for the White Sphinx Project, a secret military time-travel experiment. (How times change! For H. G. Wells, the White Sphinx could be reached by a private inventor; for Bishop, the White Sphinx is something only the military could afford.) White Sphinx sends Poe-quoting Kampa to Africa in the early Pleistocene, two million years ago. Kampa jumps from a twentieth-century scaffold to an ancient family tree. He consummates his lusts with a hairy primeval hominid he names Helen. "Helen was a human being in my sight, and our love was not bestial but sublime. I insist upon this because there are so many people whose prejudices force them to deny what to me was self-evident from the moment of our first coupling."[48]

Historical fiction pounces with Sphinxes on the past. In David Pownall's *The Sphinx and the Sybarites* (1993), Kallias, alias Sphinx, is a Greek diviner, the best in the Greek world of 510 BC He sinks deeply into the present and emerges, gasping for breath, in the future. "All is chance," he says. "The ultimate Hell lies in knowing the future," he says.[49] Like a Sphinx he destroys a city, washes it off the face of the earth.

The Sphinx of Giza is a favorite stop for time travelers visiting the past: apelike Alley Oop (1948), suffering Superman (1958), Tarzan, the Ape Man (1975), young Matthew in Vilott's *Secret of the Sphinx* (1985), and the time criminal Viridiporcus Rex of S. P. Somtow's romping *Aquiliad* (1988). The Sphinx itself was a time machine for Kang the Conqueror.[50]

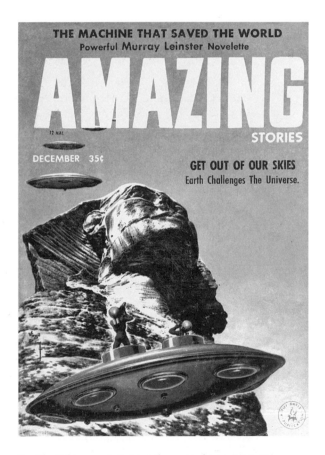

8.4. The Sphinx meets UFOs on the cover of *Amazing Stories*, December 1957.

"The record of the future broods in me," said the Sphinx to Francis Saltus.[51] Old as he is, Horemakhet still looks forward: as guardian of the sun, he is the guardian of life here tomorrow, a future more urgent than an afterlife somewhere else.

GODS AND GODDESSES

The Sphinx, says Alain in *The Gods*, "in one way or another, prefigures the ancient gods." Horemakhet was worshipped as a god himself and was a sacred site for Rā and Horus. Apollo consorted with Sphinxes. F. C. S. Schiller asserts, "There has been no age when the Sphinx could be evaded."[52] The same sun that cooks Horemakhet breaks through a stained-glass Sphinx into the National Cathedral in Washington DC.

Sphinxes were symbols of three great goddesses of the Mediterranean: Hathor, Astarte, and Isis. Hathor votaries declared her to be "the mother of the gods, and the creators of the heavens and the earth, and of everything which is in them." She assumed the powers of "every solar god." When Rā, the sun god, was displeased with humans he asked Hathor to slay them all. She did. In the Hathor style the hair divides into two equal curls falling below the shoulders onto the breast.[53] The Hathor style is traceable to the Middle Kingdom of Egypt (about 2500 BC) and Sphinxes that wear their hair like Hathor are found in Crete, Hittite Anatolia, and Syria.[54]

Astarte and Isis were also called the mother of gods. Both were tenders of death and resurrection. Temples of Isis in Egypt, Greece, Italy, and Spain were guarded by Sphinxes.[55]

HISTORY

A Sphinx sits at the feet of Clio, Muse of history, on the side of a sarcophagus in Porte Torres.

On July 14, 1860, Hugo wrote to Jules Michelet to congratulate him for the latest volume in his *Histoire de France*, "Since the centuries are so many Sphinxes, we must have our Oedipuses to face them down. You come to these dark riddles, and you speak the dread word."

Emerson wrote: "The Sphinx must solve her own riddle. If the whole of history is in one man, it is all to be explained from individual experience."[56] And if not?

ICE

Within "La beauté" Baudelaire finds a "heart of snow . . . enthroned in the azure like an incomprehensible sphinx." Gautier described a "Madonna of snow / A white sphinx sculpted by winter." Vignola's last lithograph for Fragerolle's *Le Sphinx* (1896) forecasts Horemakhet's future: dead in a dead world, covered with snow. Jules Verne installed an immense *Sphinx*

8.5. Amédée Vignola's final Sphinx for Fragerolle's *Sphinx* song cycle, 1896.

8.6. Illustration by George Roux from Verne's *Le Sphinx des glaces*, 1897.

des glaces (1897) at the South Pole; at the North, Albert White Vorse heard the "Arctic Sphinx," whose laughter, loud as cannon, is the crack of icebergs breaking into the sea.[57] Jack London's *White Fang* (1906) begins in "the savage, frozen-hearted Northland Wild": "There was a hint in it of laughter, but of a laughter more terrible than any sadness — a laughter that was as mirthless as the smile of the Sphinx."

IGNORANCE

Martin Luther interpreted the Sphinx of Thebes as murderous ignorance, equivalent to the testimonies of misunderstood scripture (specifically Psalm 119:144) that kills "those who do not understand them." In his influential *Emblemata* (1531) Andrea Alciati defined the Sphinx as the symbol of ignorance.[58]

KINGS AND QUEENS

Horemakhet had kittens. Sphinxes certified pharaohs for two thousand years, from about 2600 BC to 660 BC. The stone eyes of Djedefre, Kafre, Ammenemes I, II, and III, Sesotris I, Mentuhotpe VII, Amenhotep I and III, Thutmose I, II, III, and IV, Hatshepsut, Ramses I and Ramses the Great, Sethos I, Siamun, and Taharqa peer from Sphinx faces. A Sphinx of Schepenupet II, sister of Pharaoh Taharqa, lies in the Staatliche Museen zu Berlin.[59]

When Rome ruled Egypt the Sphinx was stamped on coins: Tiberius, Caligula, Claudius, Hadrian, and Domitian minted Sphinxes.[60] Augustus briefly used a signet ring engraved with a Sphinx to sign his letters and edicts. The ring was a gift from his mother, an Oedipal identification not lost on the wits of Rome, who joked that "the Sphinx brings its problems." Augustus was not amused. He abandoned the Sphinx signet and replaced it with a signet of Alexander the Great. The Sphinx moved to his coinage.[61]

Voltaire thought the Sphinx a good symbol for Augustus because it is a symbol of deceit.[62] Deceit is the least of it. Emperor Diocletian (245–313 AD) stole Sphinxes from the pharaohs for his own mausoleum.[63]

The presiding authority of George Bernard Shaw's *Caesar and Cleopatra* is a Sphinx. Though small enough to fit the Chicago stage where it debuted in 1901, it might be taken at first glance to be playing the role of the Great Sphinx of Giza. Through cat messengers Cleopatra confides her secrets to this Sphinx. She flees to it when she's in trouble. Cleopatra meets Caesar at the Sphinx, he addressing it privately, or so he believes, and she hidden by it. Shaw's Caesar says:

> Sphinx, you and I, strangers to the race of men, are no strangers to one another: have I not been conscious of you and of this place since I was born? Rome is a madman's dream; this is my Reality. These starry lamps of yours I have seen from afar in Gaul, in Britain, in Spain, in Thessaly, signalling great secrets to some sentinel below, whose post I could never find. And here at last is their sentinel — an image of the constant and immortal part of my life, silent, full of thoughts, alone in the silver desert. Sphinx, Sphinx. . . . My way hither was the way of destiny; for I am he of whose genius you are the symbol.

Shaw's dramatic irony emerges with Cleopatra. She shows herself to Caesar and tells him this Sphinx is not the Great Sphinx but rather a "dear little kitten of a Sphinx."[64] The grandeur of his speech, the acuity of his recognition and his faith in it, and the greatness of his comparisons abruptly deflate. A kitten of a Sphinx fooled vain Caesar.

Then Napoleon and Teddy Roosevelt.

While emperor of France, Napoleon III was known as "the Sphinx." Deposed, despised, and exiled, he followed the steps of Oedipus.[65]

Sphinxes also symbolized female rulers, most famously the self-portrait Sphinxes of Hatshepsut, ruler of Egypt in the early Eighteenth Dynasty, only 3,500 years ago.[66]

MAGIC

The "great god Heka," god of magic in pharaonic Egypt, was depicted as a Sphinx.[67] Theater magicians promoted themselves as Sphinxes, a Sphinx magic kit was sold for beginners, and professional magicians vied for fame

8.7. Hatshepsut as Sphinx in red granite, circa 1460 BC.

in the *Sphinx*, their trade magazine. Sphinxes pop up as props on magicians' posters. "Magic: The Gathering," an international card game, featured a flying "Petra Sphinx."

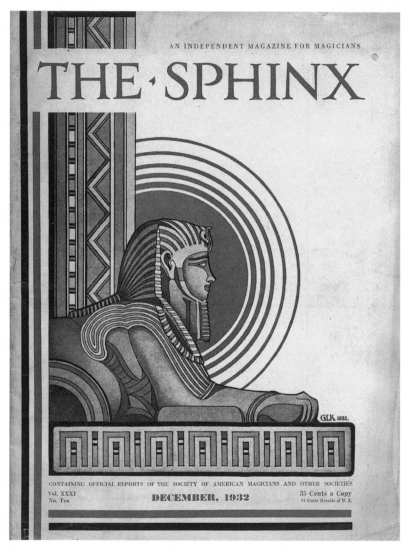

8.8. Cover of *Sphinx: An Independent
Magazine for Magicians*, December 1932.

MARRIAGE

Novels with "Sphinx" in their title tend to be romances and thus about the complications of courtship and marriage. Examples abound: Danby's *The Sphinx's Lawyer*, Erlenbusch's *Die Sphinx*, Flemming's *Cupid and the Sphinx*, Rennliw's *Sphinx Amor*, Vernier's *Un Sphinx du demi-monde*, and many more. Oedipus married a woman old enough to be his mother. Kelly's *Why the Sphinx Smiles* and Chantpleure's *Sphinx blanc* marry a woman to a man old enough to be her father.

MELANCHOLY

The Sphinx lives in the depths of solitude. In *Aurora Leigh* (1856), her novel in verse, Elizabeth Barrett Browning wrote: "In order to discover the Muse-Sphinx, / The melancholy desert must sweep round."[68]

"The ultimate secret, that which the Sphinx seems to have known for so many centuries, but to have withheld in melancholy irony, is this: that all these dead men and women who sleep in the vast necropolis below have been fooled, and the awakening signal has not sounded for a single one of them; and that the creation of mankind—mankind that thinks and suffers—has had no rational explanation, and that our poor aspirations are vain, but so vain as to awaken pity"—Pierre Loti, 1909.[69]

MEMORY

Twain called the Sphinx "the type of an attribute of man—of a faculty of his heart and brain. It was MEMORY—RETROSPECTION—wrought into visible, tangible form." Characters in Harford Flemming's *Cupid and the Sphinx* (1878) converse: "It seems as if those eyes had been looking out across the Desert ever since the memory of man."

"Ah! So it is!" said Leopold, "that they have watched the changes in the heavens, and the shifting of the sands until the brain has grown so wise that the silence of this Sphinx is eloquent—like the strange speech of an Oracle, and fills one with knowledge drawn from all that she has seen!"[70]

8.9. Sphinx on silver coin of Chios, 400 BC.

8.10. Sphinx on Roman silver denarius, 46 BC.

8.11. Sphinx, Central Bank of Egypt, 100 pounds, 1997.

MENACE

Alexandre Dumas (1802–70) died before he could complete *Le Sphinx rouge*, his historical novel on that devil, Cardinal Richelieu. The title was taken from Jules Michelet's *Histoire de France* (1858) which, like Dumas's novel, invites its readers to contemplate Philippe de Champaigne's portrait of Richelieu in the Louvre: "He looks at you from the depth of his mystery, the sphinx in a red robe. I do not dare to say from the depth of his deceit. For, contrary to the sphinx of antiquity, who died if it was divined, he seems to say, 'Who divines me will die.' "[71]

MONEY

Metal of the sun, gold has an affinity for Sphinxes. So do coins and cash.

   Coins entered European history about 700 BC; Sphinxes appeared on them shortly thereafter. With unsurpassed longevity, wealthy Chios minted Sphinxes in silver and bronze for about eight hundred years. Ancient Samothrace, Cyprus, Cilicia, Pamphylia, and Samaria minted Sphinxes. Imperial, patriotic, xenophobic, socialist, colonial, and capitalist Sphinxes guarded coins by firmly sitting on them.

Sphinxes adorned the coins of later Roman emperors: Trajan, Hadrian, and Antoninus Pius. Cymbeline minted Sphinxes in Britain. Egypt is a good place for spending Sphinxes. Introducing its currency in 1898 the National Bank of Egypt issued 50-piaster Sphinxes. When Egypt became a British protectorate in 1914 a new series of 50-piaster Sphinxes followed. Smaller Sphinxes appeared on the National Bank of Egypt's £10 note from 1952 to 1960 and on the Central Bank of Egypt's 25-piastre note from 1976 to 1978. Horemakhet reappeared on the Central Bank's £100 note of 1994 and on the Arab Republic of Egypt's 10-piastre notes of 1997 and 1998. In the 1950s Horemakhet's face looked out from Egypt's coinage in six denominations, from one millième to twenty piastres. Egypt minted a £100 gold Horemakhet in 1990, a £50 gold image in 1993 and £5 silver strikes in 1993 and 1994.[72]

NATIONAL SOCIALISM

Joseph Goebbels, head of Hitler's public relations, called the Nazi Party a Sphinx. The bishop of Cologne promptly reminded German Catholics that the Sphinx was a monster.[73]

NATURE

Carlyle looked at nature for himself and saw the Sphinx, too. "Nature, like the Sphinx, her emblem, with her fair woman's face and neck, showed also the claws of a lioness. Now too her Riddle had been propounded; and thousands of subtle disputatious Schoolmen were striving earnestly to rede it, that they might live, morally live, that the monster might not devour them." Returning to nature for his second series of essays, Emerson found the Sphinx forever the victor at the riddle scene. "Her secret is untold. Many and many an Oedipus arrives; he has the whole mystery teeming in his brain. Alas! the same sorcery has spoiled his skill; no syllable can he shape on his lips."[74] The answer to the riddle of the Sphinx is unspeakable. Understand a Sphinx perfectly and still the answer is unspeakable.

Philosophy adds: "Nature is demonic, as Aristotle said, but not godly. δαιμόνια, ου θεία. Its symbol is the Sphinx, under whose nourishing breasts the tearing claws are visible." "The riddle of nature," says Nietzsche, is "that Sphinx of two species."[75]

A Freemason writes: "the gigantic form of that huge Sphinx, which has hollowed its deep bed in the sand" is "the symbolic key of Nature."[76]

Sphinx = Nature: one riddle exchanged for another.

Natural Law

Sphinxes patrol social strata. In *The Riddle of the Sphinx* (1892) N. B. Ashby protests that the conditions of the turn-of-the-century American farmer would have appeared to the nation's founders as "a monster more terrible than the sphinx which depopulated Thebes, waiting an answer to its enigma."[77] For Ashby the monster was a combination of monopolies.

"The cold shadow of the stone image of destruction is now beginning to cover the world with its desolation, and we must make haste or we will likewise perish," Henry Rawie warned in his *Sphinx Catechism* (1911). "Over the ruins of Empire the brooding and Sardonic Sphinx has been propounding her riddle, offering to give to man a heaven upon earth if he answers correctly, but failing to answer he will be destroyed." To "this Sphinx of History . . . we put questions that the riddle may be answered and our civilization may be saved."[78]

Ashby and Rawie give the same answer to the different Sphinxes: nature. Corporate and government impediments must be removed in order to let the laws of nature thrive, creating wealth and promoting industry.

Natural Selection

In an 1883 sermon M. J. Savage brought the evolution of the Sphinx up-to-date: "The sphinx is only the old way of expressing that which Mr. Darwin calls the struggle for life, the survival of the fittest, the law of natural selection—that underneath the calm face and the beautiful smile nature is going inexorably forward."[79]

NILE

Horemakhet began as a limestone outcrop in the way of the view and became a face facing sunrise. His location, position, and shape assisted him do his duty to Egypt: to mark the rising of the Nile.

Why does the Nile flood at the summer solstice, when there is no rain? Herodotus cited and rejected various suggestions about the origin of the Nile, river of riddles—including the right one, snowmelt upriver—but he gave up the problem as timeless and insoluble.[80] For the life and prosperity of Egypt nothing in the world was more important than its rising. The builders of the great pyramids of Pharaohs Khufu and Kafre built a causeway beside the Great Sphinx, linking it directly to the Nile. In an Alexandrian statue (circa 200 BC) the Nile is portrayed as a reclining hero leaning upon a Sphinx.[81]

In the mid-seventeenth century Kircher piled the weight of his erudition on the "Sphynx Memphitica" (Horemakhet) to discern its meanings. The Great Sphinx, he concluded, represented the flooding of the Nile. He believed that the ancient Egyptians gave credit to the Sphinx for the flood and its benefits: the fruit, fertility, fish and animals of the Delta were gifts from the Sphinx.[82]

PAST

Hawass and Lehner agree: Horemakhet is "an archetype of antiquity."[83] F. C. S. Schiller declared in 1891 that "the material Sphinx is perhaps the oldest of the extant monuments of human labour, and was a mystery even to the old-time builders of pyramids. But the spiritual Sphinx, its archetype, is older still; it is as old as reflection, as old as knowledge, and, we may be assured, will last as long."[84] So long.

8.12. The Nile reclining on a Sphinx, circa 200 AD, at the Vatican Museum.

PRIDE

In Victor Hugo's *La légende des siècles* (1859), the triumphant Egyptian sultan Zim-Zizimi dreams of ten marble Sphinxes. He brags that "Pride is my valet" and asks them to sing to him about glory. They respond one by one, naming Nitocris, Cyrus, Alexander the Great, Cleopatra, and others—haughty pharaohs, kings, and conquerors now bones, ash, and dust. Silent attendants of Horemakhet study his silence; others put words in his mouth. "To some it speaks the language of passion, to others, words of hate. For one, it smiles, full of delicious promises; for another, it sneers, its forehead heavy with impending revenge. . . . Our sphinx has spoken. It has pronounced only one word: pride!"—Maurice Dekobra, 1930.[85]

PROGRESS

In *Les misérables* (1862) Hugo prophesied, "Yes, the enigma shall say its word, the Sphinx shall speak, the problem shall be resolved. Yes, the people, rough-hewn by the eighteenth century, shall be completed by the nineteenth. An idiot is he who doubts it! The future birth, the speedy birth of universal well-being, is a divinely fatal phenomenon."[86] Divinely fatal.

REGRESSION

The Sphinx is reversible, it can be read front to back, as humanity slipping back into bestiality and excuse. "You wake in me each bestial sense, you make me what I would not be," said Oscar Wilde to his Sphinx.[87]

REVOLUTION AND COUNTERREVOLUTION

After devoting much of *Les misérables* to explaining the French Revolution of 1832, Victor Hugo admits "revolutions are Sphinxes." Escaping the massacre of Paris, December 4, 1851, Hugo asked, "What was the meaning of it all? To what purpose was this monstrous promiscuous murder? No one could understand it. The Massacre was a riddle. . . . We were in the Sphinx's Grotto."[88]

SCIENCE

In his *The Wisedom of the Ancients* (1609) Sir Francis Bacon portrays science as a Sphinx:

> Science may not absurdly be termed a monster, as beeing by the ignorant and rude multitude alwaies held in admiration. It is divers in shape and figure by reason of the infinite variety of subjects wherein it is conversant. A maiden face and voice is attributed unto it for its gratious countenance and volubilitie of tongue. Wings are added because Sciences and their inventions, doe passe and flie from one to another, as it were in a moment. . . . Elegantly also is it fained to have sharpe and hooked talents [talons], because the Axioms and arguments of Science doe so fasten upon the mind.[89]

Bacon takes the Sphinx to market: after answering the riddle Oedipus pulled his sword, killed the Sphinx, skinned her, and threw her pelt on an ass to show off in triumph. Bacon's Sphinx is a bloody hybrid, the violence made when ideas cease to be the playthings of the Muses and are put into practice. The Sphinx is the crossover from contemplation to experiment.

After Bacon Western science wears the Sphinx like a thinking cap and looks where the Sphinx looks, in the sky, in the silence, in the sun, in equations. The Sphinx is symbolically interviewed in the *Revue mensuelle des questions récréatives* of Brussels (1931–39) and in Étienne Klein's *Conversations with the Sphinx: Paradoxes in Physics* (1996).

SUN

Horemakhet was a site of a sun worship. As the pharaoh was the living symbol of the sun god, so the pharaoh-faced Sphinx was officially the symbol of a symbol. Mediterranean Sphinxes often appear beside Apollo, the sun god. "It was Apollo, Apollo," Oedipus cries, "who accomplished these cruel, cruel sufferings of mine!"[90]

THEFT

The Sphinx of Thebes was not always thought to be winged or divine. Her riddle, her power, and her body were explained away long ago as embellishments about a highway robber. Palaephatus (fourth century BC) reported that "Sphinx" was the name of an Amazon robber woman, whose raids terrorized Thebes. According to Palaephatus, King Cadmus offered a reward to anyone who would slay her. A bounty hunter named Oedipus succeeded.[91]

Oedipus himself was thought to be a thief. When his father King Laius encountered him at the forking road, he mistook him for a robber (as in Hofmannsthal's *Ödipus und die Sphinx*). The lone witness who saw Oedipus slay Laius blamed a gang of thieves.[92]

In several versions of Oedipus, including Sophocles', Oedipus believes that Creon will take advantage of civic distress to steal the throne. His fears about insurrection accelerate his haste. In Dryden's *Oedipus* Creon is a cringing hunchbacked schemer, Richard III in a chiton. The fear of a coup is magnified in Centofanti's *Edipo Re* (1829): Creon, a revolutionary patriot, boldly insults Oedipus to his face. In a short soliloquy he tells Oedipus "you were a bandit from the first morning."[93]

That Phix also would be taken for a robber is yet another vestige of her presumed descent from Egypt. Fast-moving plots of the Greek romances often depend on the untimely appearance of Egyptian pirates or robbers. Aulus Gellius and Diodorus of Sicily reported an Egyptian thieves' association, governed by rules and recognized by the government, with which it would negotiate for taxes and the return of stolen goods.[94]

The legend of a treacherous male against a treacherous female gathered followers until, five centuries later, it was his gang against hers. Pausanias wrote, "Roving with a force of ships on a piratical expedition she [the Sphinx] put in at Anthedon, seized the mountain I mentioned, and used it for plundering raids until Oedipus overwhelmed her by the superior numbers of the army he had with him on his arrival from Corinth."[95] From this root grew Byzantine versions.

In an address to the Roman police in 533 AD, Cassiodorus said, "We consider it easier to comprehend the riddles of the Sphinx than to discover the presence of a fleeing thief."[96]

The gigantic lodestone Sphinx in Jules Verne's *Sphinx des glaces* (1897) is called a "thief" because its magnetism yanks objects out of seamen's hands. G. Gordon Liddy, a state-sponsored burglar, was dubbed the "Sphinx" of Watergate.[97] Thieves and Sphinxes keep each other's secrets. The more valuable the intelligence, the better the secret.

Sphinxes do not tattle. The editors of *The Sphinx: An Independent Magazine for Magicians* were obliged to disclaim any responsibility for unscrupulous advertisers who stole and sold other people's tricks and apparatus. "The *Sphinx* offers a fair field and no favor, and does not assume to instruct dealers or individuals in morals or ethics."[98]

TIME

Sphinxes keep time in seconds and centuries. A Sphinx flies merrily among monsters in the illuminations of *The Book of Hours* of Jean, Duke of Berry (1409). Carlyle wrote in 1833, "The Universe . . . was a mighty Sphinx-riddle, which I knew so little of, yet must rede, or be devoured. . . . Chronos, or what we call TIME, devours all his children." In 1835

Heine wrote, apropos the decline of Roman Catholicism, "Every epoch is a sphinx that plunges into the abyss as soon as its riddle has been solved."[99]

The "real" Sphinx is a clock, wrote García Lorca. The Sphinx of Giza is a cosmic clock, wrote Lysianne Delsol. The Tiffany Company made Sphinx clocks, hands on Swatch watches swept a Sphinx face. His bed of sand shifting on a spinning globe, his image on almanacs and calendars, Horemakhet daily acquires more authority as a symbol of time.[100]

TOBACCO

For decades Egyptian tobacco competed successfully for the international market. Tobacco of other nations claimed Egyptian connections, a vestige still seen in Camel cigarettes. Sphinxes were enlisted to certify customs taxes and advertise brands. Quick as a flick Sphinx matches and Sphinx lighters enflamed Sphinx cigarettes and tobacco.

8.13. The Sphinx on a Duke cigarette card, 1888. At the time Duke cigarettes outsold every other brand and advertised that tobacco improved health. Numerous other brands also had Sphinx cards.

8.14. Egypt customs tax stamp, 1893.

TRADITION

Sphinxes reached the Renaissance from three channels: from libraries; from carved and sculpted Sphinxes stolen or inherited from Egypt, Greece, and Rome; and from travelers' reports from Egypt. In the Renaissance the Sphinx was in vogue and more querulous than perilous. "There was a revival of exotic architecture, and Egyptianizing sphinxes jostled with stone or wooden pyramids in European gardens."[101]

TRUTH

At the opening of *Beyond Good and Evil* Nietzsche asks why philosophers are still tempted by the will to truth and its "strange, wicked, questionable questions!" "Is it any wonder that we should finally have become suspicious, lose patience, and turn away impatiently? That we should finally learn from this Sphinx to ask questions, too? *Who* is it really that puts questions to us here? *What* in us really wants 'truth'? . . . The problem of the value of truth came before us — or was it we who came before the problem? Who of us is Oedipus here? Who the Sphinx? It is a rendezvous, it seems, of questions and question marks."[102]

WAR

Athenaeus (circa 228 AD) cited the Sphinx as a simile for military conscription: "That Sphinx which crushes, not Thebes but all Hellas — the Aetolian [League] who sits upon the cliff, even as the Sphinx of old, and snatches up and carries off all our men." Robert L. O'Connell's "Dialogue with the Sphinx" inquires about the origin of weapons. Erasmus wrote in 1529: "Oh, if we believe Oedipus, four-footed and three-footed as well as two-footed men are found. Often they come back from the wars with one foot, sometimes with none."[103]

WASTE

Robert Burton's *Anatomy of Melancholy* (1628) lists "madde labours," including "Labirinths and Sphinges, which a company of crowned asses, *ad ostentationem opum* [to display their wealth] vainly built, when neither the Architect nor King that made them, or to what use or purposes, are yet knowne."[104]

WATER

Debussy, le père de la mer, deemed the sea a "great blue Sphinx." Marshall Goold elaborated: "The sea is the great Sphinx in her womanly beauty and her inhuman cruelty . . . the sea with long, shadowy flanks and rending claws, and the cruel patience that wears out her victims; the mighty, inscrutable sea."[105] Plastic Sphinxes settle quiet as anemones in home aquariums. Twelve stone Sphinxes swim with the fishes in the harbor of Alexandria.[106]

Sphinxes rule the waves. The British Navy's *Sphinx* bombarded the Sudan in 1884. In Operation Crossroads, July 1, 1946, off Bikini Atoll, the United States tested an atom bomb, the U.S. Navy's *Sphinx* standing by.

8.15. Sphinx insignia for the British Lincolnshire Regiment in Egypt, 1941.

A Sphinx called "Endurance" was a hot water bottle and syringe ideal for enemas, made by the Faultless Rubber Company of Ashland, Ohio. Lambert Products spun Sphinx toilet tissue in 1,000-sheet rolls.

Out of the erosion of the Sphinx of Giza, Colin Wilson constructed an analogy: "The water erosion of the Sphinx is to history what the convertibility of matter into energy is to physics," he wrote, with the bold hyperbole favored by Sphinxes.[107] Comparisons can be enigmas: if (a word built like a valve) the "water erosion of the Sphinx is to history what the convertibility of matter into energy is to physics," will history explode or decay? A convertibly eroded Sphinx would heat the core, throw off ions, charge and ricochet, recharge and irradiate. Sphinx erosion lit up Egyptology something like that in 1992.

WISDOM

An Austrian noble in an American novel says that the Sphinx "is said to embody all that is most wise."[108] He is correct: according to Chaeremon, an Alexandrian of the first century AD, "Egyptian wisdom is to say all things symbolically, to conceal the images of the gods in little boxes and to hang from walls only the Sphinx."[109] Wherever a Sphinx is, is hidden wisdom.

WONDER OF THE WORLD

The *Laterculi Alexandri* (second century BC) began a tradition by naming the seven wonders of the world. The seven of antiquity were the lighthouse of Alexandria, the colossus of Helios at Rhodes, the hanging gardens of Semiramis, the statue of Zeus at Olympus, the temple of Artemis in Ephesus, the mausoleum of Halicarnassus, and the pyramids of Giza. Modern depictions of the ancient wonders often feature the Sphinx with the pyramids as backdrops. Lists of the seven *modern* wonders include the Sphinx and pyramids, now in the company of the Eiffel Tower, Great Wall of China, and Taj Mahal.

WORLD

D. M. Thomas's three-part *Sphinx* (1986) pays homage to Pushkin in the form of a novel, a play, and a poem. It leaps from the Sphinx of Giza to "Russia, the Sphinx," then to a larger Sphinx. Thomas writes, "The world's unquestionably a sphinx; / with Europe's brutal, abstract head," Africa's breasts, and Russia's "Mongol eyes."[110]

8.16. Ever vigilant over empire, this Sphinx of Amen-hotep III (circa 1391–53 BC) is one of two conveyed to St. Petersburg by Czar Nicholas I in the 1830s. The two face each other along the Neva River in front of the Academy of the Arts. The two Sphinxes are featured in D. M. Thomas's *Sphinx*.

ZODIAC

Some say the Sphinx is a hybrid symbol hidden in the zodiac, a super-sign that combines the sign for Leo the lion (July–August) and Virgo the maiden (August–September), which together make the life-giving season of the sun. Catholic Kircher published this interpretation in the 1650s, citing Aven Vaschia, an Arab of Egypt. He explained that the Sphinx was watchman of the summer solstice, the season of the flooding of the Nile. The Sphinx was the symbol of fertility and renewal, brought by the rising water that sometimes lapped at its feet.[111] The lion brought the sun, the virgin brought the water.

A German Jesuit speculating about Greek symbols flying through Egyptian nights is the sort of scene a Sphinx smiles above. Look at the stars go by: Leo first, then Virgo. If the body of a Sphinx begins with a maiden's face and ends with a lion's tail, Kircher's Sphinx moves forever backward, hello, good-bye, and back again.

Sydney Watson rediscovered the Sphinx zodiac and published it as if it were news in 1900. Watson wrote that the Sphinx represented a maiden and was a sign of redemption. He looked at a ceiling of the Hathor temple of Denderah and saw a Sphinx "actually set between the two signs of VIRGO and LEO." Le Sar Péladan, the same year, published the identical observation: the Sphinx "unites the Sign of the Virgin with that of Leo."[112]

Did the Nile flood in the summer? Yes. Did the ancient Egyptians have a lion in their constellations? Yes, they did. But the constellation of the lion of Egypt and the stars of the lion of the zodiac are in different parts of the sky.[113] The Kircher explanation supposes that the Greek zodiac (still with us in horoscopes) was the same zodiac the Egyptians used. The zodiac that Watson saw is relatively recent, carved in a temple ceiling built by the Ptolemies, the last pharaohs, Greek descendents of Alexander the Great. Napoleon's expedition removed it and took it to Paris.[114]

SUBTOTAL

Every feature of Horemakhet contributes vivid symbolism. As human, he is intelligent; his head held high, he is noble; as a lion, he is powerful and able to slaughter. His keen gaze watches the horizon tirelessly, his body forever at rest. His silence is a symbol of the ineffable; his firmness, a symbol of eternity; his sunlit face, the symbol of contemplation of the unseen. Quiet Horemakhet does his duties resolutely, with unblinking blank eyes, patiently awaiting the solar resurrection. Théophile Gautier thought it lay like a dog on the grave of its master.[115]

In arts and philosophy Sphinxes are symbols within symbols, visible symbols of invisible striving, symbols of patience and petrification, of loins and pelts, symbols of terrible secrets and unspeakable needs. The Sphinx takes the measure of man.

"Confused and associated with what is other than itself," Hegel's hyperthyroid Super Sphinx symbolizes everything in sight, up to and including the limits of symbols. At the lip of a chasm or the edge of a desert or overlooking the bloodshot sunrise, Sphinxes are symbols of study, contemplation, and fatigue. The Sphinx is an "ensemble of symbols" (Hegel again) simultaneously stopped and kinetic.[116] With spectacular ease, by doing nothing, Horemakhet depicts humanity arising from life and life arising from rock.

Battalions of Sphinxes muster on shop shelves in Cairo and Athens. What is the modern Sphinx made of? Ivory, plaster, porcelain, clay, blown and molded glass, gold, silver, platinum, brass, bronze, iron, copper, plastic, paper, cardboard, concrete, granite, marble, porphyry, quartz, coal, amber, resin, wood, sugar, and ice. Sphinxes descend like other religious symbols: bigger than life, revered, secularized, brought down to size, and merchandised as pins and cufflinks.

A Sphinx can be an environment. Sphinx Summit faces the Jungfrau in the Swiss Alps, Sphinx Mountain rises high in the Madison Range of Montana. There are Sphinx peaks in the Carpathians and Cascades. Formations in the Dardanelles are called Sphinxes. A Sphinx overlooks Muir Woods, twin Sphinxes erode in South Dakota Badlands, Sphinx Glacier cools British Columbia. A Sphinx juts into the Bay of Trestraou. In Colorado the Denver and Salt Lake Railroad blasted a tunnel through Sphinx Head Rock. Another Sphinx Head Rock gazes over Lake Superior. Lake Erie laps Sphynx Head on Gibraltar Island. One Sphinx Rock looks down from the heights of the Catskills, another from the Olympics, another above Chatsworth Park Canyon, another above boulders in Newport, Oregon. A Sphinx Rock quizzes the Apostle Islands, a Sphinx Rock stares from the shoreline of La Jolla, California. A Sphinx scowls on Lake Hopatcong, New Jersey; a Sphinx guards a hill near Ponta Grossa, Brazil; a Sphinx watches shipping at Cape Ann, Massachusetts.

Imaginary Sphinxes are real properties, deeded and titled. Sphinxes are registered trademarks of Hollywood Pictures and Sphinx Records. Sphinx is the name of hotels, clubs, pubs, and restaurants. Sphinx is the imprint of publishers in Basel, Berlin, Bern, Krakow, Leipzig, Lima, Montreal, New York, Paris, and Prague. Le Sphinx of Paris specializes in crime fiction; the Sphinxes of Basel and New York prefer the occult. *Sphinx* entitles books, menus, magazines, learned journals, college and high school yearbooks.

Sphinx is the trade name of a hair dryer, paraglider, sewing machine, artificial intelligence speech recognition program, and line of computers. It is the trademark of a drug company, a papermaker, a recording label, and a brand of fishhooks. Sphinx Benzene fueled Mideuropa. Sphinx is a cocktail, a knife, a composite bow, a drill.[117] For Sphinx coffee and Sphinx tea, there are Sphinx china cups.

A Sphinx can be as close as your fingertips or catch in your throat. Sphinxes adorn bookends, cabinets, inkwells, candleholders, andirons, drapery, apparel, and dinnerware. An undertakers' supply company in Syracuse, New York, sold Sphinx Fluid for embalming. Buckstaff, a bottler in Oshkosh, Wisconsin, labeled his booze "Sphinx embalming fluid" for those who wanted to embalm themselves. A Sphinx can be a bead, bracelet, button, brooch, cufflink, earring, ring, or amulet.

8.17. Sphinx Head Rock, Briggs Landing, Oregon, 1920.

8.18. Sphynx cat on an Afghanistan stamp, 1996.

Sphinxes are actual animals, flesh and blood, as dependent on oxygen as you and I. There are Sphinx species of monkey, harem-forming fruit bat, and almost furless purebred cat.[118] There is a Sphinx moth, lipid, and gene.[119]

8.19. *Sphingidae:* from top to bottom, death's
head hawk moth (*Acheronta atropos*), bind-
weed hawk moth (*Sphinx vonvolvuli*), and
privet hawk moth (*Sphinx ligustri*) from
F. O. Morris, *A History of British Moths,* 1903.

Sphinx is the name of word games, board games, chess and mathematical puzzles, computer games, magic kits, and fortune-telling cards. Until the nineteenth century, the chariot card of most tarot decks showed a chariot pulled by horses. Éliphas Lévi put a black Sphinx and white Sphinx in harness on his chariot card. The popular Oswald Wirth deck did the same. The chariot in the Aleister Crowley tarot is pulled by four Sphinxes.[120]

Sphinx bicycle, Sphinx spark plugs, Sphinx automobile. In Egypt Sphinxes carried gods on their backs: Thoth, Horus, Harpocrates. Two Sphinxes pull the chariot of Athena up the arch of Marcus Aurelius in Tripoli.

If Sphinxes could carry gods, what could they not carry?[121]

8.20. Sphinxes on the
chariot card from
the Oscar Wirth tarot,
1896.

9 : Exit

Truth bathed in myth, or like the Sphinx imbued with
wisdom's sunset gleam,
Mountain strange, with face of stone, that stands amid the
gale of time,
And still today before the world an undeciphered riddling
rhyme,
Rears up its head of towering rock amidst the clouds'
unending stream.

Mihai Eminescu

In October 1981 parts of a hind paw of the Great Sphinx of Giza fractured and fell off. The oldest monument in the world paid its dues to time.

PREDATRIX

Sphinxes watch combat on vase paintings of classical Greece. They parade with a battle column and observe duels to the death. In the collection of the Metropolitan Museum of Art, a Sphinx watches Hercules kill Nessos; two more Sphinxes, nose to nose, watch Achilles kill Memnon, king of Ethiopia.[1]

The story of Phix grew independently. Pottery paintings of a Sphinx chasing Thebans appeared in the sixth century BC, before depictions of Phix with Oedipus. Once on the scene, Oedipus conquered the style: the pursuing Sphinx disappears.[2]

The oldest words about the slaying Sphinx are found on a fragment from Corinna of Tanagra (first century BC). Part of her poem is preserved in a commentary on Euripides: "According to some authorities his own mother was slain by Oedipus and according to Corinna he slew not only the Sphinx, but also the Teumesian fox."[3] Oedipus, according to some authorities, was triply deadly: parricide, plague, Sphinxicide.

Euripides, 409 BC: "The Sphinx bore down our city with her raids."[4] Phix attacked Thebes like a lion in rage, laying waste and inspiring terror. She could kill everyone at once, destroy everything, reduce Thebes to desolation. But she kept to her method: raid the city, ruin crops, swoop and taunt, and stick to a serial diet, one ripe Theban at a time. She slept till she was hungry and hunted again.

The future of Thebes came down to arithmetic: how fast would she eat young men? She could catch a man of her choice unless someone volunteered. It would be lucky for Thebes if wanderers and suitors came to risk their lives at her rock and riddle. They'd keep her busy and satiated.

PLAGUE

Since Moses, Egypt has been reputed to be a place of plagues: frogs, flies, lice, locusts, mortal fever. Robert Burton wrote in his *Anatomy of Melancholy* (1621) that every third year three hundred thousand people died of plague in Cairo. Edward Gibbon wrote, "Aethiopia and Egypt have been stigmatized in every age, as the original source and seminary of the plague."[5] Napoleon's Army of Egypt conquered Egypt then sickened and died.

Thebes was built on infected ground. "The first to occupy the land of Thebes are said to have been the Ectenes. . . . The Ectenes perished, they say, by plague," wrote Pausanias.[6] In Ovid's *Metamorphoses* the curse of the Sphinx is immediately followed by the curse of the Teumesian fox, whose tail was a torch that set fields afire. After the fox came plague.[7]

Sophocles introduces Oedipus as the king of a sick city and countryside. A priest pleads, "A blight is on the buds that enclose the fruit, a blight is on the flocks of grazing cattle and on the women giving birth, killing their offspring; the fire-bearing god, hateful Pestilence, has swooped upon the city and harries it."[8]

Seneca blames the plague of Thebes on contamination by the Sphinx's corpse.[9]

The slaughtering Sphinx is explained as divine retribution; she is the agent of an angry god, Hera or Apollo, punishing pederasty. She fulfills the curse King Pelops put on King Laius when Laius stole Pelops's son, Chrysippus, for sex. Or the Sphinx is the curse come true of the Chalcidians, whose supplications for food and water were met by shut gates at Thebes. Unwelcome, they left their corpses there and plague came out of them. The Sphinx came, too. The seer Tiresias says to Thebes: "The corruption of flesh engendered the horrible plague; / the corruption of hearts gave birth to monsters. / The Sphinx is a child of Thebes!"[10]

The Sphinx catches like a cat, the Sphinx catches like a cold. "In 1933, while enjoying herself in Florence, the Sphinx became ill. When she returned to England pneumonia developed and caused her death."[11]

The great white Sphinx of H. G. Wells's *The Time Machine* is so far in the future it is already old when the Time Traveler sees it up close:

> I saw the white figure more distinctly. It was very large, for a silver birch tree touched its shoulder. It was of white marble, in shape something like a winged sphinx, but the wings, instead of being carried vertically at the sides, were spread so that it seemed to hover. The pedestal, it appeared to me, was of bronze, and was thick with verdigris. It chanced that the face was towards me; the sightless eyes seemed to watch me; there was the faint shadow of a smile on the lips. It was greatly weather-worn, and that imparted an unpleasant suggestion of disease.[12]

POISON

Octave Feuillet wrote two Sphinxes: a play and a novel. In 1872, a year after the death of the Second Empire, Feuillet's *Le Sphinx* debuted in Paris. Its rich and miserable heroine, Blanche de Chelles, wears a ring with a Sphinx on it and poison in it. Blanche says, "Amid all my amusements, there are moments when I feel so weary, so *ennuyée,* that I have a desire to ask my sphinx for its secret."[13] Accused of betrayal, she takes the poison and dies.

Playing Blanche, Sarah Bernhardt poisoned herself wonderfully in English and French. A death specialist, Bernhardt expired as Camille, Cordelia, Desdemona, Doña Sol, Phaedra, Tosca, Joan of Arc, Zaïre, and two versions of Cleopatra. Of the eight plays Bernhardt chose for her tour of the United States, four include death by poisoning.[14] One was Feuillet's *Sphinx.*

The Sphinx of Feuillet's novel is Julia de Trécœur. Like Blanche, she is torn between her husband and the man she loves. Julia kills herself by galloping her terrified horse off a cliff.

HOW A SPHINX DIES

Sophocles, Seneca, Hyginus, and Apollodorus agree that Phix killed herself when her question was answered. But why? "Inexplicably," says Edith

Hamilton.[15] Carl Robert wrote that the supposed suicide of the Sphinx is a "handgreifliche Absurdität" [an obvious absurdity]. The suicidal Sphinx is absent in Statius (92 AD) but forgetful, fallen, and mangled in Apollodorus's *Library* (first century BC). Sphinxes die in droves in poems and novels.

Ovid says she threw herself into an abyss, crashed on the rocks below. By the Renaissance this was a commonplace.[16] The abyss becomes part of the Sphinx as the labyrinth became part of the Minotaur.

The death of the Sphinx is an auxiliary riddle. A Sphinx commit suicide? Long before the Sphinx sold pistols and tobacco, the symbol of symbols spared no one, killing others and itself. Accounts, of course, disagree.

1. *She disappears after Oedipus answers her riddle.*[17]

Henry Bauchau's *Oedipus on the Road* (1990) describes Oedipus's youth in Corinth, his rising courage, his profitable trade with Egypt, his swelling pride. Bachau's Oedipus falls immediately in love with the Sphinx, "Aphrodite's dark pet," and she loves him, perhaps, a little. He remembers that when the Thebans found him, she was gone.[18]

She goes elsewhere to ask her riddles now. Back to Egypt in L'Engle's *Sphinx at Dawn,* to Washington DC, for Masterton's *The Sphinx,* to Atlantic City for Friesner's *Sphynxes Wild,* and *toujours* to Paris, City of Sphinxes.

2. *She kills herself in anger.*

The woman-breasted Sphinx, with wings drawn back,
Folded her lion paws, and looked to Thebes.
There blanch the bones of whom she slew, and these
Mixt with her own, because the fierce beast found
A wiser than herself, and dashed herself
Dead in her rage.[19]

— Alfred Tennyson

3. *She kills herself in madness.*

The tradition emphasizes that the solving of the riddle was enough to drive the Sphinx wild, enough to cause her to fling herself down an abyss and die. Edmund Spenser, for instance:

> that Monster, whom the Theban Knight,
> The father of all that fatall progeny,
> Made kill her selfe for very hearts despight,
> That he had red her Riddle.[20]

The insanity caused by the discovered secret appears twice in the Oedipus legend. First the Sphinx goes mad when he answers her riddle. Then Oedipus goes mad when he answers his own. Rank is right: "The outbreak of madness after the revelation of the secret is to be emphasized as a crucial feature of the Greek legend."[21]

4. *She kills herself to end pain.*

In 1400 a Florentine scholar declared that the Sphinx felt such pain — "per dolore" — from Oedipus's answer that she threw herself down the mountain in agony. Disappointment kills, failure kills.[22]

5. *She dies worn out.*

In Hugo Von Hofmannsthal's *Ödipus und die Sphinx* (1906) the Sphinx kills herself for weariness, glad that Oedipus has arrived at last to put an end to her horrible work. Recognizing him with a bone-burning gaze, she doesn't bother to ask a riddle, but greets him sadly as "he who dreams the deep dream," then tumbles down the rocks with a shriek.[23]

6. *She dies of fright.*

The Sphinx of Péladan's *Œdipe et le Sphinx* (1903) recognizes Oedipus as the infamous parricide. She retreats in horror and falls to her death.

9.1. Oedipus slays the Sphinx on an Etruscan gem, third or fourth century BC.

9.2. *Oedipus and the Sphinx* by François Léon Sicard, 1903.

7. She dies laughing.

Georges Enescu wrote music for a Sphinx to sing. In his *Œdipe* (1936; libretto by Edmond Fleg), the Sphinx awaits Oedipus "Aux demeures sans voix de mon rêve éternel" [in the voiceless abode of my eternal dream]. She asks him to name something greater than destiny. He says "Man!" and she dies, weeping and laughing. Enescu wrote, "I had to invent its last scream, to imagine the unimaginable. When I put down my pen after finishing this scene I thought I would go mad."[24]

8. Oedipus kills her.

Fresh from murdering his father, Oedipus would have no compunction about killing the Sphinx. The typical battle between hero and beast is replaced by the riddle scene, a life-or-death contest hanging on a word. In either case, according to rule, the beast must die.

Goux concludes that the Sphinx's suicide is an Oedipal failure: had Oedipus been true to the male monomyth of triumph over monsters—Perseus slew Medusa, Hercules killed the Hydra, Theseus killed the Minotaur—Oedipus would have drawn his sword and slain the Sphinx rather than accept her conditions.[25] In fact, Attic vase paintings, Byzantine legends, and modern books finish the story as Goux would prefer, not with suicide, but with Oedipus killing the Sphinx with club, sword, or spear.

Examples abound. Jean-Marc Moret assembled plentiful evidence that iconographers introduced the slain Sphinx in the second half of the fifth century BC. Vases showing Oedipus preparing to attack the Sphinx or in combat with her postdate the literary texts and thus may show a later or independent version of the legend. Moret establishes independent artistic traditions—one literary, one pictorial—for the death of the Sphinx, traditions that eventually crossed.[26]

In Lydgate's *Fall of Princes* (circa 1438) Edippus slew the Sphinx with "myhti violence." In Helene Guerber's story for schoolchildren (1896), Oedipus draws his sword and forces the Sphinx back "until it fell over a precipice, on the sharp stones below, and was dashed to pieces." Aignan clubs her in Georges Perec's *A Void* (1969). In Philippe Sollers's *H* (1973) Oedipus kills the Sphinx twice. In Ted Hughes's "Song for a Phallus" (1971) Oedipus splits the Sphinx with an axe.

> The answers aren't in me, he cried
> Maybe your guts have got em[27]

That's about as ugly as it gets: because Oedipus is stupid the Sphinx must die.

Stories end with dead Sphinxes. The glowing desert romance in Abel Hermant's *Deux Sphinx* (1896) is cut short when Marika, an Egyptian Sphinx, is massacred by French soldiers.

Count no man happy until he is dead, says Hecube at the end of *The Trojan Women.* Then what do you count? How balance the years? How many points does Oedipus get for surviving two fatal encounters—first with his father and his father's bodyguards, then with the Sphinx—death scenes that exalt him? Oedipus was raised as the son of a king; when he became king he did a king's work as leader and judge. Suddenly he discovers he has married his mother, his children are the fruit of incest, and his family, power, and pride crumble to nothing or worse than nothing—grief, blame, self-revulsion. Old Oedipus is a has-been, accursed, criminal, bitter, lame, and homeless. Speaking for himself, he concludes that Thebes would have been better off if he hadn't been born. At the end of the day Oedipus comes to his father's point of view.

Defeating the Sphinx is his claim to fame and defining achievement. Looking back with blind eyes, he hears his triumphant words about the defeated Sphinx snap like the catch of a trap. Had he died a day before he found out who he was, Oedipus would have died with his pride intact and his conscience clear. Oedipus is an archetype of this and that and the other thing, including the man who lives too long. He lived too long, then lived long enough to believe that he had nothing to lose by living longer. In Sophocles' *Oedipus at Colonus* his suffering is rewarded after he dies: as a kind of human sacrifice, his body radiates blessings to nearby Athens. His life proceeds in three parts and three cities: Thebes to Corinth, Corinth

9.3. Drawing of the murdered Marika by
Mittis from Hermant's *Deux Sphinx*, 1896.

to Thebes, and Thebes to Athens. Athens, the last stop, a city he never enters, wins.

9. *The Sphinx is immortal.*

Or the Sphinx hasn't died yet. In fact, it is reproducing. It changes, very much, but it still kills and questions.

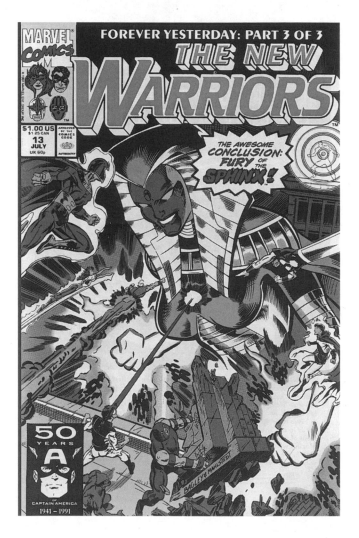

END

Sphinxes attend apocalypses, in Yeats's "The Second Coming" (1920) for one:

> somewhere in sands of the desert
> A shape with lion body and the head of a man,
> A gaze blank and pitiless as the sun,
> Is moving its slow thighs, while all about it
> Reel shadows of the indignant desert birds.

The Great Sphinx speaks: "I have thought so hard that I have nothing left to say."[28] In the thousands of years since its lips were carved, so much has been said for and about Horemakhet that its silence is ever more meaningful and consolatory.

Emerson's poet mocked a drowsy Sphinx. The Sphinx arose merry and contradictory, as a cloud, a flame, a voice promising, "Who telleth one of my meanings, / Is master of all I am."[29] Her promise is bait. Who wants to go to the trouble to be her "master" and what is "all" of a Sphinx?

The Sphinx of Giza and the Sphinx of Thebes were first symbols of labor and light, then of prejudice and superstition. What next? If Horemakhet had a brain as large as his cranium and a memory to match, what thoughts could he hatch but the same old thing, same old thing? An item on the checklist of the thorough world traveler, the Sphinx is a symbol of the vacation.

Who now resembles Oedipus the King at the moment Sophocles begins his play, glad to live in an undeluded world free of demons and monsters, confident that all dangers can be defeated, that catastrophes will be brief, and that the best defense is a good offense? In a fast era full of long waits and unexpected stops, a busy brain will have time to wonder, "What does the Sphinx ask me?"

9.4. "A World for the Winning," the cover of *The New Warriors*, July 1991.

Before the Great Sphinx big questions evaporate like futile beads of sweat, so much wasted worry. Thoughts as personal as "What do I think?" only repeat what numberless others have thought, thinking about themselves, thinking about the Sphinx, thinking about thinking about it, so many drops in the sand, gone without a trace, but not without a little helpless sympathy. Enormous, ancient, and exposed, the Sphinx spites the ordinary.

Science has millions of exhibits unknown to pharaohs, caesars, and prophets to remind us of distance, duration, and death: fossils, viruses, radioactivity, exploding stars. The Sphinx is off the clock. Thousands of years of people have passed beneath the Sphinx feeling little and lucky to be alive: it is a monument to patience, and to modesty, a royal reminder of how much we are alike.

Today the Sphinx of Giza is threatened by acid rain and a rising water table. The current great riddle is what to do about its deterioration — repair it, enclose it, or leave it to the sun and wind.[30]

Sphinxes are with us now, on shelves, on stamps and labels, in poems and private places. Prince Pantagruel saw Sphinxes on his voyages. Faust and Mephistopheles conversed with Sphinxes (Goethe, ever the biologist, could not see an animal without imagining a species). When one Sphinx song fades another begins.

Sphinx situations still occur: the snoopy stranger in the next seat, the unblinking monitor at an audition or exam, the judge who demands the truth, the bad-tempered hotel clerk who doesn't understand your language or your name, the lover whose love hangs on a question. The Sphinx is not done.

James Joyce wrote, "Sphoenix," a one-word story with a happy ending.[31]

Sphin xyz

ZZZZZZZZZ

Acknowledgments

With paw held high, *Book of the Sphinx* salutes those who made it possible. William Kohlhaase was the first to get all the way through it; his survival and recovery were heartening. My brother Phil, my twin, my *ka,* deserves thanks from Dante:

> O Sol che sani ogni vista turbata,
> tu mi contenti sì, quando tu solvi,
> che, non men che saver, dubbiar m'aggrata.

My thanks to Anthony Esolen for this translation:

> O sun who clear and cure all troubled sight,
> you please me so much when you solve these things—
> no less than knowledge, doubt is a delight!
> *Inferno* 11.91–93

Thanks to my father for my mother, to my mother for my father, and to my sisters, Diane and Margot, for a hundred years of woman lessons.

While I was out chasing Sphinxes, Liz Dulany and Margo Chaney fed my cats. In a righteous world my cats could claim coauthorship. Warm Zeno, calico Roma, the Mighty Bud, Sultan Suleiman, and Trajan Aurelius are past the Sphinx now. Zephyr, Krishna, and Ramses the Great oversaw final revisions.

Thanks to Marc Shell for emergency kindness and to the Department of Comparative Literature at Harvard for a gasp of freedom. Thanks to Dominique and Julia Chéenne for saving my life, and to William Kinderman and Katherine Syer for sustaining it. Thanks to Milad Doeuihi, John Irwin, Warren Motte, Paul Olson, Avital Ronell, and Liliane Weissberg for reading early drafts. Thanks to Sander Gilman for steadfast encouragement.

Praises upon the beautiful *Egyptomania* of the Toronto Museum of Art and upon Jean-Marc Moret's indispensable *Œdipe, la Sphinx et les*

Thébains. Grateful and amazed, I thank Heinz Demisch for his *Die Sphinx, the* Book of the Sphinx. *Book of the Sphinx* lauds nine prior Sphinx scholars: Carl Robert, Johannes Ilberg, Selim Hassan, Marie Delcourt, Ursula Schweitzer, Lowell Edmunds, Mark Lehner, Zahi Hawass, and Christiane Zivie-Coche. Paul Jordan's *Riddles of the Sphinx,* with John Ross's photographs, honors Horemakhet in a style befitting a king.

This *Book of the Sphinx* comes in the line of the *Livre de Sphinx* of Le Sar Péladan (1886), August Thiemann's *Das Buch der Sphinx* (1926), and Colin Naylor's *The Book of the Sphinx* (1974). The second-best justification for this book is that it points to better books. The best justification is that it gave Richard Eckersley the wherewithal to make a Book of the Sphinx.

Thanks to Lindsay Waters, Sylvia Manning, Thomas M. Eakman, William C. Ackermann, Richard Schacht, Judy Rowan, and Robert Wedgworth for plugging me back into university circuits. Thanks to James Dengate for his casts of Greek coins. Thanks to Betsy Hearne and Michael Claffey for a semester in residence. Thanks to the Walters Art Museum in Baltimore for happy hours. Thanks to Johns Hopkins University for its world-class faculty and press. Thanks to Rex Wallace and Maureen Ryan for help through the Latin Renaissance. Thanks to Steve Lehmann for answers to odd questions. Thanks to Paul Arroyo and Roger Buchholz for timely help preparing images. Thanks to Petra Fiero for recommending Heine, to David Fiero for Borges, and to Venera Clujeanu for Eminescu. Thanks to Jeanine Teodorescu for Ionesco's puzzles and the Sphinxes of Balzac.

Thanks to Bill Sisler for Philo and friendship, and to Elaine Sisler for moral support. Thank you, Bill Germano, for the pilgrimages to Berlioz, Bernini, and Uchida. Thank you, Michael Jensen, for coffee, camaraderie, foresight, and trust.

Thanks to the University of Illinois for its librarians, faculty, and administration. Thanks to the University of Illinois Press for the rest of my life.

Thanks to the City of Bellevue and the University of Nebraska for public education. Thanks to the University of Nebraska Press for giving the Sphinx a start and a rock to rest on. Thanks to Jonathan Culler and Gregory Nagy, who read an earlier version for UNP, for generous criticism. Without Ladette Randolph, my editor, *Book of the Sphinx* would still be loose and mangy. I thank her for taking the risk seriously.

The last person to meet my Sphinxes before they became a book was Robin DuBlanc, my copyeditor, who cared for them like an ideal veterinarian. Robin firmly disciplined the documentation, let in fresh air, and found space for more Sphinxes. Thank you, Robin.

And thank you, reader, for stopping here. May your Sphinxes be as audacious as you.

B1. Curt Liebich's
tailpiece for Richard Voss's
Sphinx, 1913.

B2. Place de Châtelet, Paris.

Notes

1. PHIX AND HOREMAKHET

The epigraph reads in the original: "Sitzen vor den Pyramiden, / Zu der Völker Hochgericht," *Faust,* part 2, lines 7245–46 [*Goethe's "Faust,"* 2:68].

1. The name Horemakhet became current in the Eighteenth Dynasty, circa 1500–1300 BC, Lehner, "Archaeology of an Image," 92.

2. Serres, *Hermes,* 47.

3. "Interim Sphinx Typhonis in Boeotiam est missa, quae agros Thebanorum vexabat. Ea regi Creonti simultatem constituit, si Carmen quod posuisset aliquis interpretatus esset, se inde abire: si aut datum Carmen non solvisset, eum se consumpturam dixit, necque aliter de finibus excessuram. Rex re audita, per Graeciam edixit, qui Sphingae Carmen solvisset, regnum se & Iocasten sororem ei in coniugium daturum promisit: cum plures regni cupidine venissent, & a Sphinge essent consumpti, Oedipus Lai filius venit & carmen est interpretatus. Illa se praecipitavit," Hyginus, *Fabularum Liber,* 24 [*Myths,* 66].

4. Goethe, *Faust,* part 2, line 7198.

5. Dessenne, *Le Sphinx,* 2, 29, 116.

6. "De quel troupeau invisible ces grands sphinx accroupis comme des chiens qui guettent sont-ils les gardiens, pour ne fermer jamais la paupière et tenir toujours la griffe en arrêt? qu'ont-ils donc à fixer si opiniâtrement leurs yeux de pierre sur l'éternité et l'infini? quel secret étrange leurs lèvres serrées retiennent-elles dans leur poitrine?" Gautier, *Une nuit de Cléopâtre,* 747 [*One of Cleopatra's Nights,* 5].

7. Hegel, *Aesthetik,* 12:480 [*Aesthetics,* 1:360].

8. Hegel, *Philosophie der Religion,* 15:472 [*Philosophy of Religion,* 2:639].

9. Horemakhet is the Sphinx of Ashby's *Riddle of the Sphinx* (1890), Barbarin's *Énigme du Grand Sphinx* (1947), Gardner's *Riddles of the Sphinx* (1987), and Jordan's *Riddles of the Sphinx* (1998).

10. Martineau, *Eastern Life,* 205; Douglas, "The Sphinx," 11.

11. Flaubert, *Voyage en Égypte,* 208 and *Salammbô,* chapter 10, "Le serpent." As Flaubert revised his travel notes for publication, he steadily intensified his terror of the Sphinx (see Naaman, *Débuts de Flaubert,* 254).

12. Fogg, *Arabistan*, 70.

13. Sphinx villains fought Dick Tracy, Doll Man, the Incredible Hulk, Mickey Mouse, the New Warriors, Nova, Superman, Tarzan, and Wonder Woman. The Riddler manipulates a Sphinx in the *Batman Chronicles* (#3, 1996). Horemakhet as a monstrous machine appears in *Weird War Tales* (#98, 1981). Comic-book Sphinx heroes also occur: Bob Burden's Mysterymen, a parodic band of super-heroes, has a Sphinx. The Sphinx in *Big Bang Comics* (August 1997) changes from hero to heroine.

14. Schmidt, *Sphinx Prophet*, 119; one Sphinx soldier asks the famous riddle to two CIA men; when they cannot answer he cuts off their heads (148).

15. Philo of Alexandria, "On the Sacrifices of Abel and Cain," 2.48. Amenophis I and Ramses the Great were named "Aa-nerw" [He who inspires great terror], Grimal, *History of Ancient Egypt*, 202.

16. "A Lyon wiping out with its Tail the impressions of its Feet, was the *Hieroglyphick* of the great Creator, covering over the marks of his Divinity by the works of Nature, and hiding his immediate Power by the visible Agency of inferior Beings," Assigni, *Hieroglyphicks*, 180.

17. The city of Leontopolis in the northern delta of the Nile was the center of a lion cult in the New Empire, and lions were kept in reverent captivity throughout temples in Egypt. Aelian (170–235 AD) described lions kept at Heliopolis, fed to the accompaniment of singing priests (see Budge, *Gods of the Egyptians*, 2:360). On the Sphinx temple see Heick-Hansen, "Sphinx Temple."

18. Champollion, *Lettres et journaux*, 121. The image is suggested by the diorite hawk standing upon the diorite shoulders of Kafre in the Cairo Museum. For the headdress as "wings" see Carrington, *Great Pyramid of Egypt*, 42.

19. Hawass and Lehner, "The Sphinx," 32.

20. Farrington, *Facing the Sphinx*, 14.

21. West, *Serpent in the Sky*, 219; Heath-Stubbs, "The Sphinx," 6.

22. Casson, *Travel in the Ancient World*, 284.

23. Albright, "What Were the Cherubim?" Demisch, *Die Sphinx*, 213–16; "Les Cherubim bibliques qui veillaient sur l'arche n'étaient probablement, dès les dernières années du second millénaire," Dessenne, *Le Sphinx*, 181. Lexicographers dispute whether there is a connection between the Hebrew *kerubim* and the Assyrian *kirubu*, an epithet for the winged bull.

24. Sarna, *Genesis*, 375.

25. Gaffarel, *Curiositiez inovyes*, 15–25. Gaffarel concluded that Cherubim

were winged bulls, like those of Assyria. On the great stela of Amenhotep II at Giza, Horemakhet was honored as "the living Horus, Strong Bull, Great in vigor." The "Strong Bull" epithet persisted for centuries. For the bull-sphinxes of the Near East see Demisch, *Die Sphinx,* 43–63; for the stela of Amenhotep II see Lichtheim, *Ancient Egyptian Literature,* 2:39–41; Hassan, *The Sphinx,* 176–86.

26. Von der Osten, *Ancient Oriental Seals,* item 331. "Es läßt sich ferner nachweisen, daß in der Tradition vom Lebensbaum genau dieselbe Verdichtung vor sich gegangen ist wie in der Sphinxepisode des Oedipusmythus und daß jener in der biblischen Erzählung dieselbe scheinbar nebensächliche Rolle spielt wie die Sphinx in der griechischen" [In the tradition of the Tree of Life precisely the same condensation has occurred as in the Sphinx episode of the Oedipus myth . . . in the biblical narrative the Tree plays the same apparently subsidiary role as the Sphinx in the Greek legend], Reik, "Oedipus und die Sphinx," 131 ["Oedipus and the Sphinx," 332]. See also Demisch, *Die Sphinx,* 228–30. The blessed monk John Cassion, who sojourned in Egypt for seven years, wrote in 426 AD that "Cherubim mean a multitude of knowledge," *Conferences,* 14.10, in Schaff and Wace, *Nicene and Post-Nicene Fathers,* 11:440.

27. The whirring wheels of Ezekiel's vision are moved by Cherubim (Ezekiel 1:7 and 10:1–19; see also Ginzberg, *Legends of the Jews,* 6:52–53). The Lord flies "on the back of a cherub" (2 Samuel 22:11) and is enthroned on cherubim (Psalms 80:1 and 99:1). For the two Cherubim on the Ark of the Covenant see Exodus 26:1, 31 and 36:8, 35. Tertullian noted two exceptions to the prohibition against sacred images: the brass serpent of Moses and the Cherubim of the Ark, each "totally remote from all conditions of idolatry" (*Against Marcion,* 2.22). King Hezekiah (who did what was "right in the sight of the LORD") destroyed the serpent because it had acquired a name, Nehushtan, and a cult. When handed a letter demanding his surrender he puts it on the Ark and prays for an answer, speaking to the God of Israel, who "dwellest between the cherubims" (2 Kings 18 and 19). Saint Bonaventure interpreted the two Cherubim allegorically as the Old and New Testaments (*Hexaemeron* 3:11, 9:11, 9:19, and 15:11).

28. Enoch 61:10; also Enoch 20:7 and 2 Enoch 19:6; *Shemot Rabbah,* 9:11. See Ginzberg, *Legends of the Jews,* 5:104, note 94. Angels destroy Sodom (Genesis 19: 12–26) and at the last minute the Lord stops an angel from destroying Jerusalem (2 Samuel 24:16). Joshua meets the captain of the "army of the Lord" (Joshua 5: 13–15), elsewhere named Michael (Daniel 12:1 and Apocalypse 12:7). See Tavard, *Les anges,* 13–15.

29. "Tu es reine et tu es déesse; comme les anges tu as les côtes attachées en avant, et la substance de ton cerveau diffère aussi peu de la mienne que la semence femelle du sperme du mâle. Parce que tu es femme, tu reflètes infiniment et representes le monde, et sais ce qui échappe aux yeux mortels," Jarry, *César-Antechrist*, 329.

30. "Où l'ange involé se mêle au sphinx antique," Baudelaire, "Avec ses vêtements," *Fleurs du mal* [*Flowers of Evil*, 410]; "Nous avons au paradis des chérubins ou kéroubs en forme de taureaux ailés; mais ce sont là les lourdes inventions d'un Dieu qui n'est pas artiste," France, *Révolte des anges*, 102; Von Hornstein, *Sphinx und der Sadist*, 123.

31. Humbert, Pantazzi, and Ziegler, *Egyptomania*, 486–87.

32. Thomson, *The City of Dreadful Night*, 47–49 (section XX).

33. "ein weibliches Wesen mit einem männlichen Glied," Rank, *Inzest-Motiv*, 267 [*Incest Theme*, 216]. Forrest supposes Phix "might have been some species of hermaphrodite," *Divine Days*, 1095. See Moret, *Œdipe*, 1:11.

34. Mann, *Joseph und seine Brüder*, 2:88 [*Joseph and His Brothers*, 498].

35. Kircher, *Sphinx Mystagoga*, 224; Herberer von Bretten, *Aegyptica Servitus*, 131; Twain, *Innocents Abroad*, 498. Twain later recounted his travels to the Holy Land in a course of public lectures. His description of the Sphinx was especially admired.

36. See Brosi's *"Kuß der Sphinx"* and the monster mothers in Dijkstra's *Idols of Perversity*, 327–32. Both books are well illustrated. Dijkstra's trip to the Sphinx passes expiring poems and paintings of fatal love, pages and pages of death eroticized.

37. Rosegger, *Frau Sphinx*, 105–6.

38. Rukeyser, "Myth," 1787–88.

2. SECRETS

The epigraph reads in the original: "Le Sphinx qui dévore est énigme. / Et son véritable mot n'est pas: *Devine, ou je te dévore!* Mais: *Devine pourquoi je te dévore!*" *Cahiers*, 2:650.

1. Philo of Alexandria, *Congressu Quaerendae Eruditionis Gratia*, section 16, Loeb *Philo*, 4:501; "viduata numinum," Hermes Trismegistus, "Asclepius," 24.7, in *Corpus Hermeticum*, 2:327; "*Aegyptus* hic mundus est qui diversis cladibus affligit populum christianum; sed Domini virtute potentiaque terretur. Aegyptus autem significat afflictionem, qui non aliter dimittit animas fideles, nisi in ipso duris laboribus ingraventur," Cassiodorus, *Explanation of the Psalms*, 3.345.

2. Breasted, *Ancient Records of Egypt,* 2:320–24. The story of Thutmose IV is no secret (Spence, *Myths and Legends,* 85–86; Jordan, *Riddles of the Sphinx,* 28; Lehner, *Complete Pyramids,* 132). Thomas Mann relates it in *Joseph und seine Brüder,* 2:85–86 [*Joseph and His Brothers,* 498–99].

3. Brunton, *Search in Secret Egypt,* 25.

4. "Ante est sphinx vel magis narranda, de qua siluere, numen accolentium. Harmain regem putant in ea conditum et volunt invectam videri; est autem saxo naturali elaborate," Pliny, *Natural History,* 36.17.

5. Vyse, *Operations Carried on at the Pyramids,* 3:118.

6. Hassan, *The Sphinx,* 8.

7. There are possible exceptions. The sculpted head of Pharaoh Djedefre (2510–2485 BC), Kafre's immediate predecessor, excavated at Abu Rawash, may be "the first surviving example of a royal sphinx," Grimal, *History of Ancient Egypt,* 74. Or the first Sphinx may be female and small (see Jordan, *Riddles of the Sphinx,* 80).

8. Jordan, *Riddles of the Sphinx,* 100; Hawass and Lehner, "The Sphinx."

9. "σφίγγας ἐπιεικῶς ἱστάντες, ὡς αἰνιγματώδη σοφίαν τῆς θεολογίας αὐτῶν ἐχούσης," Plutarch, "Isis and Osiris," 354C.

10. Proclus, *Platonis Timaeum,* 1.30; Pico, *De Hominis Dignitate,* 581.

11. Quintilian, *Institutio Oratoria,* 6.3.98.

12. Athenaeus, *Deipnosophists,* 5.197a. On sarcophagic Sphinxes see Demisch, *Die Sphinx,* 57–59, 85–88; Pfuhl and Möbius, *Ostgriechischen Grabreliefs,* 837, 890, 891, 965, 1032, 1075. For modern Sphinx furniture see Proust, *Le côté de Guermantes* and *Sodome et Gomorrhe,* *À la recherche du temps perdu,* 2:519, 689.

13. Thevet, *Cosmographie de Levant; Pilgrimage to Mecca,* 337; Sanderson, *Sundrie the personall Voyages,* 418; Radzivilius, *Hierosolymitana Peregrinatio,* 325. Steeple pyramids appeared in Kircher's *Sphinx Mystagoga* (1676).

14. For summaries of early depictions of the Sphinx see Greener, *Discovery of Egypt;* Jordan, *Riddles of the Sphinx,* 110–11; Lehner, *Complete Pyramids,* 43.

15. Norry, *Account of the French Expedition,* 35. Page copied his engraving from *L'expédition d'Égypt* by Dominique Vivant Denon (1802).

16. For an overview of the history of excavations of the Sphinx see Lehner, "Archaeology of an Image," 30–86. Caviglia also found two stelae from Ramses II. "All these remains, as well as the masonry of the Temple, were painted red," Hassan, *The Sphinx,* 11.

17. Vyse, *Operations Carried on at the Pyramids*, 1:274. Vyse thought the Sphinx had deteriorated badly in its first twenty years of exposure (3:116).

18. Naaman, *Débuts de Flaubert;* the Sarony and Major lithograph of the "Sphynx" in Francis L. Hawks's *The Monuments of Egypt* (1850) copies Vyse. Vyse's drawing and a Du Camp photo are reproduced in Jordan, *Riddles of the Sphinx*, 112, 113.

19. Jordan, *Riddles of the Sphinx*, 100. Pharaonic Sphinxes are still being unburied. Dr. Mohammed Al Sager found thirty-four more in Luxor in 1997 (*Arabic News*, 13 October, 1997).

20. Maspero, cited by Hassan, *The Sphinx*, 16.

21. Hassan, *The Sphinx*, 8; Jordan, *Riddles of the Sphinx*, 94. Jordan cites additional evidence of the Saites (96).

22. Hawass and Lehner, "The Sphinx," 30–41.

23. Cayce, *Egypt at the Time of Ra Ta*, 59, 297–300, and *Edgar Cayce on Prophecy*, 106. Unperturbed by rumors of Araaraart, Mary Stolz gives credit to the stonecarvers father and son, Zekmet and Senmut (*Zekmet*, 20–30). In *The Secret of the Sphinx*, Oscott includes the ouija testimony of its architect, Aftaly Kyepur, who says it had been covered in gold (33–34).

24. Wynn, *Sphinx Unveiled*, 79, 85, 67, 76.

25. Jeffers, *Great Sphinx Speaks*, 55, 65, 36–37. Jeffers prophesies the Second Coming of Christ in 1953 (154).

26. Barbarin, *Énigme du Grand Sphinx*, 166, 20.

27. In the Summer 1992 issue of KMT, geologist Robert M. Schoch ignited a Sphinx controversy by proposing that erosion patterns in the stone justified a date perhaps before 9000 BC. Rebuttals appeared in KMT 5 (Summer 1994): 70–74; KMT 5 (Fall 1994): 40–47; *Science*, February 14, 1992, 5046; *Archaeology* 47 (September–October 1994): 44–47; *Omni* (August 1992); *New York Times*, March 10, 1992, B7; and other journals. On the basis of the Sphinx alone, Schuré found "preuve irrécusable" [irrecusable proof] of a vanished red race, *Grands initiés*, 117 [*Great Initiates*, 133]. On the Atlantids as Sphinx makers see Brunton, *Search in Secret Egypt*, 34; Wilson, *From Atlantis to the Sphinx*. On Mars and beyond see von Daniken, *Eyes of the Sphinx;* Robert Bauval and Graham Hancock, "The Mysterious Structures That May Upstage NASA's Evidence of Martian Life," *London Daily Mail*, August 17–19, 1996.

28. Southey cites Sir William in his *Common-Place Book*, 4:255. Demisch found no leonine Sphinxes in India older than the first century AD (*Die Sphinx*, 206–8).

29. M. Virginia Donaghe, "Questioner of the Sphinx."

30. Rostand, *Secret du Sphinx,* 6, 21.

31. Hancock and Bauval, *Message of the Sphinx,* 59, 71. Their book kicked up sand by accusing American archeologists and the Egyptian government of concealing secrets of the Sphinx, including an underground chamber. The authors speculate logically, paralogically, and analogically, concluding that the Sphinx and its alignment point to a "First Time," 10,500 BC, more or less.

32. "J'ai mes questions. Elle, elle a ses étoiles!" Rostand, *Secret du Sphinx,* 17.

33. Hassan, *The Sphinx,* 82. Hassan cites it as no. 2274 of the Arabic MSS in the Bibliothèque Nationale.

34. "Die Morgen von Jahrtausenden, ein Volk von Winden, der Aufstieg und Niedergang unzähliger Sterne, der Sternbilder großes Dastehen, die Glut dieser Himmel und ihre Weite war da und war immer wieder da, einwirkend, nicht ablassend von der tiefen Gleichgültigkeit dieses Geschichtes, so lange, bis es zu schauen schien, bis es alle Anzeichen eines Schauens genau dieser Bilder aufwies, bis es sich aufhob wie das Gesicht zu einem Innern, darin alles dieses enthalten war und Anlaß und Lust und Not zu alledem. Und da, in dem Augenblick, da es voll war von allem Gegenüber und geformt von seiner Umgebung, war ihm auch schon der Ausdruck hinausgewachsen über sie. Nun wars, als ob das Weltall ein Gesicht hätte, und dieses Gesicht warf Bilder darüber hinaus, bis über die äußersten Gestirne hinaus, dorthin, wo nie noch Bilder gewesen waren," Rilke, letter to Clara Rilke, January 20, 1907. Also "der erhabene Sphinx . . . der Menschen Gesicht / auf die Waage der Sterne gelegt" [the lofty Sphinx . . . the human face / on the scale of the stars], *Duino Elegies,* 209.

35. Berman, *Glands Regulating Personality,* 22, 232–51, 12.

36. Berman, *Glands Regulating Personality,* 271.

37. Berman, *Glands Regulating Personality,* 19, 287–89.

38. Lewis, *Time and Western Man,* 332–337, 137–38.

3. CONFRONTATIONS

The epigraph reads in the original: "La ruse, les enigmas, une precision presque cruelle, une finesse implacable et quasi bestiale; tous les signes de l'attention féline et d'une féroce spiritualité sont visibles sur les simulacres de ces dures divinités. Le mélange habilement mesuré de l'acuité et de la froideur cause dans l'âme un malaise et une inquiétude particulière. Et ces monsters de silence et de lucidité, infiniment calmes, infiniment éveillés; rigides et qui semblent doués d'immanence, ou d'une souplesse prochaine, apparaissent comme l'Intelligence elle-même, en tant que bête et animal impénétrable, qui tout pénètre," *Eupalinos; ou, L'architecte,* 147 [*Eupalinos; or, The Architect,* 107].

1. Prince Oedipus's path maps his thinking. He travels from Corinth to Delphi, then from Delphi to Thebes. In *Oedipus Tyrannus* he explains that he could not go back to Corinth for fear he would kill Polybus, his presumed father, but in walking to the crossroads where he slew Laius he was moving *toward* Corinth. Laius came along at exactly the wrong moment, when Oedipus was making a hard decision. At the crossroads Oedipus discovered how easily he could kill. Only then did he turn from Corinth.

2. "Asclepius," 21–29, *The Nag Hammadi Library,* 334.

3. *Acts of Andrew and Matthias,* in Elliott, *The Apocryphal New Testament,* 288–89. On this apocryphos in the history of the Sphinx see Demisch, *Die Sphinx,* 120–21.

4. For other works that link the Sphinx directly to Jesus see Farrington, *Facing the Sphinx,* v; Dreyer, *Secret of the Sphinx,* 97–101; Wynn, *Sphinx Unveiled,* 58, 185; Jeffers, *Great Sphinx Speaks,* 35, 60–61, 131–32, 143, 154.

5. For example, Chamberlain's novel *Sphinx in Aubrey Parish* (1889) is a thinly disguised polemic on Christian obedience.

6. L'Engle, *Sphinx at Dawn,* 45. Wise beyond his years, young Jesus astonishes the Sphinx by quoting Shakespeare's *As You Like It* (2.7.174–176), 42.

7. Philo of Alexandria, "On the Sacrifices of Abel and Cain," 2.131. For the Holy Family in Egypt, see Matthew 2:13–15.

8. Philo of Alexandria, "On the Posterity and Exile of Cain," 2.337. Small statues of Tutu (or Tithoes) are in the collections of the Metropolitan Museum of Art and the Chicago Institute of Fine Arts.

9. Clement *Stromata* 1.6 [*Stromata,* 307].

10. Clement, *Exhortation to the Heathen,* 181.

11. In *The Recognitions* of Clement of Rome, Aquila asks, "And what shall we say of the books of the poets? Ought not they, if they have debased the honorable and pious deeds of the gods with base fables, to be forthwith cast away and thrown into the fire?" Saint Peter ambiguously replies, "All things are done by the good providence of God," 10.38–39 [translation 8.202].

12. Clement *Stromata* 1.8, 1.1 [*Stromata,* 309, 301].

13. Clement *Stromata* 1.1 [*Stromata,* 300].

14. Clement *Stromata* 1.10 [*Stromata,* 311].

15. In chapter 12 of his *Exhortation to the Heathen* Clement compared Odysseus tied to the mast to Christians "bound to the wood of the cross."

16. The Oedipus/Odysseus comparison returns in Nietzsche: "To see to it that man henceforth stands before man as even today, hardened in the discipline of science, he stands before the *rest* of nature, with intrepid Oedipus eyes and sealed Odysseus ears," *Beyond Good and Evil,* section 230. In his *Odyssey: A Modern Sequel,* Nikos Kazantzakis places Odysseus face-to-face with the Sphinx of Giza, first in an interrogatory Oedipal pose, then caught up in rapture (9.435–55).

17. Clement *Stromata* 1.1, 1.12 [*Stromata,* 302–3, 312].

18. Clement *Stromata* 1.1 [*Stromata,* 302].

19. "αἰνιγματώδους τοῦ περὶ θεοῦ λόγου καὶ ἀσαφοῦς ὄντος," Clement *Stromata* 5.7, 5.5.

20. Clement *Stromata,* 5.8 [*Stromata,* 455].

21. Merson painted several versions (see Humbert, Pantazzi, and Ziegler, *Egyptomania,* 496–97). "O Sphinx, abrite sous ton ombre / Le saint enfant," Fragerolle, *Le Sphinx,* 26.

22. Wallace, *Repose in Egypt,* 104–6.

23. "Regarde-moi, dit-il, je suis le Sphinx-Nature. Ange, aigle, lion et taureau, j'ai la face auguste d'un Dieu et le corps d'une bête ailée et rugissante. . . . *je suis, je vois, je sais* depuis toujours. Car je suis un des Archétypes éternels qui vivent dans la lumière incréée"; "Les Kaldéens, les Égyptiens et les Hébreux sculptaient par analogie les Kéroubim sous le symbole du Taureau, du Lion, de l'Aigle et de l'Ange (ou de l'Homme). Ce sont les quatre animaux sacrés de l'arche de Moïse, des quatre Évangélistes et de l'Apocalypse de saint Jean. Le Sphinx égyptien les résume en une seule forme, symbole merveilleusement adapté de la Nature visible et invisible, de toute l'évolution terrestre et divine," Schuré, *Évolution divine,* 24, 32 [*From Sphinx to Christ,* 15, 32].

24. "il m'est défendu de parler autrement que par ma presence"; "Elle symbolize toute l'evolution de l'âme humaine, sa descente dans la chair et son retour à l'Esprit. Grâce au Christ, le voile du sanctuaire est déchiré, l'énigme du Sphinx est résolue," Schuré, *Évolution divine,* 4, 408 [*From Sphinx to Christ,* 15, 264]. Others who argue that the Sphinx and pyramids foretold the coming of Christ include Wynn, *Sphinx Unveiled* (1928); Jeffers, *Great Sphinx Speaks* (1942); Barbarin, *Énigme du Grand Sphinx* (1946); Holt, *Sphinx and the Great Pyramid* (1977).

25. Ida, Countess Hahn-Hahn, *Letters,* 3:221.

26. Freud inserted this idea in the 1919 edition of *The Interpretation of Dreams,* chapter 6, section E.

27. Melville, *Moby Dick,* chapter 70.

28. Renard, "Sphinx à masque funéraire"; Demisch, *Die Sphinx,* 115.

29. Moret, *Œdipe,* 1:52, 82.

30. Twain, *Innocents Abroad,* 502.

31. "Ils faut être habitué à la fatalité et à ses rencontres pour oser lever les yeux quand de certaines questions nous apparaissent dan leur nudité horrible. Le bien ou le mal sont derrière ce sévére point d'interrogation. Que vas-tu faire? Demande le sphinx," Hugo, *Les misérables,* 1090 [*Les Misérables,* 1195].

32. "El remedio es considerarlo cara a cara, fija la mirada en la mirada de la Esfinge, que es así como se deshace el maleficio de su aojamiento," Unamuno, *Sentimiento trágico de la vida,* 170 [*Tragic Sense of Life,* 48].

33. Hassan, *The Sphinx,* 81–82.

34. *Pilgrimage to Mecca,* 337; Wansleben, *Sammlung der merkwurdigsten reisen in den Orient,* quoted in Hassan, *The Sphinx,* 83.

35. Ludwig, *Napoleon,* 121. Colrat revisits Gérôme's scene of Napoleon and the Sphinx in French red, white, and blue (*Sphinx bafoué,* 127–35).

36. The original painting is in the collection of the Hearst San Simeon State Historical Monument, California. The painting was engraved for books and wall hangings, parodied, and adopted as an emblem for the letterhead of *Sphinx,* the magazine for magicians. Wojciech Kossak (1857–1942) included the encounter as part of his Napoleon series.

37. Melville, *Clarel,* 4.35.3–11.

38. Twain, *Innocents Abroad,* 503; Lowell, "Sonnet," 404.

39. Harvey, "By Trolley to the Sphinx," 340.

40. Roosevelt came to Africa to kill. Who but ancient kings could know how Roosevelt felt when he boasted three thousand animal trophies, including five elephants, seven hippos, nine lions, and thirteen rhinos?

4. RIDDLES

The epigraph is from "Language," chapter 4 of "Nature" [1836], 25.

1. This is the form given in *The Library* of Apollodorus, 3.5.9. The Greeks told the riddles in numerous forms, some longer (such as Asclepiades chapter 2, note 1), some shorter (Diodorus of Sicily, 4.64.3). For a survey of the riddle and its variations in ancient Greek literature see Lesky, "Rätsel der Sphinx."

2. "She was more inscrutable in her childish ignorance than the Sphinx propounding childish riddles to wayfarers," Conrad, *Lord Jim*, 187; Kerényi and Hillman, *Oedipus Variations*, 59; "childishly simple," Symonds, *Oedipus and the Sphinx*, 24; Benjamin, "Der Erzähler," section 16; Lawrence, *Apocalypse*, 77; De Quincey, "Theban Sphinx," 140.

3. Vilott, *Secret of the Sphinx*, 20. J. K. Rowling's Harry Potter encounters a Sphinx in *Harry Potter and the Goblet of Fire* but it asks him a logogriph (628–30).

4. Seneca, *Oedipus*, 92–109.

5. "frivole e effrayante; elle est divertissante, aimable et mortelle. . . . La question la plus profonde est telle qu'elle ne permet pas qu'on l'entende; on peut seulement la répéter," Blanchot, *Entretien infini*, 22 [*Infinite Conversation*, 18].

6. Edmunds, *Sphinx in the Oedipus Legend*, 1.

7. Cocteau, *Machine infernale*, 1. A teenage shepherd returns from the Sphinx babbling and idiotic in Friesner's *Sphynxes Wild*, 14.

8. Du Bois, *John Brown*, 172. Chapter 12 is entitled "The Riddle of the Sphinx."

9. Collier, *Life Magnet*, 1:7–8.

10. For legs and feet in later version of the riddle see Aarne, *Vergleichende Rätselforschungen*, 27:7–23.

11. L'Engle, *Sphinx at Dawn*, 38.

12. Pausanias, *Description of Greece*, 9.26.2. Gide's Oedipus admits, "je le tenais prêt dès avant d'avoir entendu l'énigme" [I had it [the answer] ready even before I heard the riddle"], *Œdipe*, 80 [*Oedipus*, 28].

13. Euripides, *The Heracleidae*, 748.

14. Apollodorus, *Library*, 3.5.8.

15. Peirce, quoted in Brent, *Peirce: A Life*, 4.

16. Peirce, "A Guess at the Riddle," 187–88, 201–2.

17. Lawrence, *Apocalypse*, 79.

18. Gide, *Œdipe*, 80 [*Oedipus*, 28].

19. Kerényi and Hillman, *Oedipus Variations*, 15–16. Hegel made the same connection in his *Aesthetik*, 12:480 [*Aesthetics*, 1:361]).

20. Dickens, "A Riddle without an Answer," *Our Mutual Friend*, 339.

21. Heidfeld, *Sphinx Philosophica*. The full title translates as "The Philosophic Sphinx, Disclosing and Proposing Erudite and Subtle Enigmas or Riddles, compiled from Various Authors both Sacred and Profane, Marvelously providing Wisdom, exercising and sharpening honorable characters, and forming the judgment of the studious." Copies are rare. A fifth edition (1608) is on microfilm:

"For the fifth time Reborn, Renewed, and also Considerably more Embellished as the Newly Improved Theologicophilosophical Sphinx." At the hub of the boom Flitner published a German translation, *Sphinx Theologico-philosophica*.

22. See Friedreich's *Geschichte des Rätsels* (1860), 84–89.

23. Examples are *The New Sphinx* (circa 1810); Zucktschwerdt, *Sphinx und Harmonia* (1813); *The New Sphinx* (1840); C. C. and E. C., *The Sphynx* (1867); *The Modern Sphinx* (1873); Berloquin, *Le jardin du sphinx* (1981); Gardner, *Riddles of the Sphinx* (1987), Mayfield, See, et al., *Lair of the Sphinx* (1999).

24. Bird, *Booke of Merrie Riddles*, 16.

25. The name of the author of *Sphinx Incruenta* is a riddle, its answer to riddle 30 is "Nothing," and its answer to riddle 57 is blank.

26. "Sfinge d'illustri marmi, / U' la gelida salma indi chiudesse / Funesta, altera tomba, / Amasi il rege di Canòpo eresse. / Stabil viepiù rimbomba / Tua SFINGE in fragil carta, e negri carmi, / Sfinge, senza drizzar mole superba, / Che ti trae dal sepolcro, e in vita serba," Malatesti, *La Sfinge*, v. Hanns Meinke's *Terzinen von der Sphinx* is in terza rima.

27. Edmunds, *Sphinx in the Oedipus Legend*, 6–9.

28. Statius, *Thebaid*, 1.67; Bacon, *Wisedom of the Ancients*, section 28.

29. De Quincey, "Theban Sphinx," 151, 147. See also Velikovsky: "Were it my misfortune to stand before the Sphinx with the dire prospect of never entering Thebes, I should reply to her riddle: 'It is Oedipus,'" *Oedipus and Akhnaton*, 207.

30. De Quincey, "Theban Sphinx," 148–49.

31. Ahl, *Sophocles' Oedipus*, 261.

32. Parkes's Sphinx paintings include *Dark Sphinx, Designing the Sphinx, Rainbow Sphinx, Sphinx #1, Sphinx #2, The Sphinx*, and *White Sphinx*.

33. Delcourt, *Œdipe*, 127–28. See also Moret, *Œdipe*, 1:84.

34. Emerson, *Huntress and the Sphinx*, 152, 180, 218. Emerson parodies the famous riddle on 203.

35. Erasmus reprises the Boetians' reputation as dullards in his *Adages*, 3.2.48. The Broughs' Mercury recites that Thebans "are such sad fools. . . . Pooh! The fact's well known; it's taught in schools," *The Sphinx*, 5.

36. Ronell, *Stupidity*, 55.

37. Euripides, *Phoenician Women*, 1730.

38. *Oedipus Chymicus* is Becher's German translation of his *Institutiones Chimicae Prodromae* (1664). On Becher's life, work, and search for work, see Smith's *Business of Alchemy*, 181, 280.

39. Iversen, *Myth of Egypt*, 94.

40. Kircher interprets the hieroglyphs on the side and back of a marble Sphinx then in the museum of Gerardus Reinstius of Amsterdam, and a Sphinx in the Villa Burghesia.

41. Kircher cites Aven Vaschia in *Oedipus Aegyptiacus*, 224, 460. He thought obelisks were "idearum idea," *Sphinx Mystagoga*, 20a. On "summa significationis" see *Oedipus Aegyptiacus*, 224; *Sphinx Mystagoga*, 55a.

42. Kircher reminds his reader how hard he works, how much he knows, and how his many big books connect. Grafton calls Kircher the "maddest of polymaths" (*Defenders of the Text*, 159); Harris describes him as "the whipping boy of Egyptology" (*Legacy of Egypt*, 191). Godwin reminds us that Kircher was a happy man, curious, industrious, honored, famous, and ecstatic in a universe full of divine symbols (*Athanasius Kircher*). See also Stolzenberg, *Great Art of Knowing*.

43. Byron, *Don Juan*, canto 13, stanza 12.

5. BODY

The epigraph reads in the original: "Le sculpteur fait surgir, en des poussières claires, / Un Sphinx qui, sous ses mains, comme un spectre évoqué, / S'éveille du sommeil des granits séculaire," *Âme du Sphinx*, 37.

1. Eichler, "Nochmals die Sphinxgruppe aus Ephesos." For other reproductions see Demisch, *Die Sphinx*, 84; Moret, *Œdipe*, 2:plates 16.1 and 16.2.

2. For Hatshepsut's granite Sphinxes see Tefnin, *Statuaire d'Hatshepsout*, 102–20.

3. Fielding, *Face on the Sphinx*, 59–60; Bibesco, *Sphinx of Bagatelle*, 112–117.

4. Two marble female Sphinxes console each other celestially on the Lycian sarcophagous (circa 425 AD), now in the Archaeological Museum of Istanbul. They bare their breasts, withdraw their claws, and point their wings to heaven.

5. "Dort vor dem Tor lag eine Sphinx, / Ein Zwitter von Schrecken und Lüsten, / Der Leib und die Tatzen wie ein Löw, / Ein Weib an Haupt und Brüsten. // Entzückende Marter und wonniges Weh! / Der Schmerz wie die Lust unermeßlich! / Derweilen des Mundes Kuß mich beglückt, / Verwinden die Tatzen mich gräßlich. // "O schöne Sphinx! / O liebe! was soll es bedeuten, / Daß du vermischest mit Todesqual / All deine Seligkeiten?"; "Vorrede zur dritten Auflage," Heine, *Buch der Lieder*, 14–15 [*Complete Poems*, 7–8]. Heine's poem inspired Franz von Stuck's *The Sphinx's Kiss* (see illustration 6.1).

6. Pliny, *Natural History*, 36.iv.22–23.

7. Moret sees such seeing as anachronistic: "Toute interprétation érotique du motif doit être écartée," *Œdipe*, 1:11.

8. "There had been no figure more prominent in the world she frequented. In oil and in pastel, in water-colour, and black and white, she had graced the walls of winter and summer exhibitions, the pages of illustrated magazines, the weekly editions of fashion papers," Frankau, *Sphinx's Lawyer*, 31; "The physical perfection of a beautiful woman," Hume, *Woman*, 32; "The most beautiful woman she had ever seen," Annesley, *Sphinx in the Labyrinth*, 8; "Elsa was wearing a bikini that left very little to the imagination, and I had to admit I could find no fault with what I saw," Robin, *Cruise of the Sphinx*, 33; Erika Baron is "the perfect catalyst for the fantasies of all the men who watched her," Cook, *Sphinx*, 28.

9. This is necessary vocabulary for *The Sphinx Golden Jubilee Book of Magic* (see Christopher).

10. See Brosi, *"Kuß der Sphinx"*; Demisch, *Die Sphinx*, chapter 10. The Sphinxes of Adamson's *Spotted Sphinx* and Bell's *Tomorrow's Sphinx* are cheetahs. For domestic Sphinxes see Repplier's *Fireside Sphinx*.

11. Leyhausen and Tonkin, *Cat Behavior*, 18–19.

12. Leyhausen and Tonkin, *Cat Behavior*, 14–15, 30–31, 39, 55, 110–13. The etymology of *Sphinx* traces to "death by strangling," Liddell and Scott, *Lexicon*, 1741a.

13. The Testament of Solomon 18:1. In *Roman de la momie* Gautier describes his heroine smiling and mysterious, "comme un masque de sphinx," 525.

14. Bartholomaeus, *Orderici Vitalis Angligenae Coenobii Uticensis Monachi Historiae Ecclestasticae*, book 2, chapter 15 (see Dartmouth Dante Project); Tasso, *Gerusalemme liberata*, 4.5.2; Mandeville, *Fable of the Bees*, 2.232 [266]; Shelley, *Prometheus Unbound*, 1.346–48. Gautier's poem "Sphinx" describes a "Chimère antique" in the royal garden, 255.

15. "Et dans le silence de la nuit, l'admirable dialogue de la Chimère et du Sphinx commença, récité par des voix gutturales et profondes, rauques, puis aiguës, comme surhumaines," Huysmans, *À Rebours*, 148.

16. Goux, *Oedipus, Philosopher*, 61–67.

17. Diodorus of Sicily, 4.64.3; Kircher, *Oedipus Aegyptiacus*, 127; De Quincey, "Theban Sphinx," 144; Wilde, "The Sphinx," 155.

18. Apollodorus, *Library*, 3.5.8; see also Hyginus, *Fabularum Liber*, 24 [*Myths*, 66].

19. Hesiod, *Theogony*, 295–329.

20. Aristophanes, *Ranae*, 1287 [*Frogs*, 127].

21. The Sphinx in Anouilh's *Œdipe* is a dog. Mickey Mouse's pet dog, Pluto, was ensphinxed in *Plutopia* (1941). Snoopy, the dog from the comic strip *Peanuts*, appeared as a Sphinx in an advertisement for Metropolitan Life Insurance.

22. Sophocles, *Oedipus Tyrannus*, 391; comte de Marcellus, *Souvenirs d'Orient* (1839), cited in Carré, *Voyageurs*, 1:209. See also "corpus canis," Conti, *Mythologiae*, 286; "corpore canis," Picinelli, *Mundus Symbolicus*, 169; Tooke, *Pantheon*, 307.

23. Brownell, "The Sphinx," 247.

24. Apollodorus, *Library*, 3.5.8; Ausonius's *Griphus Ternarii Numeri* is "a lengthy riddle on the number three, full of Pythagorean doctrine," Conte, *Latin Literature*, 656; Conti, *Mythologiae*, chapter 17. The five-part Sphinx of Clearchus was the favored description of the Renaissance—for example, "the face and voice was like a Girls, the body like a Dog, the tail as a Dragons, and the claws like a Lyons, with great wings upon the back," Gautruche, *Poetical Histories*, 174; see also Alciati, *Emblemata*, 796.

25. Staatliche Museen zu Berlin, *Ägyptisches Museum*, 204–5; Lydgate, *Fall of Princes*, line 3354; Bird, *Booke of Merrie Riddles*, 16; Wilde, "The Sphinx," 13–16; Henry, "The Sphinx Apple," 211–22.

26. Wynn, *Sphinx Unveiled*, 58.

27. Dryden and Lee, *Oedipus*, 145. "The Sphinx bore down our city with her raids," Euripides, *Phoenician Women*, 45.

28. "Il admire sa face camarde et le large sourire épanoui sur ses lèvres épaisses comme une ironie éternelle de la fragilité des chose humaines; ses oreilles, sur lesquelles retombent les gaufrures des bandelettes sacrées, et qui ont entendu, comme la chute d'un grain de sable, l'écoulement de tant de dynasties!" Gautier, *L'Orient*, 2:253. See also Ampère, "Sa grande oreille semble recueillir les bruits du passé; ses yeux tournés vers l'orient semblent épier l'avenir," quoted in Rawlinson, *History of Ancient Egypt*, 1:277.

29. Lowell, "The Sphinx."

30. For reproductions of the changing faces of the Great Sphinx see Lehner, *Complete Pyramids*, 43; Jordan, *Riddles of the Sphinx*, 110–12.

31. For a thorough description of the Sphinx's face and the damage done to it see Lehner, "Archaeology of an Image," 177–83; Péju uses the term "une leper," *La part du Sphinx*, 224.

32. In Plato's *Phaedo*, 71a–c Socrates teaches Cebes that opposites generate opposites.

33. Alciati, *Emblemata*, 801; Valeriano Bolzani, *Hieroglyphica*, 14.

34. Withers, *Egypt*, 37.

35. Bouvet, *Smile of the Sphinx*, 332.

36. "une langue de sphinx, aux syllabes de granit," Gautier, *Roman de la momie*, 623–25.

37. Brontë, *Jane Eyre*, 122; Flemming, *Cupid and the Sphinx*, 2.

38. Schuré, *Évolution divine*, 24 [*From Sphinx to Christ*, 15]; Enel, *Message from the Sphinx*, 9–11; Péladan, *Terre du Sphinx*, 340.

39. Besant, *Sphinx of Theosophy*, 3.

40. "l'univers est rond comme un zéro," Rostand, *Secret du Sphinx*, 19; Brunton, *Search in Secret Egypt* 285; MacLeish, "What Riddle Asked the Sphinx"; Enel, *Gnomologie*, 221–22.

41. Kinglake, *Eothen*, 286; Eldridge, *And the Sphinx Spoke*, xv.

42. Milton, *Prolusions*, 229. See Ronell on the Sphinx, sphincter, and Oedipedagogy (*Finitude's Score*, 108–9).

43. Sophocles, *Oedipus Tyrannus*, 36 and 130.

44. Homer, *Odyssey*, 24.60; Apollodorus, *Library*, 3.5.8; Wegner, *Musensarkophage*, 40, 70–71, plates 21, 128–30.

45. *Love's Labor's Lost* 4.iii.337. For the Apollo amphora see Moret, *Œdipe*, 2: plate 60.

46. *amousotataisi* is the feminine plural dative superlative of *amousos:* "without taste, unrefined, inelegant, rude, gross," Liddell and Scott, *Lexicon*, 85b.

47. On dactylic hexameters as the customary meter for oracles, see Lesky, "Rätsel der Sphinx," 318; Segal, "Music of the Sphinx," 154; Delcourt, *Œdipe*, 134.

48. It is the missing piece. Mendelssohn's incidental music for Sophocles' *Antigone* (opus 55) and *Oedipus at Colonus* (opus 93) were completed and performed in 1841 and 1845 respectively.

49. "Manon, Manon, Sphinx étonnant, / Véritable sirène! Coeur trois fois féminine!" Massenet, *Manon,* libretto by Henri Meilhac and Philippe Gille, act 4, scene 2.

50. Leiris, *Âge d'homme*, 213.

51. Valentine and Harper, *Red Sphinx*, 83, 86, 259. In Joseph-Renaud's *Sphinx bleu* the jilted seductress Sita vows to choke her rival to death (103).

52. "Wie bedeutsam ist es nun, daß gerade dieser Oidipus das Räthsel der Sphinx gelöst hatte! Er sprach im Voraus seine Rechtfertigung und seine Verdammung zugleich selbst aus, da er als den Kern dieses Räthsels den Menschen

bezeichnete. Aus dem halbthierischen Leibe der Sphinx trat ihm zunächst das menschliche Individuum nach seiner Naturunterworfenheit entgegen: als das Halbthier aus seiner öden Felseneinsamkeit sich selbstzerschmetternd in den Abgrund gestürzt hatte, wandte sich der kluge Räthsellöser zu den Städten der Menschen, um den ganzen, den sozialen Menschen, aus seinem eigenen Unter- gange errathen zu lassen," Wagner, *Oper und Drama,* 4:57 [*Opera and Drama,* 183].

53. Wagner wrote in a letter to Mathilde Wesendonk (August 1860) that Kun- dry would be "sphinxartig."

54. See Schauffler, *Florestan,* 71, 290–91. In a 1928 recording Alfred Cortot broke with convention and played the Sphinxes aloud, to announce what the Sphinxes would sound like if they sounded at all. The Cortot recording was released on compact disk #296 by the Piano Library, Fono Enterprise, 1999. Mitsuko Uchida revived the idea, with more mystery (*Carnaval,* Philips 442 777–2, 1995).

55. Lear's lyrics provoke the Sphinx episode in Garreta's *Sphinx,* 116–19.

6. EROS

The epigraph is from *The Sphinx,* 79.

1. Chekhov, *The Seagull,* act 3.

2. Novalis, *Henry von Ofterdingen,* 132–40. It is relatively rare in Western lit- erature for a Sphinx to ask questions of a girl.

3. According to Carl Robert, the commission from Hera was a relatively late addition to the story. In other accounts the Sphinx was sent by Dionysos, Ares, or Hades (*Oidipus,* 1:155, 157–58, 394, 495; 2:62.

4. "un grande sphinx de marbre noir, accroupi sur un bloc de granit," Zola, *La curée,* 74 [*The Kill,* 45]. "Renée agenouillée, penchée, avec des yeux fixes, une atti- tude brutale qui lui fit peur. Les cheveux tombés, les épaules nues, elle s'appuyait sur ses poings, l'échine allongée, pareille à une grandee chatte aux yeux phos- phorescents. Le jeune homme, couché sur le dos, aperçut, au-dessus des épaules de cette adorable bête amoureuse qui le regardait, le sphinx de marbre, dont la lune éclairait les cuisses luisantes. Renée avait la pose et le sourire du monstre à tête de femme, et, dans ses jupons dénoués, elle semblait la soeur blanche de ce dieu noir," *La curée,* 199–200 [*The Kill,* 167]. "Elle était toute gonflée de vo- lupté, et les lignes claires de ses épaules et de ses reins se détachaient avec des sécheresses félines sur la tache d'encre dont la fourrure noircissait le sable jaune

de l'allée. Elle guettait Maxime, cette proie renversée sous elle, qui s'abandonnait, qu'elle possédait tout entire," *La curée,* 203 [*The Kill,* 170].

5. Fitzgerald, "Bernice Bobs Her Hair," 135; "Qu'elle était belle, blanche et noire, dans la profondeur souriante ey comme on espérait / Qu'après le premier voile, il y en aurait un autre, toujours d'autres indéfiniment. / Il n'y a rien de plus que l'énigme, la grande enigma qui vous aime et qui sans fin se renouvelle. . . . Mes yeux de sel ont vu cette fille des forêts, habilée par la fleur sauvage / On pressentait ses formes franches, sous sa robe on voyait de grandes courbes animals / Et l'on voulait passionément adorer, déchirer, arracher sa fourrure," Bauchau, *Œdipe sur la route,* 163–64 [*Oedipus on the Road,* 131].

6. Howard, "The Encounter," 78. Vladimir Propp notes that in some folklore versions Oedipus deprives the Sphinx "of her power just as the princess-sorceress in fairy tales is deprived of hers—by sexual intercourse," "Oedipus in the Light of Folklore," 109.

7. Wilde, *Sphinx,* stanza 22. Wilde's Sphinx loves a lion, kills it, then takes "a tiger to mate," stanzas 71–73.

8. Lawrence, "New Eve and Old Adam," 87; *Complete Poems,* 603, 604.

9. Friesner, *Sphynxes Wild,* 257.

10. Gautier, *Une nuit de Cléopâtre,* 742, 743, 747, 754, 762, 768 [*One of Cleopatra's Nights,* 2, 5, 9, 13, 17, 23].

11. Joncières, *Âme du Sphinx,* 49–52.

12. "Les deux pointes de sa poitrine / Haletant me poignardaient, / Ses prunelles d'aigue-marine / —Deux soleils qui me regardaient—/ / Semblaient jeter en une flamme, / A travers mes yeux éblouis, / / Toute son âme dans mon âme! / —O ma chérie! ô mon idole! / Demain pas plus qu'hier, qu'aujourd'hui, / Je ne pourrai lire en ton âme. / / Et je chercherais vainement: / Tu garderas l'enigme, ô femme, / Sphinx exaspérant et charmant," *Âme du Sphinx,* 160–61.

13. For more on Cleopatra's seductions see Humbert, Pantazzi, and Ziegler, *Egyptomania,* 552–81.

14. Reade, *The Cloister and the Hearth,* 524.

15. "Sphinx! . . . ô toi, le plus ancien des dieux! . . . murmura la belle vierge prométhéene, je sais que ton royaume est semblable à des steppes arides et qu'il faut longtemps marcher dans le désert pour arriver jusqu'à toi. L'ardente abstraction ne saurait m'effrayer; j'essaierai. Les prêtres, dans les temples d'Égypte, plaçaient, auprès de ton image, la statue voilée d'Isis, la figure de la Création; sur le socle, ils avaient inscrit ces paroles: 'Je suis ce qui est, ce qui fut, ce qui

sera: personne n'a soulevé le voile qui me couvre.' Sous la transparence du voile, dont les couleurs éclatantes suffisaient aux yeux de la foule, les initiés pouvaient seuls pressentir la forme de l'énigme de pierre, et, par intervalles, ils le surchargaient encore de plis diaprés et mystérieux pour mettre de plus en plus le regard des hommes dans l'impuissance de la profaner. Mais les siècles ont passé sur le voile tombé en poussière; je franchirai l'enceinte sacrée et j'essaierai de regarder le problème fixement," Villiers de L'Isle-Adam, *Isis*, 133, 149–50.

16. James, "The Beast in the Jungle." Marcher sought from May "an answer to his long riddle," 519.

17. Hugo's love Sphinx is "le sombre sphinx Nature," "Ténèbres," 638; "Je connais un baiser qui ne finit jamais," Rostand, *Secret du Sphinx*, 22; Bibesco, *Sphinx of Bagatelle*, 11.

18. Caesar and Cleopatra meet at a Sphinx in Shaw's play. See also Corelli's *Ziska*, 7–10; Erlenbusch's *Die Sphinx*, 123–26.

19. Goux, *Oedipus, Philosopher*, 47–59.

20. Kierkegaard, *Either/Or*, 2:45. Walter Lowrie writes that Kierkegaard broke his engagement with Regina Schlegel for sublime reasons, that she understood his reasons and loved him the more for them, and that he loved her till his death (*Kierkegaard*, 1:191–231). In his pure and troubled heart Kierkegaard distrusted introspection: "The poet understands everything, in riddles, and marvelously explains everything, in riddles, but he cannot understand himself, or understand that he himself is a riddle," *Works of Love*, 45. In one persona he advised, "One ought to be a riddle not only to others but also to oneself," *Either/Or*, 1:26; in another he responded that Nero (who died quoting *Oedipus Rex*) was such a person after he set Rome afire, "He is a riddle to himself, and anxiety is his nature; now he will be a riddle to everybody and rejoice over their anxiety," *Either/Or*, 2:187.

21. Chamberlain, *Sphinx in Aubrey Parish*, 481.

22. Balzac, "Petites misères de la vie conjugale," *La comédie humaine*, 12:31.

23. Cartland, *Moonlight on the Sphinx*, 114, 115, 180.

24. Péladan lashed out at Zola and his "prétentions scientifiques" in his third volume of *La décadence latine* (1887): "sait-il que l'ouvrière que les ovaires sains chantera en travaillant? que le blasement vient de l'affaiblissement testiculaire et le parlage sempiternal, de l'irritation glandulaire," *L'initiation sentimentale*, 9.

25. Péladan, *Curieuse!* (1886) and *La vertu suprême* (1900), 398. The first pages of *La vertu suprême* and *À coeur perdu* (1888) mirror the first pages of *La vice*

suprême. For the several Sphinxes drawn and painted by Rops (1833–98) see Brosi, *"Kuß der Sphinx,"* 48–50, 218, plates 17 (*Die Sphinx,* 1874) and 18 (*Parallel,* 1896). Péladan wrote an homage to Rops in Arsène, *Félicien Rops.* For a Rops overview, see Rouir, *Félicien Rops.*

26. "Sa pensée tourne ces pages du livre du sphinx qui bruissent comme un écho affaibli de baisers nombreux et sourds et d'où glissent les signets: fleurs séchées moins vite que les ardeurs qui les ont échangées; billets jaunis, survivants des amours mort-nés, gardant sur leur vélin le parfum et la caresse des corsage. Dans un lointain perdu, le choeur des poètes chante l'hymne d'amour éternelle et les oreilles humaines sont tendues à ces concerts qui semblent ceux mêmes des anges," Péladan, *La vice suprême,* 89.

27. Péladan, *La vice suprême,* 119, 126, 337.

28. Haggard, *Ayesha,* 98–99. Haggard's heroes find "the grandest allegorical work of Art that the genius of her children has ever given to the world," a statue of Truth, a woman naked except for a sculpted veil, a colossal winged beauty reaching for the ignorant world, in an abandoned temple in the ruins of Kôr (*She,* 175–76).

29. Haggard, *She,* 18, 26.

30. Haggard, *She,* 188.

31. Corelli, *Ziska,* 215–16, 334–49. Asked if he understands that Princess Ziska is a fiend, Gervase answers, "It would take Oedipus himself all his time to do that," 280.

32. "Le sfingi concentra / la donna nel cuore; / chi l'ama non c'entra, / chi l'ange ci muore," Lanciarini, *Sphinx,* 22–23. The Sphinx's Italian shows her age.

33. "Il eut peur de l'infini et du mystère plus encore que de la solitude," Hermant, *Deux Sphinx,* 173; Nichols, *Smile of Sphinx,* 57.

34. "Cette complexité même de la femme l'enchante: voilà un merveilleux domestique don't il peut s'éblouir à peu de frais. Est-elle ange ou démon? L'incertitude en fait un Sphinx. C'est sous cette égide qu'était placée une des maisons closes les plus renommées de Paris. A la grande époque del la Féminité, au temps des corsets, de Paul Bourget, d'Henri Bataille, du french-cancan, le thème du Sphinx sévit intarissablement dans les comédies, les poésies et les chansons: 'Qui es-tu, d'où viens-tu, Sphinx étrange?' " de Beauvoir, *Le deuxième sexe,* 1:303–4 [*The Second Sex,* 217].

35. "Les fiancées brillaient aux fenêtres, éclairées d'une seule branche indiscrète, et leurs voix, alternant avec celles des jeunes hommes qui brûlaient en

bas pour elles, mêlaient aux parfums déchaînés de la nuit de mai un murmure inquiétant, vertigineux comme celui qui peut signaler sur la soie des déserts l'approche du sphinx," Breton, *L'amour fou*, 737 [*Mad Love*, 69].

36. "Qui suis-je?"; "Elle, je sais que dans toute la force du terme il lui est arrivé de me prendre pour un dieu, de croire que j'*étais* le soleil. Je me souviens aussi . . . de lui être apparu noir et froid comme un home foudroyé aux pieds du Sphinx"; "une question qu'il n'y a que moi pour poser. . . . Qui êtes-vous?"; "ce sphinx qui nous avait épargnés l'un après l'autre"; "pour moi c'était de toute éternité devant toi que devait prendre fin cette succession d'énigmes. . . . Je dis que tu me détournes pour toujours de l'énigme," Breton, *Nadja*, 647, 714, 688, 691, 752 [*Nadja*, 11, 111, 78, 71, 158]. One Sphinx in D. M. Thomas's novel *Sphinx* is named Nadia.

37. In New York by Julius Schmid, in Los Angeles by A & M Accessories. Both are defunct.

38. Athenaeus, *Deipnosophists*, 13.558d.

39. Herodotus, *Histories*, 2:134–35; Murtada ibn al-Afif, *Egyptian History*, 54–55.

40. Radzivilius, *Hierosolymitana Peregrinatio*, 325. He confuses two names from Herodotus: Naucratis was the city where Rhodopis established her reputation.

41. Sandys, *Relations of Africa*, 206–7. Sandys's image of the Sphinx was perhaps influenced by Herodotus, who wrote that Cheops had financed construction of his great pyramid by prostituting his daughter (*Histories*, 2:126–27).

42. Picinelli, *Mundus Symbolicus*, 169:

43. Hugo, "Love in Prison," section 4.

44. "Là où se poursuit l'activité la plus equivoque des vivants, l'inanimé prend parfois un reflet de leurs plus secrets mobiles: nos cités sont ainsi peuplées de sphinx méconnus qui n'arrêtent pas la passant rêveur, s'il ne tourne vers eux sa distraction meditative, qui ne lui posent pas de questions mortelles. Mais s'il sait les deviner, ce sage, alors, que lui les interroge, ce sont encore ses propres abîmes que grace à ces monsters sans figure il va de nouveau sonder," Aragon, *Paysan de Paris*, 18, "putains" 133 [*Nightwalker*, 9–10, 88–89]. For a similar account see Soupault's *Dernières nuits de Paris*.

45. Nin, *Diary*, 16 (Winter 1931–32); Miller, *Tropic of Cancer*, 191.

46. "Tout voir, tout entendre et ne rien dire," "le Sphinx avait reveille le quartier Montparnasse qui était à moitié mort depuis des années," "ils apportaient au Sphinx des têtes de morts ou des tibias et sortaient de leurs poches des mains

découpées sur des cadavers," "Plus j'ai d'hommes en même temps dans mon lit et mieux je chante le lendemain," Lemestre, *Madame Sphinx*, 151, 168, 211, 233 [*Madame Sphinx*, 103, 114, 141, 157]; Leiris, *Fourbis*, 183 [*Scraps*, 183].

47. "Plus j'ai d'hommes en même temps dans on lit et mieux je chante le lendemain," Lemestre, *Madame Sphinx*, 233 [*Madame Sphinx*, 157].

48. Wilson, *Sphinx in the City*, 8.

49. Carr, *Sleeping Sphinx*, 206, 218.

50. *Parabhram* is also an epithet of Vishnu (see *Vishnu Purāna*, 1:170).

7. MIND

The epigraph is from "The Approach to Thebes," 340.

1. White, *From Sphinx to Oracle*, 1. Compare Baudelaire's "La beauté," an incomprehensible Sphinx as "un rêve de pierre."

2. Gay, *Freud*, 104.

3. Freud, *Traumdeutung*, 2:116 [*Interpretation of Dreams*, 4:111].

4. Lacan studied this case in his "Dream of Irma's Injection" (*Seminar*, book 2), highlighting the Jewish features of Freud's dream. It is the dream as dream, rather than Freud's recollection of it, that interests Lacan.

5. Freud, *Traumdeutung*, 2:235 [*Interpretation of Dreams*, 4:230].

6. Jones, *Life and Work of Sigmund Freud*, 10. Other psychoanalysts agree that the Oedipus complex exists, but they do not accept its universality or its biological basis. For example: "The question remains, however, as to whether fixations in the parents arise in a child for biological reasons or whether they are the product of describable conditions. I firmly believe the latter is true," Horney, *New Ways in Psychoanalysis*, 82; "This so-called Oedipus complex is not a 'fundamental fact,' but is simply a vicious unnatural result of maternal over-indulgence," Adler, *Social Interest*, 22.

7. Freud's letter to Wilhelm Fliess, October 15, 1897, in *Complete Letters*, 272.

8. The locus classicus for the Oedipus complex is Freud's *Traumdeutung*, 2: 268 [*Interpretation of Dreams*, 4:263]. Lowell Edmunds queries why Freud concentrated only on the events in Sophocles' *Oedipus Tyrannus*, ignoring *Oedipus at Colonus* (*Oedipus*, 3–5). Equally intriguing is why Freud passed by the riddle scene so swiftly.

9. Freud and Jung, *Letters*, 33.

10. Freud and Jung, *Letters*, 266.

11. Freud, *Three Essays on Sexuality,* 194–95; "Woher kommen die Kinder?" 95. Reaffirmed in *Autobiographical Study,* 37.

12. Wittels, *Freud,* 114. Freud himself provided this detail; see his letter to Wittels, December 18, 1923, *Gesammelte Werke,* 19:758.

13. Laistner, *Rätsel der Sphinx,* 1:ii. Róheim, *Riddle of the Sphinx,* 3.

14. Freud and Jung, *Letters,* 441; Freud, *Future of an Illusion,* 70–71.

15. Gubel, *Sphinx de Vienne,* 1993.

16. "Eine vollständige Rekonstruction der ursprünglichen Fassung ist uns nicht möglich," Reik, "Oedipus und die Sphinx," 120 ["Oedipus and the Sphinx," 319].

17. "Die Zusammensetzung der Sphinx aus weiblichen und männlichen Bestandteilen würde so ebenfalls eine unbewußte Strömung gegen den Vatergott widerspiegeln, Impulse der Auflehnung, welche gegen die auf homosexuellen Bindungen beruhende Religion die heterosexuellen Libidotendenzen in Treffen führen. Wir würden diese aggressive Strömung mit einer in der Spätantike einsetzenden Zurückdrängung und einer veränderten Beurteilung der homosexuellen Betätigung zusammenstellen, als deren letzte Überreste wir noch die Verspottung der Homosexualität bei griechischen und römischen Satirikern ansehen," Reik, "Oedipus und die Sphinx," 130 ["Oedipus and the Sphinx," 330–31].

18. A useful survey is in Vogt's *Psychoanalyse zwischen Mythos und Aufklärung,* 45–101.

19. Jung, *Symbols of Transformation,* 179; "mère phallique," "Mère des Animaux," Lévi-Strauss, *Anthropologie structural,* 238 [*Structural Anthropology,* 231].

20. Jung, *Symbols of Transformation,* 182.

21. Schiller, *Riddles of the Sphinx,* 109.

22. Rank, *Trauma of Birth,* 144–45.

23. Mott, *Universal Design,* 239.

24. For Dante's *Purgatory* see Demisch, *Die Sphinx,* 169–70, figure 466; Cooke, *Sphinx's Children,* 12,17, 24. Charles's Baby Sphinx is restive but harmless (*Story of the Baby Sphinx,* 3–5). "Daughters of Sphinx" is one degree of the Masonic sisters, Eastern Star.

25. "in unserem Sinne nur eine nachträgliche Doublierung der Mutter wäre. Eine neugriechische Rätselwette bei Schmidt . . . läßt tatsächlich Jokaste und die Sphinx als eine Person erscheinen, was auch Schmidt im Hinblick darauf für ursprünglicher halt, daß in allen ähnlichen Überlieferungen die umworbene Köni-

gin selbst die Aufgeberin des Rätsels ist," "Daß Sphinx und Mutter ursprünglich zusammenfielen," "homosexuellen Neigung," Rank, *Inzest-Motiv,* 268, 272, 273; *Incest Theme,* 216, 220, 221]; Róheim, *Riddle of the Sphinx,* 7.

26. Hesiod, *Theogony,* 309–29.

27. Pausanius, *Description of Greece,* 9.26.3–4.

28. Jung, *Man and His Symbols,* 181; Jung, *Symbols of Transformation,* 182. Jung explains that because Oedipus was male, the Sphinx he encountered had to be female; there are male Sphinxes, too, he acknowledges, conveying the same warning to women.

29. Freud, *On the History of the Psychoanalytic Movement,* 62–63.

30. Delcourt, *Œdipe,* 106–8, 105.

31. Moret, *Œdipe,* 1:69–75; Hoffelner, *Sphinxsäule,* 15.

32. Sophocles, *Oedipus Tyrannus,* 1525.

33. Freud, "Charakter und Analerotik," 203. Freud inserted this equation in the fifth edition of *The Interpretation of Dreams* (1918).

34. See Weissberg, "Circulating Images," 117–24.

35. Thoreau, *Walden,* 287. "Whoever discovered this solution spoke the essence of Apollo, on whose temple in Delphi already in Sophocles' era had been carved 'Know thyself'—a riddle whose solution was 'That you are a man,'" Kerényi and Hillman, *Oedipus Variations,* 15.

36. May, *Power and Innocence,* 212.

37. "si se non noverit," Ovid, *Metamorphoses,* 3.346.

38. "Cuadrúpedo en la aurora, alto en el día / y con tres pies errando por el vano / ámbito de la tarde, así veía / la eterna esfinge a su inconstante hermano, / el hombre, y con la tarde un hombre vino / que descifró aterrado en el espejo / de la monstruosa imagen, el reflejo / de su declinación y su destino./ Somos Edipo y de un eterno modo / la larga y triple bestia somos, todo / lo que seremos y lo que hemos sido. / Nos aniquilaría ver la ingente / forma de nuestro ser; piadosamente / Dios nos depara sucesión y olvido," Borges, "Edipo y el enigma."

39. "¡Pobrecillo! Quieres latir en todo y con todo: palpitar con el universo entero; recibir y devolver su savia eterna, la que viene de los infinitos mundos y a ellos vuelve. ¡Y con tanto anhelar derramarte me ahogas. . . , sí . . . , me ahogas!" Unamuno, *La Esfinge,* act 1, scene 13; Unamuno's ellipses. Based on parallels between *La Esfinge* and Unamuno's diaries, Unamuno scholars have concluded that in *La Esfinge* Unamuno looks at himself (see Andrés Franco, *El teatro de Unamuno* [Madrid: Ínsula, 1971], 72–83).

40. Disraeli, *Endymion,* 114; "No cerréis, pues, los ojos a la Esfinge acongojadora, sino miradla cara a cara," Unamuno, *Sentimiento trágico de la vida,* 406 [*Tragic Sense of Life,* 43].

41. Fuller, "Mythological Sonnets," XIII, *Collected Poems,* 206–7.

42. Bion, *Experiences in Groups,* 8, 162; Sturdy, "Questioning the Sphinx," 46.

43. Jones, *Beoni the Sphinx,* 154; Von Hornstein, *Sphinx und der Sadist,* 120–21.

44. Hume, *Woman,* 32, 310–11.

45. Lindsay, *Sphinx,* 39.

8. SYMBOL OF SYMBOLS

The epigraph is from *Wittgenstein's Lectures,* 28.

1. Schiller, *Riddles of the Sphinx,* 472.

2. For the history of the Sphinx symbol see Demisch, *Die Sphinx* (all of it). Todorov credits Clement of Alexandria for the first signs of sign study, *Theories of the Symbol,* 32.

3. The symbols embodied in the Sphinx are taken apart in Hagenbach and Bertschi, *Sphinx 10.*

4. Plato, *Cratylus,* 414d.

5. "die Sphynx mit dem menschlichen Gesichte aus dem Thierleibe erst nachherausstrebt," Wagner, *Judenthum in der Musik,* 80 [*Judaism in Music,* 95].

6. Hegel, *Enzyklopädie,* section 459 [*Philosophy of Mind,* 215].

7. Deuteronomy 10.14; Psalms 148.4; Milton, *Paradise Regained,* 1.406–20; also I Kings, II Chronicles, and Nehemiah; Goethe, *Maxims and Reflections,* section 1192; Cayce, *Egypt at the Time of Ra Ta,* 278, 298.

8. Group μ, *General Rhetoric,* 15, 39, 90.

9. Nietzsche, *Daybreak,* section 173; Husserl, *Ideas,* section 24; Levinas, *Nine Talmudic Readings,* 30–50.

10. A small sample: "signifier of the signifier," "mediation of mediation," "science of science," "interior of the interior," "exterior of the exterior," "catastrophe of the catastrophe," "the trace of the trace" (*Of Grammatology,* 7, 12–13, 27, 43, 126, 148, 295); "the truth of the truth," "the category of the category," "the man of man," "the circle of circles," "lesson of the lesson" (*Margins,* 66, 120, 182, 248, 268); "the law of the law," "mourning of mourning" (*Of Hospitality,* 65, 93); "philosophy of philosophy," "the right of right," "law of law," "science of science," "truth of truth" (*Who's Afraid of Philosophy?* 33, 59, 61, 62, 122).

11. *Mishna,* Aboth 3.1.

12. This term might be a riddle to readers, who will find no assistance in their dictionaries (so far has rhetoric fallen), though it often occurs with an *x* of *x*s: *antanaklasis* is a figure of speech in which the same word is used with two different meanings (Quintilian, *Institutio Oratoria,* 9.3.68). The *logos* of the Gospel of John is a notorious example. In our exempla "writing" may be both the act of writing and what is written; "lesson" may be both a session for instruction and the instruction itself.

13. Derrida, *Of Grammatology,* 135.

14. And a translation of a translation—from Hebrew *hébel hébel'm* [wind of winds]. Unamuno, *Sentimiento trágico de la vida,* 169–70 [*Tragic Sense of Life,* 42]; see Ecclesiastes, 1:2.

15. Kafka, *Letters to Milena,* June 23, 1920.

16. "Der Weltkrieg ist ein tausendmal rätselhafteres Ungeheuer. . . . Ich sehe darin die uralte Sphinx," "Auch die thebanische Sphinx hatte die Lieblichkeit einer Jungfrau mit zarter Weiberbrust und liebendem Weibherzen. Aber gleichzeitig war sie ein furchtbares Raubtier, so dass in demselben Leibe die hartnächigsten Feindgefühle mit der Menschenliebe untrennbar verwachsen wohnten," Hauptmann, *Uralte Sphinx,* 13, 20.

17. "Die Sphinx bin ich selber!" Hauptmann, *Uralte Sphinx,* 22.

18. "Aber keins der Sinnbilder, die die Einbildungskraft der Menschen sonst gebar, hat je die innerste Quelle aller Übel des Menschengeschlechts so restlos und klar leibhaftig gemacht, als das Sinnbild der Sphinx.

"Es ist der Mensch, der drohend durch alle Zeiten der Menschheit ragt. Das uralte Rätselwesen mit dem liebenden Weibherzen und den harten Pranken und grausamen Krallen am Raubtierleibe. Aus dessen Munde der ewige Weltalb, die Erz- und Urfrage ausgeht, die uns allen heute wieder leidenschaftlicher als je am herzen frist und den Atem abdrückt: Wo kommt du her? Wo gehst du hin? Welchem Sinne bist du eigentlich ergeben?" Hauptmann, *Uralte Sphinx,* 24–25.

19. "Das alte Sphinxbild, das Leben, vergewaltigt uns innen und aussen," Hauptmann, *Uralte Sphinx,* 27.

20. Sandys, *Relations of Africa,* 206. On the Sphinx's Ethiopian origin see Robert, *Oidipus,* 1:157–59; Fogg, *Arabistan,* 69; Flaubert, letter to Louis Bouilhet, January 15, 1850.

21. Sheldon Peck, "Sphinx May Really Be a Black African," *New York Times,* July 18, 1992.

22. Prestre, *Sphinx d'ébène,* 70.

23. Von Zahn's *Schwarze Sphinx* concerns German coal.

24. Du Bois, *Darkwater*, 52–55. Disgusted and discouraged by racism in the United States, Du Bois (1888–1963) spent the last years of his life in Ghana.

25. Briey, *Sphinx noir*, 3–5, 14, 104, 115, 329, 331, 333. On German colonies see chapter 2, "Le Pangermanisme colonial," 17–48.

26. Du Bois, *Suppression of the African Slave-Trade*, 197.

27. Farrakhan, quoted by Mary Lefkowitz in "Louis Farrakhan's Challenge," *Chronicle of Higher Education*, December 1, 1995, A60.

28. "Si del todo morimos todos, ¿para qué todo? ¿Para qué? Es el ¿para qué? de la Esfinge, es el ¿para qué? que nos corroe el meollo del alma, es el padre de la conjoga, la que nos da el amor de esperanza," Unamuno, *Sentimiento trágico de la vida*, 170 [*Tragic Sense of Life*, 43].

29. "die Einführung der Sphinx statt, in der sich die durch den Verdrängungs-vorgang geschaffenen Angstaffekte in Anlehnung an die Traumerfahrung niederschlagen," "den schwierigen Rätselfragen der ängstliche Examen-und Alptraum zu Grunde liege," Rank, *Inzest-Motiv*, 272, 268 [*Incest Theme*, 219, 216].

30. "Je ne pense pas que personne puisse l'être comme lui. Il vous brise l'esprit d'un mot, et je me vois comme un vase manqué que le potier jette aux débris. Il est dur comme un ange.... '*Lumineux nons-sens!* ... *Mystique sans Dieu!* ... *Pourquoi pas un Hippogriffe, un Centaure!*' '— *Pourquoi pas un Sphinx?*'" Valéry, *Monsieur Teste*, 85–86, 106 [*Monsieur Teste*, 23, 31–32].

31. "tristesse de sphinx ennuyé de regarder perpétuellement le desert, et qui ne peut se detacher du socle de granit où il aiguise ses griffes depuis vingt siècles," Gautier, *Une nuit de Cléopâtre*, 742 [*One of Cleopatra's Nights*, 2]; "Bah! à quoi bon? autant ça qu'autre chose! la vie n'est pas si drôle!" Flaubert, *Éducation sentimentale*, 150 [*Sentimental Education*, 130].

32. Bakunin, "The Workers and the Sphinx," 18.

33. Burleigh, "The Sphinx."

34. Gügler, *Ziffern der Sphinx*, 92; Pike, *Morals and Dogma*, 8 and 727–28.

35. Descartes, *Regulae ad Directionem Ingenii*. Descartes wrote nothing but titles for rules 19, 20, and 21, and nothing at all for the final fifteen. See Dugald Murdoch's preface to *Philosophical Writings*, 7.

36. James, *Pragmatism*, 591; see also 509.

37. "L'aile immense est à l'aigle et l'oeil perçant au lynx. / L'homme a pour vis-à-vis formidable le sphynx," Hugo, *Chantiers*, 286; "La vérité lui était apparue sous la figure d'un sphinx. Maintenant le sphinx lui disait: Je suis le Doute! Et la

bête ailée avec sa tête de femme impassible et ses griffes de lion l'emportait pour le déchirer dans le sable brûlant du désert," Schuré, *Grands initiés,* 139 [*Great Initiates,* 152]. Colrat finds on the Sphinx of Egypt "symboles attrayants du doute sacré," *Sphinx bafoué,* 221.

38. Shawqi, quoted by Hourani, *History of the Arab Peoples,* 342–43.

39. Petrie, *History of Egypt,* 1: 52.

40. Christ from Browning, "A Drama of Exile," 93; Sphinx from Hudson, *The Sphinx and Other Poems,* 11–14.

41. "Aus der dumfen Stärke und Kraft des Thierischen will der menschliche Geist sich hervordrängen, ohne zur vollendeten Darstellung seiner eigenen Freiheit und bewegten Gestalt zu kommen, da er noch vermischt und vergesellschaftet mit dem Anderen seiner selber blieben muss," Hegel, *Aesthetik,* 12:480 [*Aesthetics,* 1:361].

42. On Rimbaud as Sphinx see Miller, *Books in My Life,* 90.

43. "Umsphinxt," Nietzsche, "Unter Töchtern der Wüste," *Also sprach Zarathustra,* 4:16 [*Thus Spoke Zarathustra,* 419].

44. Kaplan, *Encyclopedia of Tarot,* 2:312, 393.

45. Loye, *Sphinx and the Rainbow,* 6.

46. Clarke, *Seeker of the Sphinx,* 127. See also Repp, "Sphinx of the Spaceways"; Woodcott, *Martian Sphinx;* Limat, *Sphinx des nuages;* Doherty, *Area 51: The Sphinx.*

47. Aliens = other races, other species. Other races are respected in *Star Trek* and taken for granted in *Star Wars.* Race trouble much like America's erupts in Samuel Delany's sci-fi Neveryon series and *Babel-17.* Alien tourists photograph the Sphinx of Giza on the cover of *Amazing Stories* (December 1957).

48. Bishop, *No Enemy But Time,* 167. Bishop's novel won the Nebula Award for best science-fiction novel of 1982. Bishop responds to H. G. Wells's *The Time Machine* on 276–77 and 391.

49. Pownall, *The Sphinx and the Sybarites,* 183, 193.

50. For Alley Oop see Hamlin, *The Sphinx and Alley Oop;* for Tarzan see "The Ape Man Battles the Stone Sphinx"; for Kang the Conqueror see *Avengers Forever,* #3 and #4, Marvel Comics, 1998. Robin Cook's *Sphinx,* published in 1979, is set in 1980.

51. Saltus, "The Sphinx Speaks," 522.

52. "Le Sphinx, de toute façon, figure les anciens dieux," Alain, *Les dieux,* 115 [*The Gods,* 84]; Schiller, *Riddles of the Sphinx,* 12.

53. Hus, "Recherches sur la statuaire," 212–13.

54. See "Coiffures, hathoriques" in Dessenne, *Le Sphinx*, 209.

55. On Hathor see Budge, *Gods of the Egyptians*, 1:93, 2:93–94. On Astarte see Rus, "La estatuilla de alabastro de Galera." On Isis see Witt, *Isis in the Ancient World*, 32, 34, 69, 87; and the painting of the Isis temple in Herculaneum, reproduced in Witt, figure 23, and Demisch, *Die Sphinx*, 35 and figure 76. For Egyptian female Sphinxes see Hassan, *The Sphinx*, 106–10; Jordan, *Riddles of the Sphinx*, 80.

56. Wegner, *Musensarkophage*, 40 and plate 80a. Hugo, cited in Barthes, *Michelet*, 213; Emerson, "History," 237.

57. "Je trône dans l'azur comme un sphinx incompris," Baudelaire, "La beauté" from *Fleurs du mal;* "la Madone des neiges, / Un sphinx blanc que l'hiver sculpta; // Sphinx enterré par l'avalanche, / Gardien des glaciers étoilés, Et qui, sous sa poitrine blanche, / Cache de blancs secrets gelés," Gautier, "Symphonie en blanc majeur." Verne's *Le Sphinx des glaces* is a sequel to Poe's *Adventures of Arthur Gordon Pym*. Vorse, *Laughter of the Sphinx*, 15–16, 19, 22, 35. See also Kirchwey's "The Snow Sphinx" in *Those I Guard*, 44–45, and Rehn's *Weiße Sphinx*, a polar expedition novel.

58. Luther, *First Lectures on the Psalms*, 508 (1523); "pro typo & symbolo ignorantiae capitur," Alciati, *Emblemata*, 799.

59. Schweitzer, *Löwe und Sphinx*, tables 10 and 15; Evers, *Staat aus dem Stein*, plates 48–50. The lion-eared Sphinx of Ammenemes III (1928–1895 BC) is at the Cairo Museum. Sesotris (1962–1928 BC) commissioned sixty Sphinxes from the quarry of Wadi Hammamat. Mentuhotpe VII (circa 1630 BC) left two Sphinxes at Edfu (Grimal, *History of Ancient Egypt*, 164, 181, 189, 308, 318, 348). For Schepenupet II's Sphinx see Staatliche Museen zu Berlin, *Ägyptisches Museum*, 170.

60. On the list of Caesars see Paradin, *Devises héroïques*, 34–35. Augustus also wore Sphinxes on both shoulders of his armor (see Demisch, *Die Sphinx*, 112).

61. Pliny, *Natural History*, 37.4; Suetonius, *Lives*, 50; thence Alciati, *Emblemata*, lvii; Paradin, *Devises héroïques*, 34.

62. Voltaire, note to act 2, scene 1, of *Le triumvirat*, 200.

63. In Salona, now Split, on the coast of Croatia. Inscriptions on Diocletian's Sphinxes date them from the rule of Sethos I, Amenhotep III, and perhaps Thutmose I.

64. Shaw, *Caesar and Cleopatra*, 374–75.

65. As seen in Hay's "Sphinx of the Tuileries," 35–37; Zola's *La curée;* Grün's *Louis Napoleon Bonaparte*.

66. Hatshepsut Sphinxes are on display at the Cairo Museum, the Metropolitan Museum of Art in New York, and the Ägyptisches Museum in Berlin.

67. Ilberg, "Sphinx," 1303.

68. Browning, *Aurora Leigh,* 1020–21.

69. "Le Sphinx a l'air de savoir depuis tant de siècles, comme ultime secret, mais de taire avec une mélancolique ironie, c'est que, dans la prodigieuse nécropole, là en dessous, tout le people des morts aurait été leurré, malgré la piété et les prières, le réveil n'ayant encore jamais sonné pour personne; et c'est que la creation d'une humanité pensante et souffrante n'aurait eu aucune raison raisonnable, et que nos pauvres espoirs seraient vains, mais vains à faire pitié!" Loti, *Mort de Philae,* 14 [*Egypt,* 12–13].

70. Twain, *Innocents Abroad,* 502; Flemming, *Cupid and the Sphinx,* 2.

71. "Il vous regarde du fond de son mystère, le sphinx à robe rouge. Je n'ose dire du fond de sa fourberie. Car, au rebours du sphinx antique, qui meurt si on le devine, celui-ci semble dire: 'Quiconque me devine en mourra,'" Michelet, *Histoire de France,* 255. Michelet summed up his opinion of Richelieu as "le dictateur du désespoir," 295. See also Dumas, *Sphinx rouge,* 169–71.

72. Sphinxes also appeared on the coins of Bela IV of Hungary (1235–70). The United Nations issued a silver Sphinx in 1981. In 1998 France issued a 100-franc commemorative with King Tut on one side and Horemakhet on the other. Uganda minted a 2,000-shilling silver Sphinx in 1996.

73. Gerdemann and Winfried, *Christenkreuz oder Hakenkreuz?* 28–30.

74. Carlyle, "Early German Literature," 280; Emerson, "Nature" [1844], 554.

75. "Die Natur ist dämonisch, wie Aristotles sagt, aber nicht göttlich, δαιμό-νια, ου θεία [*Parva Naturalia* 463b]. Ihr Symbol ist die Sphinx, unter dem nährenden Busen liegen die zerreißenden Krallen," Paulsen, "Zukunftsaufgaben der Philosophie," 415 (William James translated most of the last sentence in *Pluralistic Universe,* 640); Nietzsche, *Birth of Tragedy,* section 9.

76. Pike, *Morals and Dogma,* 321.

77. Ashby, *Riddle of the Sphinx,* 49–50.

78. Rawie, *Sphinx Catechism,* 5–6.

79. Savage, *Modern Sphinx,* 16–17.

80. Herodotus, *Histories,* 2:18–28.

81. The pose was often copied. It appeared on Roman coins and on French medals. The statue is now in the Vatican. See Demisch, *Die Sphinx,* 37 and his illustration 81.

82. Kircher, *Oedipus Aegyptiacus*, 224, 460–64. For example, "ad connotanda reconditiora mentis sensa. Sphynges itaque sic expressae stationem Nili Aegyptum inundantis repraesentabant," 224; "Vult autem Abenvaschia [Aven Vaschia, an Arab of Egypt] hisce verbis nihil aliud dicere, nisi quod fuerit in similitudinem Sphyngis, quod apud Authores inundationis Nili symbolum reperi," 224. Also "Vult autem Aven Vaschia hisce verbis nihil aliud dicere, nisi etc.," 460.

83. Hawass and Lehner, "The Sphinx," 30.

84. Schiller, *Riddles of the Sphinx*, 9.

85. Hugo, "Zim-Zizimi," 688–90; "A celui-ci, il parle le langage de la passion; à celui-là des mots de haine. A l'un, il sourit plein de promesses délicieuses; à la autre, il ricane, le front lourd de vengeances prochaines. . . . Notre sphinx a parlé. Il n'a prononcé qu'un seul mot: orgueil!" Dekobra, *Le Sphinx a parlé*, 312 (my translation). Inexplicably the Metcalfe Wood translation (1930) omits this passage, although it is here in a scandal of cocaine that the Sphinx of the book's title explicitly speaks.

86. "Oui, l'énigme dira son mot, le sphinx parlera, le problème sera résolu. Oui, le peuple, ébauché par le dix-huitième siècle, sera achevé par le dix-neuvième. Idiot qui en douterait! L'éclosion future, l'éclosion prochaine du bien-être universel, est un phénomène divinement fatal," Hugo, *Les misérables*, 791 [*Les Misérables*, 866].

87. Wilde, "The Sphinx," 168.

88. "les révolutions sont sphinx," Hugo, *Les misérables*, 969 [*Les Misérables*, 1062]; Hugo, *History of a Crime*, 287. In 1861 Baudelaire wrote of Hugo that "surtout dans ces dernières années qu'il a subi l'influence métaphysique qui s'exhale de toutes ces choses, curiosité d'un Œdipe obsédé par d'innombrables Sphinx," *Œuvres complètes*, 709.

89. Bacon, *Wisedom of the Ancients*, section 28. In Nietzsche's myth of the origins of science, Zarathustra declares, "*Mut* dünkt mich des Menschen ganze Vorgeschichte. Den wildesten mutigsten Tieren hat er alle ihre Tugenden abgeneidet und abgeraubt: so erst wurde er–zum Menschen. *Dieser* Mut, endlich fein geworden, geistlich, geistig, dieser Menschen-Mut mit Adler-Flügeln und Schlangen-Klugheit" [*Courage* seems to me to be man's whole prehistory. He envied the wildest, most courageous animals and robbed all their virtues: only thus did he become man. *This* courage, finally refined, spiritualized, spiritual, this human courage with eagles' wings and serpents' wisdom], *Also sprach Zarathustra*, 538 [*Thus Spoke Zarathustra*, 415].

90. A Sphinx appears on either side of Apollo in a relief discovered in the Maison de Fourni in 1960 (Marcadé, *Au musée de Délos*, 164–65 and plate 28). Sophocles, *Oedipus Tyrannus*, 292; Hofmannsthal, *Ödipus und die Sphinx*, 54.

91. Edmunds, *Oedipus*, 51.

92. Sophocles, *Oedipus Tyrannus*, 292; Hofmannsthal, *Ödipus und die Sphinx*, 54.

93. "Edippo, ei stesso, / Che sia bandito alla prima alba imponga," Centofanti, *Edipo Re*, 31.

94. Aulus Gellius, *Attic Nights*, 9.18; Diodorus of Sicily, *Library*, 1.77.

95. Pausanias, *Description of Greece*, 9.26.2.

96. Cassiodorus, *Variae*, 207.

97. *Time*, April 21, 1980. See also Roubaud, *Le voleur et le sphinx*.

98. B. M. Ernst, president of Sphinx Publishing Corporation, in *The Sphinx*, November 1932, inside front cover.

99. *The Book of Hours* of Jean, Duke of Berry, plate 43; Carlyle, *Sartor Resartus*, 125, 127; Heine, "Romantic School," 132.

100. García Lorca, "La verdadera esfinge / es el reloj," *Collected Poems*, 268; Delsol, *Le Sphinx*, 117–38. A Tiffany clock is on display at the Metropolitan Museum of Art (see Bloemink et al., *The Sphinx and the Lotus*, figure 7).

101. Grimal, *History of Ancient Egypt*, 6.

102. "Wunderlichen schlimmen fragwürdigen Fragen!" "Was Wunder, wenn wir endlich einmal mißtrauisch werden, die Geduld verlieren, uns ungeduldig umdrehn? Daß wir von dieser Sphinx auch unsrerseits das Fragen lernen? *Wer* ist das eigentlich, der uns hier Fragen stellt? *Was* in uns will eigentlich 'zu Wahrheit'? . . . Das Problem vom Werte der Wahrheit trat vor uns hin—oder waren wirs, die vor das Problem hintraten? Wer von uns ist hier Ödipus? Wer Sphinx? Es ist ein Stelldichein, wie es scheint, von Fragen und Fragezeichen," Nietzsche, *Jenseits von Gute und Böse*, 567 [*Beyond Good and Evil*, 199].

103. Athenaeus, *Deipnosophists*, 6.253e; O'Connell, *Of Arms and Men*, 13–29; Erasmus, *Colloquies*, 892.

104. Burton, *Anatomy of Melancholy* ("Democritus to the Reader," 106). Burton resumes a classical tradition that considered Egyptian monuments to be ostentatious and unproductive, for example, Horace *Odes* 3.30.1 and Propertius, *Elegies*, 3.2.19–22.

105. Nichols, *Debussy;* Goold, *Sea-Sphinx*, 216–17.

106. La Riche, *Alexandria*, 68–69, 96–109, 118–19.

107. Wilson, *From Atlantis to the Sphinx*. Wilson follows a tradition established by American Ignatius Donnelly (1831–1901), whose wildly popular *Atlantis: The Antediluvian World* (1882) regards Egypt as a colony of Atlantis. See also Enel, *Message from the Sphinx*, 294.

108. Flemming, *Cupid and the Sphinx*, 173.

109. "Σοφία δὲ Αἰγυπτίων τὸ πάντα λέγειν συμβολικῶς τά τε τῶν θεῶν εἴδη ἐν κιβωτίοις ἀποκρύπτειν, τὴν Σφίγγα δὲ μόνην ἀπὸ τῶν τειχῶν ἀποκρεμαννύειν," Michael Psellus (1018–18), citing Chaeremon, in Van der Horst, *Chaeremon*, 10, 11. The Sphinx as the emblem for wise sayings is employed in Sosso's *Wisdom for the Wise*, Leysen's *Sphinx nu*, and Williams's *Riddle of the Sphinx*.

110. Thomas, *Sphinx*, 25, 226.

111. Kircher, *Oedipus Aegypticus*, 4:224, 455–56.

112. Watson, *What the Stars Held*, 58. The Dendera zodiac has been well reproduced, showing the Lion, the Scorpion, Sagittarius, and other familiar signs, but I do not find a Sphinx there. Perhaps Watson's light was bad. Péladan, *Terre du Sphinx*, 36. For a fierce restatement of the thesis, see West, *Serpent in the Sky*.

113. Jordan defends the Sphinx from zodiacal zeal in *Riddles of the Sphinx*, 135–43.

114. Wilkinson, *Complete Temples*, 150. For the *Description de l'Égypte*, Napoleon's engravers meticulously reproduced the Denderah zodiac — twice. See Gillispie and Dewachter, *Monuments of Egypt*, A.IV.21.

115. Gautier, *L'Orient*, 2:253.

116. Hegel, *Aesthetik*, 12:479–80 [*Aesthetics*, 1:360–61].

117. For more Sphinx apparitions see Humbert, Pantazzi, and Ziegler, *Egyptomania*, 22–23.

118. For more on the harem-forming fruit bat, *Cynopterus sphinx*, see Storz, Bhat, and Kunz, "Genetic Consequences of Polygeny and Social Structure in an Indian Fruit Bat," 1224.

119. Wang et al., "Origin of *Sphinx*."

120. Kaplan, *Encyclopedia of Tarot*, 2. On Lévi, see Decker, Depaulis, and Dummett, *Wicked Pack of Cards*, plate 10b. On Crowley's tarot see his *Book of Thoth*, 85, 226.

121. Demisch, *Die Sphinx*, 38. For Athena's chariot see Aurigemma, "Notizie," 45 and figure 5. For metaphors as vehicles see Richards, *Philosophy of Rhetoric*, chapter 5.

9. EXIT

The epigraph is from "Epigonii," 1.91. The lines are part of a tribute to Eminescu's beloved precursor, Eliade Rădulescu, who "built his songs from dreams":

Adevăr scăldat în mite, sfinx pătrunsă de-nțeles;

Munte cu capul de piatră de furtune detunată,

Stă ·i azi în fața lumii o enigmă nesplicată

Şi veghează—o stîncă arsă dintre nouri de eres.

1. I take "predatrix" from Conti, *Mythologiae*, 287. For reproductions of warlike Sphinxes see Demisch, *Die Sphinx*, illustrations 232 and 233.

2. Sphinxes with Oedipi appear in the fifth century BC (Moret, *Œdipe*, 1:1–2). Moret sometimes resorted to reproductions of reproductions to illustrate Sphinxes that have been lost or destroyed (1:171, 176, 180, 2:plate 55/2).

3. Time has been cruel to Corinna, who five times defeated Pindar in poetic competitions but whose works survive only in scraps (Campbell, *Greek Lyric*, 4:1–3, 48–49). Pausanias says Corinna came from Thebes.

4. Euripides, *Phoenician Women*, 45.

5. Burton, *Anatomy of Melancholy*, 125; Gibbon, *Decline and Fall of the Roman Empire*, 2:774.

6. Pausanias, *Description of Greece*, 9.5.

7. Ovid, *Metamorphoses*, 7.758–93.

8. Sophocles, *Oedipus Tyrannus*, 25–29.

9. Seneca, *Oedipus*, 92–94. Poe's 1845 tale "The Sphinx" is set amid "the dread reign of Cholera in New York."

10. "La corruption des chairs engender l'horrible peste; / la corruption des coeurs donne naissance aux monstres. / Le Sphinx est fils de Thèbes!" Péladan, *Œdipe et le Sphinx*, 30.

11. Wyndham, *Sphinx and Her Circle*, 101.

12. Wells, *Time Machine*, 16.

13. "Et pourtant, au milieu de toutes mes distractions, il y a des moments où je me sens si lasse, si ennuyée, que j'ai envie de demander à mon sphinx son secret," Feuillet, *Sphinx*, act 1, scene 10.

14. Taranow, *Sarah Bernhardt*, 207–8.

15. Hamilton, *Mythology*, 257.

16. Robert, *Oidipus*, 56; "et praecipitata iacebat," Ovid, *Metamorphoses*, 7.760; Dartmouth Dante Project.

17. Why did the Sphinx leave? Oedipus passed her test. He could go and so could she (Delcourt, *Œdipe*, 150).

18. "l'animale sombre d'Aphrodite," Bauchau, *Œdipe sur la route*, 164 [Oedipus on the Road, 132].

19. Tennyson, "Tiresias." Like Ingres's Oedipus, Tennyson's "Tiresias" was a lifetime work. Tennyson wrote it in 1833 but kept it to himself until 1883, when he recited it, aged seventy-four.

20. Spenser, *The Faerie Queene*, 5.11.25.2–5.

21. "Als ein tiefer Zug der griechisen Sage ist der Ausbruch des Wahnsinns nach Enthüliung des Geheimnisses hervorzuheben," Rank, *Inzest-Motiv*, 263 [*Incest Theme*, 213].

22. See Dartmouth Dante Project. "Es kann im Bild nichts so schrecklich sein wie in Wörtern. Sphinxe und Sirenen sind erst spät ästhetisiert. Ursprünglich ist nicht Vernichtung durch den Furchtlosen, sondern Selbstvernichtung durch die erste Erfahrung der Wirkungslosigkeit" [Nothing can be as fearsome in a picture as in words. Sphinxes and Sirens are aestheticized only at a late date. The primary process is not destruction by a fearless hero but self-destruction as a result of the first experience of ineffectiveness], Blumenberg, *Arbeit am Mythos*, 75 [*Work on Myth*, 66].

23. Hofmannsthal, *Ödipus und die Sphinx*, 162–63. The riddle scene is not staged. Instead, Oedipus describes it and behaves as if the Sphinx and her last words were the riddle for which he had no answer.

24. Enescu, quoted by Malcolm, *George Enescu*, 149.

25. Goux, *Oedipus, Philosopher*, 38, 74.

26. Moret, *Œdipe*, chapter 5, "Le combat d'Œdipe et de la Sphinx," 1:79–91.

27. Lydgate, *Fall of Princes*, line 3475; Guerber, *Story of Greece*, 34; Perec, *La disparition*, 44 [*A Void*, 28–29]; Sollers, *H*, 158; Hughes, "Song for a Phallus," 64.

28. "A force de songer, je n'ai plus rien à dire," Flaubert, *Tentation de Saint Antoine*, 191 [*The Temptation Saint Anthony*, 224]. Flaubert rewrote this novel for decades, publishing it in 1874 at the age of fifty-three.

29. Emerson, "The Sphinx," 8.

30. This was the focus of the 1992 Sphinx Symposium. See Esmael, *International Symposium*.

31. Rabelais, *Gargantua and Pantagruel*, book 5, chapter 10; Goethe, *Faust*, part 2, lines 7495–581; Joyce, *Finnegans Wake*, 473. Theodore Spencer's desert Sphinx rises and goes to Heliopolis to witness the rebirth of the Phoenix.

B3. Oedipus on the Menu, Liebig Co., Antwerp, 1902.

Bibliography

Aarne, Antii. *Vergleichende Rätselforschungen.* Vols. 26–28 of Folklore Fellows Communications. Helsinki: Suomalaisen Tiedeakatemian Kustantama, 1918–20.

Acta Andreae et Matthiae. In *Acta Apostolorum Apocrypha,* edited by Constantin von Tischendorf, 132–66. Leipzig: Avenarius & Mendelssohn, 1851. Translated by Alexander Walker as *Acts of Andrew and Matthais,* in *The Ante-Nicean Fathers,* ed. A. Cleveland Coxe (New York: Christian Literature, 1885–87), 8: 517–25.

Adamson, Joy. *The Spotted Sphinx.* New York: Harcourt, Brace & World, 1969.

Adler, Alfred. *Social Interest: A Challenge to Mankind.* London: Faber & Faber, 1938.

Ahl, Frederick. *Sophocles' "Oedipus": Evidence and Self-Conviction.* Ithaca: Cornell University Press, 1991.

Alain. *Les dieux.* Paris: Gallimard, 1934. Translated by Richard Pevear as *The Gods* (New York: New Directions, 1974).

Albright, W. F. "What Were the Cherubim?" *Biblical Archaeologist* 1 (1938): 1–3.

Alciati, Andrea. *Emblemata cum Commentariis.* A facsimile of the 1621 Padua edition, including the commentary of Claude Mignault. New York: Garland, 1976 [1531].

Annesley, Maude. *The Sphinx in the Labyrinth.* London: Mills & Boon / New York: Duffield, 1913.

Anouilh, Jean. *Œdipe; ou, Le roi boiteux.* Paris: Table Ronde, 1986.

"The Ape Man Battles the Stone Sphinx." In *Tarzan.* New York: National Periodical Publications (May 1975): vol. 8, no. 237.

Apollodorus. *The Library.* Translated by James George Frazier. Cambridge: Harvard University Press, 1921.

Aragon, Louis. *Le paysan de Paris.* Paris: Gallimard, 1926. Translated by Frederick Brown as *Nightwalker* (Englewood Cliffs NJ: Prentice-Hall, 1970).

Aristophanes. *Ranae [Batrachoi].* In *Comoediae,* edited by F. W. Hall and W. M. Geldart, 2:106–67. Oxford: Oxford University Press, 1907 [405 BC]. Translated by Dudley Fitts as *The Frogs* (New York: Harcourt, Brace, 1955).

Arsène, Alexandre, ed. *Félicien Rops et son œuvre.* Brussels: Edmond Deman, 1897.

"Asclepius." In *The Nag Hammadi Library,* 3rd ed, edited by James M. Robinson, 330–38. San Francisco: Harper San Francisco, 1988.

Ashby, N. B. *The Riddle of the Sphinx: A Discussion of the Economic Question relating to Agriculture, Land, Transportation, Money, Taxation, and Cost of Interchange: A Consideration of Possible Remedies for Existing Inequalities, and an Out-Line of the Position of Agriculture in the Industrial World.* Chicago: Mercantile Publishing and Advertising, 1890.

Assigni, Marius d'. *Hieroglyphicks.* In *The Poetical Histories,* by Pierre Gautruche. A facsimile of the 1671 London edition. New York: Garland, 1976.

Athenaeus. *The Deipnosophists.* 7 vols. Cambridge: Harvard University Press, 1928–37.

Aurigemma, Salvatore. "Notizie archeologiche sulla Tripolitania." *Notizario archeologico* 1 (1915): 47–64. Rome: Luigi Alfieri.

Bacon, Francis. *The Wisedom of the Ancients.* Translated by Arthur Gorges. A facsimile of the 1619 London edition. New York: Garland, 1976.

[Bagwell, William.] *Sphynx Thebanus, with His Oedipus; or, Ingenious Riddles with Their Observations, Explications, and Morals.* London: J. C. for Dixy Page, 1664.

Bakunin, Michael. "The Workers and the Sphinx." In *Bakunin's Writings,* edited by Guy A. Aldred, 13–18. Bombay: Modern Publishers, [1948?].

Balzac, Honoré de. *La comédie humaine.* 12 vols. Paris: Gallimard, 1976 [1834–55].

Barbarin, Georges. *L'énigme du Grand Sphinx.* Paris: Éditions J'ai Lu, 1966 [1946].

Barthes, Roland. *Michelet par lui-même.* Paris: Éditions de Seuil, 1954. Translated by Richard Howard as *Michelet* (New York: Hill & Wang, 1987).

Bauchau, Henry. *Œdipe sur la route.* Arles: Actes Sud, 1990. Translated by Anne-Marie Glasheen as *Oedipus on the Road* (London: Quartet Books, 1994).

Baudelaire, Charles. *Les fleurs du mal.* New York: David R. Godine, 1985 [1857]. Translated by Richard Howard as *Flowers of Evil* (New York: David R. Godine, 1985).

———. *Œuvres complètes.* Edited by Y.-G. Le Dantec, revised by Claude Pichois. Paris: Gallimard, 1961.

Bell, Clare. *Tomorrow's Sphinx.* New York: Macmillan, 1986.

Benjamin, Walter. "Der Erzähler." In *Gesammelte Schriften,* 2: 438–65. Frankfurt: Suhrkamp [1936]. Translated by Harry Zohn as "The Storyteller: Observations on the Work of Nikolai Leskov," in *Selected Writings, Volume 3: 1935–1938* (Cambridge: Harvard University Press, 2002), 143–66.

Berloquin, Pierre. *Le jardin du sphinx.* Paris: Bordes, 1981.

Berman, Louis. *The Glands Regulating Personality: A Study of the Glands of Internal Secretion in Relation to the Types of Human Nature.* New York: Macmillan, 1921.

Besant, Annie. *The Sphinx of Theosophy.* London: Theosophical Publishing Society, circa 1895.

Bibesco, Princess Marthe. *The Sphinx of Bagatelle.* Translated by Edward Marsh. London: Grey Walls Press, 1951.

Bion, Wilfred. *Experiences in Groups.* London: Tavistock, 1961.

Bird, Robert. *A Booke of Merrie Riddles.* London: Robert Bird, 1631.

Bishop, Michael. *No Enemy but Time.* New York: Timescape, 1982.

Black Sabbath. "Sphinx (The Guardian)." *Seventh Star.* Gimcastle. ESM CD 335. Compact disc. 1996 [1986].

Blanchot, Maurice. *L'entretien infini.* Paris: Gallimard, 1969. Translated by Susan Hanson as *The Infinite Conversation* (Minneapolis: University of Minnesota Press, 1993).

Blismon, Ana-gramme [Simon Blocquel]. *Sphinxiana: Recueil curieux d'énigmes, de charades et logogriphes dédié à tous les Œdipes présents et futures.* Paris: Delarue, 1855.

Bloemink, Barbara, Kevin Stayton, Bernadette M. Sigler, and Liese Hilgeman. *The Sphinx and the Lotus: The Egyptian Movement in American Decorative Arts, 1865–1935.* Yonkers NY: Hudson River Museum, 1990.

Blumenberg, Hans. *Arbeit am Mythos.* Frankfurt: Suhrkamp, 1979. Translated by Robert M. Wallace as *Work on Myth* (Cambridge: MIT Press, 1985).

Boccaccio, Giovanni. *Genealogie.* A facsimile of the 1531 Paris edition. New York: Garland, 1976.

Borges, Jorge Luis. "Edipo y el Enigma." In *Nueva antología personal.* Buenos Aires: Emecé, 1968.

Bouvet, Marguerite. *The Smile of the Sphinx.* Chicago: A. C. McClurg, 1911.

Brand New Heavies. "Sphynx." *Brand New Heavies.* Capitol Records. CDP 7243 8 35955 2 5. Compact disc. 1991.

Breasted, James Henry. *Ancient Records of Egypt.* 5 vols. Champaign: University of Illinois Press, 2001 [1906].

Brent, Joseph. *Charles Sanders Peirce: A Life.* Bloomington: Indiana University Press, 1993.

Breton, André. *L'amour fou.* In *Œuvres complètes,* edited by Marguerite Bonnet, 2:673–785. Paris: Gallimard, 1992 [1936]. Translated by Mary Ann Caws as *Mad Love* (Lincoln: University of Nebraska Press, 1987).

———. *Nadja.* In *Œuvres complètes,* edited by Marguerite Bonnet, 1:643–753. Paris: Gallimard, 1988 [1928]. Translated by Richard Howard as *Nadja* (New York: Grove Press, 1960).

Briey, Renaud de. *Le Sphinx noir: Essai sur les problèmes de colonisation africaine.* Paris: Berger-Levrault, 1926.

Briggs, L. B. R. *The Sphinx Garrulous.* Cambridge: Washburn & Thomas, 1929.

Brontë, Charlotte. *Jane Eyre.* Edited by Richard J. Dunn. New York: W. W. Norton, 1971 [1847].

Brosi, Sybille. *"Der Kuß der Sphinx": Weibliche Gestalten nach griechischem Mythos in Malerei und Graphik des Symbolismus.* Munster: Lit, 1992.

Brough, Robert B., and brother. *The Sphinx: A "Touch from the Ancients."* London: National Acting Drama Office, 1849.

Brownell, Henry Howard. "The Sphinx." In *An American Anthology, 1787–1900,* edited by Edmund Clarence Stedman, 247–48. Boston: Houghton Mifflin, 1900.

Browning, Elizabeth Barrett. *Aurora Leigh.* In *The Complete Poetical Works,* edited by Harriet Waters Preston, 254–410. Cambridge: Houghton Mifflin, 1900 [1856].

———. "A Drama of Exile." In *The Complete Poetical Works,* edited by Harriet Waters Preston, 67–98. Cambridge: Houghton Mifflin, 1900.

Brunton, Paul. *A Search in Secret Egypt.* New York: E. P. Dutton, 1936.

Budge, E. A. Wallis. *The Gods of the Egyptians.* 2 vols. New York: Dover Publications, 1969 [1904].

Bulfinch, Thomas. *Mythology.* New York: Thomas Y. Crowell, 1970. Originally published as *The Age of Fable,* 1855.

Burleigh, George Shepard. "The Sphinx." In *Spirit-Echoes. American Poetry 1690–1900,* microfilm, segment 2, reel 21, item 359 (p. 502, dated July 25, 1857). Research Publications, 1975.

Burton, Robert. *The Anatomy of Melancholy.* 5 vols. Edited by Thomas C. Faulkner, Nicolas K. Kiessling, and Rhonda L. Blair. Oxford: Oxford University Press, 1989–2000 [1621–51].

Byron, George Gordon, Lord. *Don Juan.* In *The Poetical Works of Lord Byron,* 635–857. London: Oxford University Press, 1904 [1819–24].

Cacciatore, Leonardo. *Nuovo atlante istorico.* 3 vols. 4th ed. Florence: Tipografia all'insegna di Dante, 1831–33 [1825–27].

Campbell, David A. *Greek Lyric.* 4 vols. Cambridge: Harvard University Press, 1992.

Carew, Henry. *The Secret of the Sphinx.* London: Hodder & Stoughton, 1924.

Carlyle, Thomas. "Early German Literature." In *Critical and Miscellaneous Essays,* 2:274–332. London: Chapman & Hall, 1899 [1831].

———. *Sartor Resartus.* Edited by Charles Frederick Harrold. New York: Odyssey Press, 1937 [1838].

Carr, John Dickson. *The Sleeping Sphinx.* New York: Harper & Brothers, 1947.

Carré, Jean-Marie. *Voyageurs et écrivains français en Egypte.* 2 vols. Cairo: Institute Français d'Archéologie Orientale, 1956.

Carrington, Hereward. *The Great Pyramid of Egypt: The Sphynx and the Religion and Magic of Ancient Egypt.* Girard ĸs: Haldeman-Julius, 1924.

Carroll, Leon. *Sphinx Rag.* Sphinx Publishing, 1912.

Cartland, Barbara. *Moonlight on the Sphinx.* New York: Jove Books, 1984.

Cassiodorus, Aurelius. *Explanation of the Psalms.* Translated by P. G. Walsh. New York: Paulist Press, 1991.

———. *Variae.* Edited by Theodor Mommsen. Berlin: Weidman, 1894.

Casson, Lionel. *Travel in the Ancient World.* Baltimore: Johns Hopkins University Press, 1994 [1974].

Castleman, Henry C. "False Sphinx." In *Two Songs.* London: Weekes, 1913.

Cayce, Edgar. *Edgar Cayce on Prophecy.* Edited by Mary E. Carter. New York: Hawthorn Books, 1968.

———. *Egypt at the Time of Ra Ta.* 2 vols. Compiled by Ann Lee Clapp. Virginia Beach ᴠᴀ: Association for Research and Enlightenment, 1989.

C. C. and E. C. *The Sphynx: A New and Original Collection of Double Acrostics.* London: Harrison & Sons, 1867.

Centofanti, Silvestro. *Edipo Re.* Florence: Tipografia Formigli, 1829.

Chamberlain. N. H. *The Sphinx in Aubrey Parish.* Boston: Cupples & Hurd / Algonquin Press, 1889.

Champollion, Jean-François. *Lettres et journaux écrits pendant le voyage d'Égypte.* Edited and annotated by H. Hartleben. Paris: Christian Bourgois Éditeur, 1986.

Chantpleure, Guy [Jeanne Violet Dussap]. *Sphinx blanc*. Paris: Calmann-Lévy, [1922?].

Charles, Lucile Marie Hoerr. *The Story of the Baby Sphinx and Other Fables*. Yellow Springs OH: Antioch Press, 1959.

Chekhov, Anton. *The Seagull*. In *The Plays of Anton Chekhov*, translated by Paul Schmidt. New York: HarperCollins, 1998 [1895].

Christopher, Milbourne. *The Sphinx Golden Jubilee Book of Magic*. New York: Sphinx Publishing, 1951.

Cioran, Emile M. *Œuvres*. Paris: Gallimard, 1995.

———. *Tears and Saints*. Translated by Ilinca Zarifopol-Johnston. Chicago: University of Chicago Press, 1995 [1937].

Clarke, Arthur C. *Seeker of the Sphinx*. In *Two Complete Science Adventure Books*, 106–42. New York: Wings, 1951.

Clement of Alexandria. *Exhortation to the Heathen*. In *The Ante-Nicean Fathers*, edited by A. Cleveland Coxe, 2:171–206. New York: Christian Literature Company, 1885.

———. *The Stromata*. In *The Ante-Nicean Fathers*, edited by A. Cleveland Coxe, 2:299–567. New York: Christian Literature Company, 1885.

Cocteau, Jean. *La machine infernale*. Paris: Éditions Bernard Grasset, 1934.

Coleman, Ornette. "The Sphinx." *The Music of Ornette Coleman: Something Else!!!* Contemporary Records. OJCCD-163-2. Compact disc. 1988 [1958].

Collier, Robert. *The Life Magnet*. 7 vols. New York: Robert Collier, 1928.

Colrat, Raymond. *Le Sphinx bafoué*. Lausanne: J. Couchoud & Fils, 1923.

Conrad, Joseph. *Lord Jim*. Edited by Thomas C. Moser. New York: W. W. Norton, 1968 [1900].

Conte, Gian Biagio. *Latin Literature: A History*. Translated by Joseph B. Solodow, revised by Don Fowler and Glenn W. Most. Baltimore: Johns Hopkins University Press, 1994 [1987].

Conti, Natale. *Mythologiae*. A facsimile of the 1567 Venice edition. New York: Garland Publishing Company, 1979 [1551].

Cook, Robin. *Sphinx*. New York: G. P. Putnam's Sons, 1979.

Cooke, George Alexander. *Modern and Authentic System of Universal Geography*. London: R. Evans, 1817.

Cooke, Rose Terry. *The Sphinx's Children and Other People's*. Cambridge MA: Houghton, Mifflin, 1897.

Corelli, Marie. *Ziska: The Problem of a Wicked Soul.* Bristol: J. W. Arrowsmith, 1897.

Costandinos, Alec R. *Sphinx: Judas Iscariot, Simon Peter.* Polydor. 2933 105. 33rpm. 1977.

Crowley, Aleister [The Master Therion]. *The Book of Thoth: A Short Essay on the Tarot of the Egyptians.* York Beach ME: Samuel Weiser, 1974 [1944].

Crowley, John. *Aegypt.* Bantam: 1987.

Dartmouth Dante Project. http://www.princeton.edu/~dante/dante2.html.

Davidson, D., and H. Aldersmith. *The Great Pyramid: Its Divine Message.* Williams & Norgate, 1926. The book went through eleven editions by 1948 and is still in print.

de Beauvoir, Simone. *Le deuxième sexe,* 2 vols. Paris: Gallimard, 1949. Translated by H. M. Parshley as *The Second Sex* (New York: Vintage Books, 1974).

Decker, Ronald, Thierry Depaulis, and Michael Dummett. *A Wicked Pack of Cards: The Origins of the Occult Tarot.* New York: St. Martin's Press, 1996.

Dekobra, Maurice. *Le Sphinx a parlé.* Paris: Baudinière, 1930. Translated by Metcalfe Wood as *The Sphinx Has Spoken* (New York: Brewer & Warren, 1930).

Delcourt, Marie. *Œdipe; ou, La légende du conquérant.* Paris: E. Droz, 1944.

Delsol, Lysianne. *Le Sphinx et le dernier âge du monde.* Paris: Éditions de Vecchi, 1977.

Demisch, Heinz. *Die Sphinx: Geschichte ihrer Darstellung von den Anfängen bis zur Gegenwart.* Stuttgart: Verlag Urachhaus Johannes M. Mayer, 1977.

De Quincey, Thomas. "The Theban Sphinx." In *The Collected Writings,* edited by David Masson, 6:139–51. Edinburgh: Adam and Charles Black, 1890.

Derrida, Jacques. *Of Grammatology.* Translated by Gayatri Spivack. Baltimore: Johns Hopkins University Press, 1976 [1967].

———. *Of Hospitality: Anne Dufourmantelle Invites Jacques Derrida to Respond.* Translated by Rachel Bowlby. Stanford: Stanford University Press, 2000.

———. *Margins.* Translated by Alan Bass. Chicago: University of Chicago Press, 1984 [1972].

———. *Who's Afraid of Philosophy?* Translated by Jan Plug. Stanford: Stanford University Press, 2002.

Descartes, René. *Regulae ad Directionem Ingenii.* In *The Philosophical Writings,* translated by John Cottingham, Robert Stoothoff, and Dugald Murdoch, 1: 7–78. Cambridge: Cambridge University Press, 1985.

Description de l'Égypt; ou, Recueil des observations et des recherches qui ont été faites en Égypte pendant l'expédition de l'armée française. 9 vols. Paris: L'Impri-merie Impériale, 1809–22.

Dessenne, André. *Le Sphinx: Étude iconographique.* Paris: Éditions de Boccard, 1957.

Dickens, Charles. *Our Mutual Friend.* Harmondsworth UK: Penguin, 1971 [1864–65].

Diderot, Denis, and Jean Le Rond d'Alembert. *Encyclopédie; ou, Dictionnaire rai-sonné des sciences, des arts et des métiers.* 28 vols. Paris: 1751–72.

Dijkstra, Brad. *Idols of Perversity: Fantasies of Feminine Evil in Fin-de-Siècle Cul-ture.* New York: Oxford University Press, 1986.

Diodorus of Sicily. *Library of History.* Vol. 3. Translated by C. H. Oldfather. Cam-bridge: Harvard University Press, 1970.

Disraeli, Benjamin. *Endymion.* In *The Bradenham Edition of the Novels and Tales of Benjamin Disraeli,* 12:1–468. London: Peter Davies, 1927 [1880].

Doherty, Robert. *Area 51: The Sphinx.* New York: Dell, 2000.

Donaghe, M. Virginia. "The Questioner of the Sphinx." *Century Illustrated Monthly Magazine,* November 1886, 37.

Douglas, Lord Alfred. "The Sphinx." In *The Sonnets of Lord Alfred Douglas,* 11. London: Richards Press, 1943.

Dreyer, Hans P. *The Secret of the Sphinx.* Kansas City MO: Burton, 1929.

Dryden, John, and Nathaniel Lee. *Oedipus.* In *The Dramatic Works of John Dry-den,* edited by George Saintsbury, 6:121–240. Edinburgh: William Paterson, 1882 [1679].

Du Bois, W. E. B. *Darkwater.* New York: Schocken Books, 1969 [1920].

———. *John Brown: A Biography.* Edited by John David Smith. Armonk NY: M. E. Sharpe, 1997 [1909].

———. *The Suppression of the African Slave-Trade to the United States of America, 1638–1870.* In *Writings,* 1–356. New York: Library of America, 1986 [1896].

Dumas, Alexandre. *Le Sphinx rouge.* Paris: Éditions Universelles, 1946.

Dylan, Bob. "Sara." *Desire.* Columbia Records. CK33893. Compact disc. 1975.

Edmunds, Lowell. *Oedipus: The Ancient Legend and Its Later Analogues.* Balti-more: Johns Hopkins University Press, 1985.

———. *The Sphinx in the Oedipus Legend.* Königstein: Verlag Anton Hain, 1981.

Eichler, Fritz. "Nochmals die Sphinxgruppe aus Ephesos." *Jahresheft des Öster-reichlichen Archealogischen Institutes in Wien* 45 (1960): 5–22.

Eldridge, Paul. *And the Sphinx Spoke.* Boston: Stratford, 1921.

Elliot, J. K. *The Apocryphal New Testament: A Collection of Apocryphal Christian Literature in an English Translation.* Oxford: Oxford University Press, 1993. A revision of the Montague Rhodes James translation (1924).

Ellis, Joseph J. *American Sphinx: The Character of Thomas Jefferson.* New York: Knopf, 1997.

Emerson, Ralph Waldo. "History." In *Essays and Lectures,* 237–56. New York: Library of America, 1983 [1841].

———. "Nature." In *Essays and Lectures,* 5–49. New York: Library of America, 1983 [1836].

———. "Nature." In *Essays: Second Series, Essays and Lectures,* 539–55. New York: Library of America, 1983 [1844].

———. "The Sphinx." In *Collected Poems and Translations,* 5–8. New York: Library of America, 1994 [1846].

Emerson, Ru. *The Huntress and the Sphinx.* New York: Boulevard Books, 1997.

Eminescu, Mihai. "Epigonii." In *Poezii,* edited by D. Murăraşu, 1.91.21–24. Bucharest: Editura Minerva, 1982. Translated by Corneliu M. Popescu as "Epigones," in *Poems* (Bucharest: Editure Cartea Românească, 1988), 123.

Enel [Scariatin]. *Gnomologie, enseignement et experiences des anciennes écoles initiaques.* Paris: Éditions des Champs-Élyssé, 1959.

———. *A Message from the Sphinx.* London: Rider, 1936.

Enescu, Georges. *Œdipe.* Orchestre Philharmonique de Monte-Carlo, Lawrence Foster. 1990. Original sound recording made by EMI France. CDS 7 54011 2. 2 compact discs.

Erasmus, Desiderius. *Adages: 2.7.1 to 3.3.100.* Translated and annotated by R. A. B. Mynors. Vol. 32 of *The Collected Works of Erasmus.* Toronto: University of Toronto Press, 1992.

———. *Colloquies.* Translated by Craig R. Thompson. Vol. 39 of *The Collected Works of Erasmus.* Toronto: University of Toronto Press, 1997.

Erlenbusch, Hans. *Die Sphinx.* Cologne: J. P. Bachem, 1900.

Esmael, Feisal A., ed. *International Symposium on the Great Sphinx, Proceedings.* Cairo: Ministry of Culture, 1992.

Euripides. *The Heracleidae.* Translated by Ralph Gladstone. In *The Complete Greek Tragedies,* 5:125–72. New York: Modern Library, 1959 [circa 430 BC].

———. *The Phoenician Women.* Translated by Elizabeth Wykoff. In *The Complete Greek Tragedies,* 7:272–342. New York: Modern Library, 1959 [circa 410 BC.

Evers, Hans Gerhard. *Staat aus dem Stein: Denkmäler, Geschichte und Bedeutung der ägyptischen Plastik während des Mittleren Reichs.* Munich: F. Bruckmann, 1929.

Farrington, Marie Lesquoy. *Facing the Sphinx.* San Francisco: privately printed, 1889.

Feuillet, Octave. *Julia de Trecœur; ou, Le Sphinx.* Translated by O. Vibeur as *The Sphinx; or, Julia de Trecœur* (New York: J. W. Carleton, 1875).

———. *Le Sphinx.* Paris: Lévy, 1874. Translated as *The Sphinx* (New York: Chickering Sons, 1881).

Fielding, Daphne. *The Face on the Sphinx: A Portrait of Gladys Deacon, Duchess of Marlborough.* London: Hamish Hamilton, 1978.

Fitzgerald, F. Scott. "Bernice Bobs Her Hair." In *Flappers and Philosophers,* 116–40. New York: Charles Scribner's Sons, 1959 [1920].

Flaubert, Gustave. *L'éducation sentimentale.* Lausanne: Éditions Recontres, 1957 [1869]. Translated by Robert Baldick as *Sentimental Education* (Harmondsworth UK: Penguin, 1964).

———. Letter to Louis Bouilhet, January 15, 1850. In *Correspondance, I (janvier 1830 à juin 1851),* edited by Jean Bruneau. Paris: Gallimard, 1973.

———. *Salammbô.* Edited by Edouard Maynial. Paris: Garnier, 1961 [1862]. Translated by J. C. Chartres as *Salammbo* (London: Dent, 1931).

———. *La tentacion de Saint Antoine.* In *Œuvres,* edited by A. Thibaudet and René Dumesnil, 1:35–302. Paris: Gallimard, 1951 [1874]. Translated by Kitty Mrosovsky as *The Temptation of Saint Anthony* (Ithaca: Cornell University Press, 1981).

———. *Voyage en Égypte.* Edited by Pierre-Marc de Biasi. Paris: Bernard Grasset, 1991.

Flemming, Harford [Harriet Hare McClellan]. *Cupid and the Sphinx.* New York: G. P. Putnam's Sons, 1878.

Flitner, Johann. *Sphinx Theologico-philosophica; oder, Theologisher und Philosophischer Zeitvertrieber.* Frankfurt: Kempffer für Jennis, 1624.

Fogg, William Perry. *Arabistan: The Land of the Arabian Nights.* Hartford CT: Dustin, Gilman, 1875.

Follett, Ken. *The Key to Rebecca.* New York: William Morrow, 1980.

Forrest, Leon. *Divine Days.* New York: W. W. Norton, 1993.

Fould, Wilhelmine Joséphine Simonin [Gustave Haller, pseud.]. *Le Sphinx aux perles.* Paris: Calmann Lévy, 1884.

Fragerolle, Georges. *Le Sphinx: Épopée lyrique en 16 tableaux.* Lithographs by Amédée Vignola. Paris: Enoch & Co. et E. Flammarion, 1896.

France, Anatole. *La révolte des anges.* Paris: Calmann-Lévy, 1914.

Franco, Andrés. *El teatro de Unamuno* Madrid: Ínsula, 1971.

Frankau, Julia [Frank Danby, pseud.]. *The Sphinx's Lawyer.* New York: Frederick A. Stokes, 1906.

Frolics of the Sphinx. Oxford: Munday & Slatter, 1812.

Freud, Sigmund. "Charakter und Analerotik." In *Gesammelte Werke,* 7:203–12. London: Imago, 1941 [1908].

———. *The Complete Letters of Sigmund Freud to Wilhelm Fliess.* Edited by Jeffrey Moussaieff Masson. Cambridge: Harvard University Press, 1985.

———. *Drei Abhandlungen zur Sexualtheorie.* Vol. 5 of *Gesammelte Werke.* London: Imago, 1942 [1905]. Translated by James Strachey as *Three Essays on Sexuality,* vol. 7 of *The Standard Edition* (London: Hogarth Press, 1953).

———. *Selbstdarstellung.* Vol. 14 of *Gesammelte Werke.* London: Imago, 1946 [1925]. Translated by James Strachey as *An Autobiographical Study,* in *The Standard Edition* (London: Hogarth Press, 1959), 20:7–74.

———. *Die Traumdeutung.* Vols. 2 and 3 of *Gesammelte Werke.* London: Imago, 1942 [1900]. Translated by James Strachey as *The Interpretation of Dreams,* vols. 4 and 5 of *The Standard Edition.* (London: Hogarth Press, 1932).

———. "Woher kommen die Kinder?" In *Gesammelte Werke,* vol. 5. London: Imago, 1941.

———. *Die Zukunft einer Illusion* [1927]. Translated by W. D. Robson-Scott as *The Future of an Illusion* (New York: Liveright, 1953).

———. *Zur Geschichte der psychoanalytischen Bewegung.* Vol. 11 of *Gesammelte Werke.* London: Imago 1944 [1914]. Translated by James Strachey as *On the History of the Psychoanalytic Movement,* vol. 14 of *The Standard Edition* (London: Hogarth Press, 1957).

———, and Jung. *The Freud/Jung Letters.* Edited by William McGuire. Princeton: Princeton University Press, 1974.

Friederich, J. B. *Geschichte des Rätsels.* Wiesbaden: Martin Sändig, 1969 [1860].

Friesner, Esther M. *Sphynxes Wild.* New York: Signet, 1989.

Fuller, Mary. "Riddles of the Sphinx." *Fate* 1 (October 1951): 8–12.

Fuller, Roy. "Mythological Sonnets." In *Collected Poems.* London: André Deutsch, 1962.

Gaffarel, Jacob. *Curiositez invoyes sur la sculpture talismanique des Persans.* Paris, 1637.

Gantz, Timothy. *Early Greek Myth: A Guide to Literary and Artistic Sources.* Baltimore: Johns Hopkins University Press, 1993.

García Lorca, Federico. *The Collected Poems: A Bilingual Edition.* Edited by Christopher Maurer. New York: Farrar, Straus & Giroux, 2002.

Gardner, Martin. *Riddles of the Sphinx and Other Mathematical Puzzle Tales.* Washington DC: Mathematical Society of America, 1987.

Garreta, Anne. *Sphinx.* Paris: Grasset, 1986.

Gautier, Théophile. *Une nuit de Cléopâtre.* In *Romans, contes et nouvelles,* edited by Pierre Laubriet, 1:739–72. Paris: Gallimard, 2002 [1838]. Translated as *One of Cleopatra's Nights, The Works of Théophile Gautier,* 1–25 (New York: Walter J. Black, 1928).

————. *L'Orient,* 2 vols. Paris: G. Charpentier, 1877 [1870].

————. *Le roman de la momie.* In *Romans, contes et nouvelles,* edited by Pierre Laubriet, 2:483–634. Paris: Gallimard, 2002 [1858].

————. "Le Sphinx." In *Poésies complètes,* 1:255. Paris: G. Charpentier, 1877 [1845].

————. "Symphonie en blanc majeur." In *Émaux et camées,* 21–23. Lille: Librairie Giard, 1947 [1852].

Gautruche, Pierre. *The Poetical Histories.* A facsimile of the 1671 London edition. New York: Garland, 1976.

Gay, Peter. *Freud: A Life for Our Time.* New York: W. W. Norton, 1988.

Gellius, Aulus. *The Attic Nights.* 3 vols. Translated by John Rolfe. Cambridge: Harvard University Press, 1927 [circa 180].

Gerdemann, Wilhelm, and Heinrich Winfried. *Christenkreuz oder Hazenkreuz?* Cologne: Katholische Tat Verlag, 1931.

Gibbon, Edward. *The Decline and Fall of the Roman Empire.* 3 vols. New York: Penguin, 1995 [1776–88].

Gide, André. *Œdipe.* Paris: Gallimard, 1931. Translated by John Russell as *Oedipus,* in *Two Legends: "Oedipus" and "Theseus"* (New York: Alfred Knopf, 1950).

Gillispie, Charles Colson, and Michel Dewachter, eds. *The Monuments of Egypt: The Napoleonic Edition.* Princeton: Princeton Architectural Press, 1987.

Ginzberg, Louis. *Legends of the Jews.* 7 vols. Baltimore: Johns Hopkins University Press, 1998 [1909–38].

Godwin, Joscelyn. *Athanasius Kircher: A Renaissance Man and the Quest for Lost Knowledge.* London: Thames & Hudson, 1979.

Goethe, Johann Wolfgang. *Faust: Der Tragödie zweiter Teil.* In *Letzte Jahre, 1827–1832.* In *Sämtliche Werke,* edited by Gisela Henckmann and Dorothea Hölscher-Lohmeyer, vol. 18, part 1, 103–351. Munich: Carl Hanser Verlag, 1997 [1831]. Translated by Leopold J. Bernays as Goethe's *"Faust"* (London: S. Low, 1839).

———. *Maxims and Reflections.* Translated by Elisabeth Stopp. Harmondsworth UK: Penguin, 1998.

Goold, Marshall N. *The Sea-Sphinx.* London: George Allen, 1911.

Goux, Jean-Joseph. *Oedipus, Philosopher.* Translated by Catherine Porter. Stanford: Stanford University Press, 1993.

Grafton, Anthony. *Defenders of the Text.* Princeton: Princeton University Press, 1991.

Greener, Leslie. *The Discovery of Egypt.* New York: Viking, 1966.

Grimal, Nicolas. *A History of Ancient Egypt.* Translated by Ian Shaw. Oxford: Basil Blackwell, 1992 [1988].

Group µ. *A General Rhetoric.* Translated by Paul B. Burrell and Edgar M. Slotkin. Baltimore: Johns Hopkins University Press, 1981 [1970].

Grün, Max. *Louis Napoleon Bonaparte, die Sphinx auf dem französischen Kaiserthron.* Hamburg: Meißner, 1859.

Gubel, E. *Le Sphinx de Vienne: Sigmund Freud, l'art et l'archeologie.* Brussels: Ludion, 1993.

Guerber, Helene Adeline. *The Story of Greece.* New York: American Book, 1896.

Gügler, Joseph Heinrich Alois. *Ziffern der Sphinx; oder, Typen der Zeit und ihr Deuten auf die Zukunft.* Solothurn: M. Schwallerschen, 1819.

Hagenbach, Dieter, and Hannes Bertschi, eds. *Sphinx 10: (Fast) alles über (die) Sphinx.* Basel: Sphinx Verlag, 1985.

Haggard, H. Rider. *The Annotated She: A Critical Edition.* Edited by Norman Etherington. Bloomington: University of Indiana Press, 1991. The text reproduces Haggard's 1888 corrected version, in preference to the first edition of 1887 and the last revision of 1891.

———. *Ayesha: The Return of "She."* New York: Dover, 1978 [1904–5].

Halbreich, Harry. Brochure for Enescu's *Œdipe*, 25.

Hamilton, Edith. *Mythology.* Boston: Little, Brown, 1942.

Hamlin, V. T. *The Sphinx and Alley Oop.* Princeton WI: Kitchen Sink Press, 1991.

Hancock, Graham, and Robert Bauval. *The Mars Mystery: The Secret Connection Linking Earth's Ancient Civilization and the Red Planet.* New York: Random House, 1998.

————. *The Message of the Sphinx: A Quest for the Hidden Legacy of Mankind.* New York: Crown, 1996.

Harris, John R. *The Legacy of Egypt.* 2nd ed. Oxford: Clarendon Press, 1971.

Harvey, Alexander. "By Trolley to the Sphinx." *Cosmopolitan,* August 1899, 339–49.

Hassan, Selim. *The Sphinx: Its History in the Light of Recent Excavations.* Cairo: Government Press, 1949.

Hauptmann, Carl. *Die uralte Sphinx.* Leipzig: Kurt Wolff, 1915.

Hawass, Zahi. *The Secrets of the Sphinx: Restoration Past and Present.* Cairo: American University in Cairo Press, 1998.

————, and Mark Lehner. "The Sphinx: Who Built It, And Why?" *Archaeology* 47, no. 5 (1994):32–41.

Hay, John. "The Sphinx of the Tuileries." In *The Complete Poetical Works,* 35–37. Boston: Houghton Mifflin, 1917.

Heath-Stubbs, John Francis Alexander. "The Sphinx." *Outposts* (Spring 1958): 6.

Heberer von Bretten, Michael. *Aegyptiaca Servitus.* Edited by Karl Teply, in *Frühe Reisen und Seefahrten,* vol. 6. Graz: Akademische Druck und Verlagsanstalt, 1967 [1706].

Hegel, G. W. F. *Aesthetik.* Vols. 12–14 of *Sämtliche Werke.* Edited by Hermann Glockner. Stuttgart: Fr. Fromanns Verlag, 1953. Translated by T. M. Knox as *Aesthetics: Lectures on Fine Art,* 2 vols. (Oxford: Oxford University Press, 1975).

————. *Philosophy of Mind.* Translated by William Wallace and A. V. Miller. Part 3 of the *Enzyklopädie der philosophischen Wissenschaften im Grundrisse* [1817]. Oxford: Oxford University Press, 1971.

————. *Vorlesungen über die Philosophie der Religion.* Vols. 15–17 of *Sämtliche Werke.* Edited by Hermann Glockner. Stuttgart: Fr. Fromanns Verlag, 1959. Translated by R. F. Brown, P. C. Hodgson, J. M. Stewart, and H. S. Harris as *Lectures on the Philosophy of Religion,* 3 vols., edited by Peter C. Hodgson (Berkeley: University of California Press, 1987).

Heick-Hansen, Bent. "The Sphinx Temple." *Sesto congresso internazionale di egittologia,* 1:243–47. Turin: International Association of Egyptologists, 1992–93.

Heidfeld, Johannes. *Quintum Renata, Renovata, ac Aliquanto Ornatius etiam, quam Nuper, Exculta Sphinx Theologicophilosophica; Promens ac Proponens Pia, Erudita, ac Arguta Aenigmata sive Scrupos, ex Variis & Quamplurimis, tum Sacris tum Profanis Authoribus Sedulo Comportatos, qui Mitissime Faciunt ad Comparandam Sapientiam, ad Exercenda & Acuenda Liberalia Ingenia, ad Formanda Judicia Ingenuamque Delectationem Philologorum Omnium.* Herbona, 1608.

————. *Sphinx Philosophica, Promens et Proponens Erudita ac Arguta Enigmata sive Scrupos, ex Variis tum Sacris tum Profanis Authoribus comportatos, qui Mirificé faciunt ad Comparandam Sapientiam, ad exercenda & acuenda liberalia ingenia, ac formanda judicia studiosorum.* Herbonae Nassoviorum: C. Corvinus, 1600.

Heine, Heinrich. *Buch der Lieder.* In *Samtliche Schriften,* edited by Klaus Briegleb, 1:7–212. Munich: Carl Hanser, 1968 [1837]. Translated by Hal Draper as *The Complete Poems* (Boston: Suhrkampf / Insel, 1982).

————. "The Romantic School." In *Selected Works,* translated and edited by Helen M. Mustard, 129–273. New York: Random House, 1973.

Henry, O. "The Sphinx Apple." In *The Complete Works of O. Henry,* 1:211–22. Garden City: Doubleday, 1953 [1904].

Hermant, Abel. *Deux Sphinx.* Paris: Librarie Borel, 1896.

Hermes Trismegistus. *Corpus Hermeticum.* 4 vols. Edited by A. D. Nock. Paris: Société d'Édition les Belles Lettres, 1945.

Herodotus. *The Histories.* 4 vols. Translated by A. D. Godley. Cambridge: Harvard University Press, 1920.

Hesiod. *The Homeric Hymns and Homerica.* Translated and edited by Hugh G. Evelyn-White. Cambridge: Harvard University Press, 1914.

Hoffelner, Klaus, and Michael Kerschner. *Die Sphinxsäule: Votivträger, Altäre, Steingeräte.* Mainz: von Zabern, 1996.

Hofmannsthal, Hugo von. *Ödipus und die Sphinx.* Berlin: S. Fischer Verlag, 1906.

Holt, Etelka. *The Sphinx and the Great Pyramid.* Los Angeles: Summit University Press, 1977.

Homer. *The Odyssey.* Translated by Robert Fagles. New York: Viking, 1996.

Horkheimer, Max, and Theodor W. Adorno. *Dialectic of the Enlightenment.* Translated by John Cumming. New York: Continuum, 1972 [1947].

Horney, Karen. *New Ways in Psychoanalysis.* New York: W. W. Norton, 1939.

Hourani, Albert. *A History of the Arab Peoples.* Cambridge: Harvard University Press, 1991.

Howard, Richard. "The Encounter." In *The Damages,* 75–79. Middletown CT: Wesleyan University Press, 1967.

Hudson, William Henry. "The Sphinx." In *"The Sphinx" and Other Poems,* 11–14. San Francisco: Elder & Shepard, 1900.

Hughes, Ted. "Song for a Phallus." In *Crow,* 63–65. New York: Harper & Row, 1971.

Hugo, Victor. *Chantiers.* Vol. 15 of *Œuvres complètes.* Edited by J. Seebacher and G. Rosa. Paris: Robert Laffont, 1990.

———. *Les contemplations.* Edited by Léon Cellier. Paris: Éditions Garnier, 1969 [1856].

———. *Histoire d'un crime: Déposition d'un témoin.* Paris: J. Hetzel, 1877. Translated by T. H. Joyce and Arthur Locker as *The History of a Crime: The Testimony of an Eye-Witness* (London: George Routledge and Sons, 1886).

———. "Love in Prison." In *Memoirs,* 97–117. London: Heinemann, 1899.

———. *Les misérables.* Vol. 2 of *Œuvres complètes.* Edited by J. Seebacher and G. Rosa. Paris: Robert Laffont, 1985 [1862]. Translated by Charles E. Wilbour as *Les Misérables* (New York: Modern Library, 1992).

———. "Ténèbres." In *La légende des siècles, Poésie III, Œuvres complètes,* 635–38. Paris: Éditions Robert Laffont, 1985 [1883].

———. "Zim-Zizimi." In *La légende des siècles, Poésie II, Œuvres complètes,* 685–94. Paris: Éditions Robert Laffont, 1985 [1859].

Humbert, Jean-Marcel, Michael Pantazzi, and Christiane Ziegler. *Egyptomania: Egypt in Western Art, 1730–1930.* Ottawa: National Gallery of Canada, 1994.

Hume, Fergus. *Woman: The Sphinx.* London: John Long, 1902.

Hus, Alain. *Recherches sur la statuaire en pierre étrusque archaïque.* Paris: Éditions E. De Boccard, 1961.

Husserl, Edmund. *Ideen zu einer reinen Phänomenologie un phänomenologischen Philosophie.* The Hague: M. Nijhoff, 1976 [1913]. Translated by W. R. Boyce Gibson as *Ideas: General Introduction to Pure Phenomenology* (London: George Allen & Unwin, 1931).

Huysmans, Joris. *À rebours.* Edited by Pierre Waldner. Paris: Flammarion, 1978 [1884].

Hyginus. *Fabularum Liber.* A facsimile of the 1535 Basel edition. New York: Garland, 1976.

———. *The Myths of Hyginus.* Translated and edited by Mary Grant. Humanistics Studies 34. Lawrence: University of Kansas, 1960.

Ida, Countess Hahn-Hahn. *Letters of a German Countess Written during Her Travels in Turkey, Egypt, the Holy Land, Syria, Nubia, &c. in 1843–4.* 3 vols. London: Henry Colburn, 1846.

Ilberg, Johannes. "Sphinx." In *Ausführliches Lexicon der griechischen und römischen Mythologie* by W. H. Roscher, 4:1298–1408. Leipzig: Teubner, 1915.

Ionesco, Eugène. *L'homme aux valises*. Paris: Gallimard, 1975. Adapted by Israel Horovitz as *Man with Bags*, based on a translation by Marie-France Ionesco (New York: Grove Press, 1977).

Iron Maiden. *Powerslave*. Capitol Records. 4969200. Compact disc. 1998 [1984].

Iversen, Erik. *The Myth of Egypt and Its Hieroglyphs in European Tradition*. Princeton: Princeton University Press, 1993 [1961].

James, Henry. *Complete Stories, 1898–1910*. New York: Library of America, 1996.

James, William. *A Pluralistic Universe*. In *William James, Writings 1902–1910*, edited and annotated by Bruce Kuklick, 625–816. New York: Library of America, 1987 [1909].

———. *Pragmatism*. In *William James, Writings 1902–1910*, edited and annotated by Bruce Kuklick, 479–624. New York: Library of America, 1987 [1907].

Jarry, Alfred. *César-Antechrist*. In *Œuvres complètes*, 1:271–344. Paris: Gallimard, 1972 [1895].

Jean, Duke of Berry. *The Book of Hours*. A facsimile edition, Musée Condé, Chantilly. New York: George Braziller, 1971.

Jeffers, James A. *The Great Sphinx Speaks to God's People*. Los Angeles: Alberty, 1942.

Joncières, Léonce de. *L'âme du Sphinx*. Paris: Alphonse Lemerre, 1906.

Jones, Ernest. *The Life and Work of Sigmund Freud*. Abridged. New York: Basic Books, 1961.

Jones, Ira L. *Beoni the Sphinx*. Privately printed, 1898.

Jordan, Charlotte Brewster. *Sphinx-Lore: A Collection of Original, Literary Ingenuities, and Historical Recreations, Interspersed with Charades, Anagrams, and Diagram and Jingle-Puzzles*. New York: E. P. Dutton, 1897.

Jordan, Paul. *Riddles of the Sphinx*. Photographs by John Ross. New York: New York University Press, 1998.

Joseph-Renaud, J. *Le Sphinx bleu*. Paris: La Technique du Livre, 1945.

Joyce, James. *Finnegans Wake*. New York: Viking, 1959 [1939].

Jung, Carl, and Marie-Louise von Franz. *Man and His Symbols*. Garden City NY: Doubleday, 1964.

———. *Symbols of Transformation*. 2nd ed. Translated by R. F. C. Hull. Princeton: Princeton University Press, 1967.

Kafka, Franz. *Letters to Milena*. Translated by Philip Boehm. New York: Schocken Books, 1990 [1952].

Kaplan, Stuart R. *The Encyclopedia of Tarot.* 2 vols. Stamford CT: U.S. Games Systems, 1978, 1986.

Kazantzakis, Nikos. *The Odyssey: A Modern Sequel.* Translated by Kimon Friar. New York: Simon & Schuster, 1958 [1938].

Kelly, Ethel Knight. *Why the Sphinx Smiles.* London: Bodley Head, 1925.

Kerényi, Karl, and James Hillman. *Oedipus Variations: Studies in Literature and Psychoanalysis.* Dallas: Spring, 1991 [1966, 1968].

Kierkegaard, Søren. *Either/Or.* 2 vols. Edited and translated by Howard V. Hong and Edna H. Hong. Princeton: Princeton University Press, 1987 [1843].

———. *Works of Love.* Translated by Howard V. Hong and Edna H. Hong. New York: Harper & Row, 1962 [1847].

King, Robert, and Harry Warren. *Sphinx.* 1926.

Kinglake, A. W. *Eothen.* Lincoln: University of Nebraska Press, 1970 [1844].

Kircher, Athanasius. *Oedipus Aegyptiacus: Hoc est Universalis hieroglyphicae veterum doctrinae temporu iniuria abolitae instauratio.* Rome: Vitalis Mascardi, 1652–54.

———. *Sphinx Mystagoga, sive Diatribe Hieroglyphica, qua Mumiae, et Memphiticis Pyramidum Adytis Erutae, & non ita pridem in Galliam transmissae, juxta veterum hieromystarum mentem, intentionemque, plena fide & exacta exhibetur interpretatio.* Amsterdam: Janssonius Waesberge, 1676.

———. *Turris Babel, sive Archontologia qua primo priscorum post diluvium hominum vita, mores rerumque gestarum magnitudo, secundo turris fabrica civitatumque exstructio, confusio linguarum, & inde gentium transmigrationis, cum principalium inde enatorum idiomatum historia, multiplici eruditione describuntur & explicantur.* Amsterdam: Janssonius Waesberge, 1679.

Kirchwey, Karl. *Those I Guard.* New York: Harcourt Brace, 1993.

Klein, Étienne. *Conversations with the Sphinx: Paradoxes in Physics.* Translated by David Le Vay. London: Souvenir Press, 1996.

Kunitz, Stanley. "The Approach to Thebes." In *The Poetry Anthology, 1912–1977,* edited by Daryl Hine and Joseph Parisi, 339–340. Boston: Houghton Mifflin, 1978.

Lacan, Jacques. "The Dream of Irma's Injection." In *The Seminar of Jacques Lacan, Book II: The Ego in Freud's Theory and in the Technique of Psychoanalysis, 1954–1955,* edited by Jacques-Alain Miller, translated by Sylvana Tomaselli, 146–71. New York: W. W. Norton, 1988 [1955].

Laistner, L. *Das Rätsel der Sphinx: Grundzüge einer Mythengeschichte.* 2 vols. Berlin: W. Hertz, 1889.

Lanciarini, Giuseppe. *Sphinx.* Florence: G. Civelli, 1898.

La Riche, William. *Alexandria: The Sunken City.* London: Weidenfeld & Nicolson, 1996.

Lawrence, D. H. *Apocalypse.* New York: Viking Press, 1966 [1931].

———. *The Complete Poems.* Edited by Vivian de Sola Pinto and F. Warren Roberts. New York: Viking Press, 1971.

———. "New Eve and Old Adam." In *Complete Short Stories,* 1:71–94. New York: Viking Press, 1968.

Lear, Amanda. *The Sphinx.* Ariola-Eurodisc. 100 037-100. 45 rpm. 1978.

Le Gallienne, Richard. *Little Dinners with the Sphinx and Other Prose Fancies.* New York: Moffat, Yard, 1907.

Lehner, Mark Edward. "Archaeology of an Image: The Great Sphinx of Giza." Ph.D. diss., Yale University. 1991.

———. *The Complete Pyramids: Solving the Ancient Mysteries.* London: Thames & Hudson, 1997.

Leiris, Michel. *L'âge d'Homme.* Paris: Librarie Gallimard, 1946. Translated by Richard Howard as *Manhood* (New York: Grossman, 1963).

———. *Fourbis.* Vol. 2 of *La règle du jeu.* Paris: Éditions Gallimard, 1955. Translated by Lydia Davis as *Scraps* (Baltimore: Johns Hopkins University Press, 1997).

Lemestre, Marthe [Martoune, pseud.]. *Madame Sphinx vous parle.* Paris: Euredif, 1974. Compiled by Antoine Giovanni and Michel Trécourt. Translated by Gale Strom as *Madame Sphinx* (New York: Ballantine Books, 1975).

L'Engle, Madeleine. *The Sphinx at Dawn.* New York: Harper & Row, 1989 [1982].

Lesky, Albin. "Das Rätsel der Sphinx." In *Gesammelte Schriften,* 318–26. Bern and Munich: Francke Verlag, 1966.

Levinas, Emmanuel. *Nine Talmudic Readings.* Translated by Annette Aronowicz. Bloomington: Indiana University Press, 1990 [1968].

Lévi-Strauss, Claude. *Anthropologie structural.* Paris: Plon, 1958. Translated by Claire Jacobson and Brooke Grundfest Schoepf as *Structural Anthropology* (New York: Basic Books, 1963).

Leyhausen, Paul, and Barbara A. Tonkin. *Cat Behavior: The Predatory and Social Behavior of Domestic and Wild Cats.* New York: Garland, 1975.

Leysen, Sylvain. *Le Sphinx nu.* Toulouse: Éditions Eché, 1987.

Lichtheim, Miriam. *Ancient Egyptian Literature.* Vol. 2, *The New Kingdom.* Berkeley: University of California Press, 1976.

Liddell, H. G., and R. Scott. *Greek-English Lexicon, with a Revised Supplement.* Oxford: Oxford University Press, 1996.

Limat, Maurice. *Le sphinx des nuages.* Paris: Éditions Fleuve Noir, 1986.

Lindsay, David. *Sphinx.* New York: Carroll & Graf, 1988 [1923].

London, Jack. *White Fang.* In *Novels and Short Stories,* 87–284. New York: Library of America, 1982 [1906].

Loti, Pierre. *La mort de Philae.* Paris: Calmann-Levy, 1909. Translated by W. P. Baines as *Egypt* (New York: Duffield, 1910).

Lowell, James Russell. "Sonnet on Being Asked for an Autograph in Venice." In *The Complete Poetical Works,* 404. Boston: Houghton Mifflin, 1897 [1875].

———. "Sphinx." In *The Early Poems,* 220–22. New York: Thomas Y. Crowell, 1892.

Lowrie, Walter. *Kierkegaard.* 2 vols. New York: Harper & Row, 1962 [1938].

Loye, David. *The Sphinx and the Rainbow: Brain, Mind, and Future Vision.* Boulder CO: New Science Library, 1983.

Lucas, St. John. *The Marble Sphinx.* London: Elkin Mathews, 1907.

Ludwig, Emil. *Napoleon.* Translated by Eden and Cedar Paul. New York: Boni & Liveright, 1926 [1925].

Luther, Martin. *Luther's Works.* Vol. 11, *First Lectures on the Psalms II: Psalms 76– 126,* edited by Hilton C. Oswald, translated by Herbert J. A. Bouman. Saint Louis: Concordia, 1976.

Lydgate, John. *Fall of Princes.* Edited by Henry Bergen. London: Early English Text Society, 1924 [circa 1438].

MacLeish, Archibald. "What Riddle Asked the Sphinx." In *The Collected Poems,* 165–66. Boston: Houghton Mifflin, 1962 [1952].

Malatesti, Antonio. *La Sfinge: Enimmi.* Florence: Alla Passione [Andrea Orlandini], for Antonio Morelli, 1683.

Malcolm, Noel. *George Enescu.* Stroud: Toccata Press, 1990.

Mandeville, Bernard. *The Fable of the Bees; or, Private Vices, Publick Benefits.* 2 vols. Oxford: Clarendon Press, 1924 [1714, 1729].

Mann, Thomas. *Joseph und seine Brüder.* Frankfurt: Fischer Verlag, 1964 [1933– 43]. Translated by H. T. Lowe-Porter as *Joseph and His Brothers* (New York: Alfred A. Knopf, 1968).

Marcadé, Jean. *Au musée de Délos: Étude sur la sculpture hellénistique en ronde bosse découverte dans l'isle.* Paris: Éditions E. De Boccard, 1969.

Martineau, Harriet. *Eastern Life: Present and Past.* Boston: Roberts Brothers, 1876.

Masterton, Graham. *The Sphinx.* Los Angeles: Pinnacle Books, 1978.

May, Rollo. *Power and Innocence: A Search for the Sources of Violence.* New York: W. W. Norton, 1972.

Mayfield, Matt, Rick Smith, Vicky Mayfield, Steve Martin, Robin Marks, Darryl See, Rod Stephens, Blake Montana, and Doug Carr. *Lair of the Sphinx.* Lafayette CO: Cloud Kingdom Games, 1999.

Meinke, Hanns. *Die Terzinen von der Sphinx.* Minden-Westfalen: I.C.C. Bruns, 1926.

Melletz, Harry, and Waltrer Welker. "Burning Sands." San Francisco: Metro, 1922.

Melville, Herman. *Clarel: A Poem and Pilgrimage in the Holy Land.* Edited by Harrison Hayford, Hershel Parker, and G. Thomas Tanselle. Evanston IL: Northwestern University Press, 1991 [1876].

———. *Moby Dick.* Edited by Harrison Hayford, Hershel Parker, and G. Thomas Tanselle. Evanston IL: Northwestern University Press, 1988 [1851].

Menzel, C. A. *Die Kunstwerke vom Alterthum bis an Gegenwart: Ein Wegweiser durch das ganze Gebiet der bildenen Kunst.* 2nd ed. 2 vols. Trieste: Lterarisch-artistische Abtheilung des Oesterreischischen Lloyd, 1857.

Michelet, Jules. *Histoire de France*, vol. 8. Lausanne: Éditions Recontre, 1966 [1858].

Miller, Henry. *The Books in My Life.* New York: New Directions, 1969.

———. *Tropic of Cancer.* New York: Grove Press, 1961.

Milton, John. *Paradise Regained.* In *The Works of John Milton*, 2/2:403–82. New York: Columbia University Press, 1931 [1671].

———. *Prolusions.* In *The Works of John Milton*, 12:117–285. New York: Columbia University Press, 1936.

The Modern Sphinx: A Collection of Enigmas, Charades, Rebuses, Double Acrostics, Triple Acrostics, Anagrams, Logogiphs, Metagrams, Square Words, Verbal Puzzles, Conundrums, Etc. London: Griffith & Farran, Gilbert & Rivington, 1873.

Moret, Jean-Marc. *Œdipe, la Sphinx et les Thebains: Essai de mythologie iconographique.* 2 vols. Rome: Institut suisse de Rome, 1984.

Morris, F. O. *A History of British Moths.* London: J. C. Nimro, 1903.

Mott, Francis John. *The Universal Design of the Oedipus Complex: The Solution of the Riddle of the Theban Sphinx in Terms of a Universal Gestalt.* Philadelphia: McKay, 1950.

Murdoch, Dugald. Preface to *The Philosophical Writings,* by René Descartes, 1: 7–8. Cambridge: Cambridge University Press, 1985.

Murtada ibn al-Afif. *The Egyptian History Treating of the Pyramids, the Inundation of the Nile, and other Prodigies of Egypt: According to the Opinions and Traditions of the Arabians. Written Originally in the Arabian Tongue by Murtadi, the Son of Gaphiphus. Rendered into French by Monsieur Vattier and thence faithfully done into English by J. Davies of Kidwilly.* London: Printed by R. B. for Thomas Basset, 1672.

Myers, Thomas. *A New and Comprehensive System of Modern Geography.* 2 vols. London: H. Fisher, son & P. Jackson, 1829.

Naaman, Antoine Youssef. *Les débuts de Gustave Flaubert et sa technique de la description.* Paris: A. G. Nizet, 1962.

Naylor, Colin. *The Book of the Sphinx.* Cullompton UK: Beau Geste Press, 1974.

The New Sphinx. London: G. Balne, 1840.

The New Sphinx: An Elegant Collection of Enigmas, Charades, Rebusses, Logogriphs, Puzzles, Transposi. London: Thorp & Birch, circa 1810.

Nichols, Robert. *The Smile of the Sphinx.* Woodcuts by Ethelbert White. Westminster [London]: Beaumont Press, 1920.

Nichols, Roger. *The Life of Debussy.* Cambridge: Cambridge University Press, 1998.

Nico. "The Sphinx." *Chelsea Girl / Live.* Aura Records. Cleo 6108-2. Compact disc. 1994 [1985].

Niemeyer, Anton. *Historisch-geographische Sphinx: Ein Geschenck für häusliche und gesellige Kreise.* Cassel: Theodor Fischer, 1853.

Nietzsche, Friedrich. *Also Sprach Zarathustra.* In *Werke in drei Bänden,* edited by Karl Schlecta, 2:275–561. Munich: Carl Hanser, 1977 [1883–85]. Translated by Walter Kaufman as *Thus Spoke Zarathustra,* in *The Portable Nietzsche* (New York: Viking, 1954), 103–439.

———. *Jenseits von Gute und Böse.* In *Werke in drei Bänden,* edited by Karl Schlecta, 2:563–760. Munich: Carl Hanser, 1977 [1886]/ Translated by Walter Kaufman as *Beyond Good and Evil,* in *Basic Writings of Nietzsche* (New York: Modern Library, 1968), 181–435.

———. *Morgenröte.* In *Werke in drei Bänden,* edited by Karl Schlecta, 1:1009–1279. Munich: Carl Hanser, 1973 [1881]. Translated by R. J. Hollingdale as *Day-*

break: Thoughts on the Prejudices of Morality (Cambridge: Cambridge University Press, 1982).

———. *Zur Genealogie der Moral.* In *Werke in drei Bänden,* edited by Karl Schlecta, 2:761–900. Munich: Carl Hanser, 1977 [1887]. Translated by Walter Kaufman as *On the Genealogy of Morals,* in *Basic Writings of Nietzsche* (New York: Modern Library, 1968), 437–599.

Nin, Anaïs. *Diary.* New York: Swallow Press / Harcourt, Brace & World, 1966.

Nordau, Max [Max Südfeld]. *Entartung.* 2 vols. Berlin: C. Duncker, 1892–93. Translated as *Degeneration* (Lincoln: University of Nebraska Press, 1993).

Norry, Charles. *An Account of the French Expedition to Egypt.* London: James Ridgway, 1800.

Novalis [Friedrich von Hardenberg]. *Heinrich von Ofterdingen.* In *Schriften,* edited by Paul Kluckhorn and Richard Samuel, 5:181–334. Darmstadt: Wissenschaftliche Buchgesellschaft, 1960 [1802]. Translated by Palmer Hitty as *Henry von Ofterdingen* (New York: Frederick Ungar, 1964).

O'Connell, Robert L. *Of Arms and Men: A History of War, Weapons, and Aggression.* New York: Oxford University Press, 1989.

Oscott, Francesco Luciano. *The Secret of the Sphinx by Pharaoh Amigdor.* Translated by Gavin Gibbons. Sudbury: Neville Spearman, 1977.

Ovid. *Metamorphoses.* 2 vols. Translated by Frank J. Miller. Cambridge: Harvard University Press, 1916 [circa 8 AD].

Paradin, Claude. *Devises héroïques.* A facsimile of the 1557 Lyons edition. Brookfield VT: Scolar Press, 1989.

Paul, M. *Die neue Sphinx: 500 Rätsel gedichtet für Alt und Jung.* Leipzig: E. Berndt, 1877.

Paulsen, Friedrich. "Die Zukunftsaufgaben der Philosophie." In *Die Kultur der Gegenwart: Systematische Philosophie,* 2nd ed., edited by Paul Hinneberg, 391–424. Berlin and Leipzig: Teubner, 1908.

Pausanias. *Description of Greece.* 5 vols. Translated by W. H. S. Jones. Cambridge: Harvard University Press, 1918–35.

Peirce, Charles Sanders. "A Guess at the Riddle." In *Pierce on Signs,* edited by James Hoopes. Chapel Hill: University of North Carolina Press, 1991.

Peju, Pierre. *La part du Sphinx.* Paris: R. Laffont, 1987.

Péladan, Joséphin [Le Sar]. *La décadence latine.* 21 vols. Geveva: Éditions Slatkine, 1979 [1886–1925].

———. *Œdipe et le Sphinx.* Paris: Société du Mercure de France, 1903.

————. *La terre du Sphinx.* Paris: Flammarion, 1900.

Perec, Georges. *La disparition.* Paris: Éditions Denoël, 1969. Translated by Gilbert Adair as *A Void* (London: Harvill, 1994).

Petrie, William M. Flinders. *A History of Egypt.* Rev. ed. 3 vols. London, 1902.

Pfuhl, Ernst, and Hans Möbius. *Die ostgriechischen Grabreliefs.* 4 vols. Mainz: Verlag Phillip von Zabern for the Deutsches Archäologisches Institut, 1979.

Philo of Alexandria. *Philo.* 10 vols., 2 supplements. Translated by F. H. Colson, G. H. Whitaker, and Ralph Marcus. Cambridge: Harvard University Press, 1929–53 [circa 20 BC–40 AD].

Picinelli, Filippo. *Mundus Symbolicus.* A facsimile of the 1694 Cologne edition. New York: Garland, 1976.

Pico della Mirandola. *De Hominis Dignitate, Heptaplus, De Ente et Uno, e Scritti Vari a Cura.* Edited by É. Garin. Florence: Vallecchi, 1942.

Pike, Albert. *Morals and Dogma of the Ancient and Accepted Scottish Rite of Freemasonry.* Charleston SC, 1871.

Pilgrimage to Mecca [*A description of the yeerely voyage or pilgrimage of the Mahumitans, Turkes and Moores unto Mecca in Arabia*]. In *The Principal Navigations, Voyages, Traffiques & Discoveries of the English Nation,* edited by Richard Hakluyt, 5:. New York: Macmillan, 1904.

Plato. *Cratylus.* Translated by Benjamin Jowett. In *Collected Dialogues,* edited by Edith Hamilton and Huntington Cairns, 421–74. Princeton: Princeton University Press, 1961 [circa 330 BC].

Pliny. *Natural History.* 10 vols. Translated by D. E. Eichholz. Cambridge: Harvard University Press, 1962.

Plutarch. "Isis and Osiris." Translated by F. C. Babbitt. In *Moralia,* 5: 1–191. Cambridge: Harvard University Press, 1936.

Pococke, Richard. *Description of the East, and some other countries,* 2 vols. London: privately printed, 1743–45.

Poe, Edgar Allan. "The Sphinx." In *Tales and Sketches,* edited by Thomas Ollive Mabbott, 2:1245–51. Cambridge: Harvard University Press, 1978.

Pond, William A., Jr. *Sphinx Galop.* Privately printed, 1877.

Popy, Francis. *Sphinx? Valse.* Paris: Paris-Musical, 1906.

Pownall, David. *The Sphinx and the Sybarites.* London: Sinclair-Stevenson, 1993.

Prestre, W. A. *Le Sphinx d'ébène.* Neuchatel: Éditions H. Messeiller, 1970.

Proclus. *In Platonis Timaeum Commentaria,* 3 vols. Edited by E. Diehl. Liepzig: Teubner, 1903–6 [circa 470 AD].

Propertius, Sextus. *Elegies.* Edited and translated by G. P. Goold. Cambridge: Harvard University Press, 1999 [circa 25 BC].

Propp, Vladimir. "Oedipus in the Light of Folklore." Translated by Polly Coote. In *Oedipus: A Folklore Casebook,* edited by Lowell Edmunds and Alan Dundes, 76–121. New York: Garland, 1984 [1944].

Proust, Marcel. *A la recherche du temps perdu.* 3 vols. Edited by Pierre Clarac and André Ferré. Paris: Gallimard, 1954 [1913–27].

Quintilian, Marcus Fabius. *Institutio Oratoria.* 4 vols. Translated by H. E. Butler. Cambridge: Harvard University Press, 1966.

Rabelais, François. *Gargantua et Pantagruel.* In *Œuvres complètes,* 2 vols., edited by Pierre Jourda. Paris: Éditions Garnier Frères, 1962 [1546–62].

Radzivilius. *Hierosolymitana Peregrinatio.* Brunsberge, 1601.

Rank, Otto. *Das Inzest-Motiv in Dichtung und Sage: Grundzüge einer Psychologie des dichterischen Schaffens.* Leipzig and Vienna: Franz Deuticke, 1912. Translated by Gregory C. Richter as *The Incest Theme in Literature and Legend: Fundamentals of a Psychology of Literary Creation* (Baltimore: Johns Hopkins University Press, 1992).

———. *The Trauma of Birth.* London: Kegan Paul, Trench, Trübner ad Co, 1929 [1924].

Rawie, Henry. *The Sphinx Catechism.* Baltimore: George W. King, 1911.

Rawlinson, George. *History of Ancient Egypt.* 2 vols. London: Longmans, Green, 1881.

Reade, Charles. *The Cloister and the Hearth.* New York: Heritage Press, 1932 [1861].

Rehn, Jens. *Die weisse Sphinx.* Herford: Koehler Verlag, 1978.

Reik, Theodor. "Oedipus und die Sphinx." *Imago* 6, no. 2 (1920): 95–131. Translated by Bernard Miall as "Oedipus and the Sphinx," in *Dogma and Compulsion* (New York: International Universities Press, 1951), 289–332.

Renard, Marcel. "Sphinx à masque funéraire." *Acta Musei Apulensis* 7, no. 1 (1973): 273–305.

Rennliw, A. M. *Sphinx Amor.* Dresden and Leipzig: E. Pierson, 1894.

Repp, Ed Earl. "Sphinx of the Spaceways." *Science Fiction* (August 1939): 10–29.

Repplier, Agnes. *The Fireside Sphinx.* Boston: Houghton Mifflin, 1939 [1901].

———. "Le repos en Egypte." In *I Sing of a Maiden: The Mary Book of Verse,* edited by Thérèse Lentfoehr, 274–75. New York: Macmillan, 1947.

Richards, I. A. *The Philosophy of Rhetoric.* London: Oxford University Press, 1936.

Rilke, Rainer Maria. *Duino Elegies.* In *The Selected Poetry of Rainer Maria Rilke,* edited and translated by Stephen Mitchell, 149–211. New York: Random House, 1982 [1923].

———. *Letters of Rainer Maria Rilke, 1892–1910.* 2 vols. Translated by Jane Bannard Greene and M.D. Herter Norton. New York: W. W. Norton, 1945.

Robert, Carl. *Oidipus: Geschichte eines poetischen Stoffs im griechischen Altertum.* 2 vols. Berlin: Weidmannsche Buchhandlung, 1915.

Robin, Liliane. Translated as *Cruise of the Sphinx.* Toronto: Mystique Books, 1979.

Róheim, Géza. *The Riddle of the Sphinx.* Translated by R. Money-Kyrle. New York: Harper & Row, 1974 [1934].

Ronell, Avital. *Finitude's Score: Essays for the End of the Millennium.* Lincoln: University of Nebraska Press, 1994.

———. *Stupidity.* Urbana and Chicago: University of Illinois Press, 2002.

Rosegger, Hans Ludwig. *Frau Sphinx: Ein bittersüßlicher Roman.* Leipzig: O. J. Schumann, [1910?].

Rostand, Maurice. *Le secret du Sphinx: Piéce in quatre actes, en vers. La petite illustration: Revue hebdomidaire* (Paris), May 24, 1924. A Flammarion edition followed in 1926.

Roubaud, Louis. *Le voleur et le Sphinx.* Paris: B. Grasset, 1926.

Rouir, Éugene. *Félicien Rops: Catalogue raisonné de l'œuvre grave et lithographie.* Brussels: C. Van Loock, 1987.

Rowling, J. K. *Harry Potter and the Goblet of Fire.* New York: Arthur A. Levine Books, 2000.

Rukeyser, Muriel. "Myth." In *The Norton Anthology of Literature by Women,* edited by Sandra M. Gilbert and Susan Gubar, 1787–88. New York: W. W. Norton, 1985.

Rus, P. J. "La estatuilla de alabastro de Galera." *Cuadernos de historia primitiva,* 5, no. 2 (1950): 113–21.

Saltus, Francis. "The Sphinx Speaks." In *An American Anthology, 1787–1900,* edited by Edmund Clarence Stedman, 522. Boston: Houghton Mifflin, 1900.

Sanderson, John. *Sundrie the personall Voyages.* In *Hakluytus Posthumus of Purchas His Pilgrimes,* edited by Samuel Purchas, vol. 9. New York: Macmillan, 1905.

Sandys, George. *Relations of Africa.* In *Hakluytus Posthumus of Purchas His Pilgrimes,* edited by Samuel Purchas, vol. 6. New York: Macmillan, 1905.

Sarna, Nahum. *Genesis: The Jewish Publication Society Torah Commentary.* Philadelphia: Jewish Publication Society, 1989.

Sauguet, Henri. *La rencontre (Œdipe et le Sphinx): Ballet de Boris Kochno.* Paris: Heugel & Cie., 1952.

Savage, M. J. *The Modern Sphinx and Some of Her Riddles.* Boston: George H. Ellis, 1883.

Schaff, Philip, and Henry Wace, eds. *Nicene and Post-Nicene Fathers.* 2nd ser., 14 vols. Peabody MA: Hendrickson, 1995 [1890–1900].

Schauffler, Robert Haven. *Florestan: The Life and Work of Robert Schumann.* New York: Dover, 1963 [1945].

Schiller, Ferdinand Canning Scott. *Riddles of the Sphinx: A Study in the Philosophy of Humanism.* 3rd ed. New York: Macmillan, 1910 [1891].

Schmidt, Dan. *The Sphinx Prophet.* New York: Bantam Books, 1991.

Schmied, Wieland. "Die Sphinx und der Weg nach Theben." In *Lebendige Literature,* edited by Frank G. Ryder and E. Allen McCormick, 1:20–25. Boston: Houghton Mifflin, 1960 [1954].

Schoch, Robert M. "Redating the Great Sphinx of Giza." KMT 3 (Summer 1992): 53–59, 66–70.

Schuré, Éduoard. *L'évolution divine du Sphinx au Christ.* Paris: Perrin, 1912. Translated by Eva Martin as *From Sphinx to Christ: An Occult History* (London: Rider, 1928).

———. *Les grands initiés.* Paris: Librarie Académique Perrin, 1983 [1889]. Translated by Gloria Raspberry as *The Great Initiates: A Study of the Secret History of Religions,* introduction by Paul M. Allen (New York: Harper & Row, 1961).

Schwabach, Kurt, and Michael Jary. "Allerdings sprach die Sphinx." Munich: Musikverlag, 1949.

Schweitzer, Ursula. *Löwe und Sphinx im alten Ägypten.* Glückstadt: J. J. Augustin, 1948.

Scott, Cyril. *Sphinx for the Pianoforte, Opus 63.* London: Elkin, 1908.

Segal, Charles, "The Music of the Sphinx: The Problem of Language in *Oedipus Tyrannus.*" In *Contemporary Literary Hermeneutics and Interpretation of Classical Texts,* edited by Stephanus Kresic, 151–63. Ottawa: Éditions de l'Université d'Ottawa.

Seneca. *Oedipus.* In *Tragedies,* translated by Frank J. Miller. Cambridge: Harvard University Press, 1917 [circa 50 AD].

Serres, Michel. *Hermes: Literature, Science, and Philosophy.* Edited by Josué V. Harari and David F. Bell. Baltimore: Johns Hopkins University Press, 1982.

Shaw, George Bernard. *Caesar and Cleopatra.* In *Complete Plays with Prefaces,* 3: 355–481. New York: Dodd, Mead, 1963.

Shelley, Percy Bysshe. *Prometheus Unbound.* In *Poetical Works,* edited by Thomas Hutchinson, 204–74. London: Oxford University Press, 1970.

Singhal, Jwala Prasad. *The Sphinx Speaks; or, The Story of Prehistoric Nations.* New Delhi: Sadgyan Sadan, 1963.

Smith, Pamela H. *The Business of Alchemy: Science and Culture in the Holy Roman Empire.* Princeton: Princeton University Press, 1994.

Sollers, Philippe. *H.* Paris: Éditions du Seuil, 1973.

Somtow, S. P. *The Aquiliad.* 3 vols. New York: Ballantine Books, 1988.

Sonnini, M. *Travels in Upper and Lower Egypt Performed in the Years 1777 and 1778.* Vol. 23 of *An Historical Account of the Most Celebrated Voyages, Travels, and Discoveries, from the Time of Columbus to the Present Period,* by William Mavor. Philadelphia: Samuel F. Bradford, 1803.

Sophocles. *Oedipus at Colonus.* In *Sophocles,* edited and translated by Hugh Lloyd-Jones, 2:409–599. Cambridge: Harvard University Press, 1994 [circa 405 BC].

———. *Oedipus Rex.* Edited by R. D. Dawe. Cambridge: Cambridge University Press, 1982.

———. *Oedipus Tyrannus.* In *Sophocles,* edited and translated by Hugh Lloyd-Jones, 1:323–483. Cambridge: Harvard University Press, 1994 [circa 425 BC].

Sosso, Lorenzo. *Wisdom for the Wise.* New York: Dodge, 1907.

Soupault, Philippe. *Les dernières nuits de Paris.* Paris: Calmann-Lévy, 1928.

Southey, Robert. *Southey's Common-Place Book.* 4 vols. 2nd ser. Edited by John Wood Warter. London: Reeves & Turner, 1876.

Spence, Lewis. *Myths and Legends of Ancient Egypt.* London: Harrap, 1915.

Spencer, Theodore. "The Phoenix." In *The Criterion Book of Modern American Verse,* edited by W. H. Auden, 213–16. New York: Criterion Books, 1956.

Spenser, Edmund. *The Faerie Queene.* Edited by Thomas P. Roche Jr. Harmondsworth UK: Penguin, 1978 [1596].

Le Sphinx, aux Œdipes présens et à venir; ou, Recueil choisi d'énigmes, charades et logogriphes modernes, par un sorcier. Paris: A. Égron, 1803. Sometimes attributed to A. F. Le Bailly.

Sphinx. *Everybody's Book of Riddles and Conundrums.* London: Saxon, circa 1890.

Sphinx Incruenta; or, Two Hundred and Twelve Original Enigmas and Charades. Edinburgh: Adam and Charles Black, 1835.

Sphinx: Monatsschrift für Seelen- und Geistesleben. Edited by Hübbe-Schleiden. Braunschweig: C. A. Schwetschke & Son, 1885–96.

Sphinx: Revue mensuelle des questions récréatives. Brussels: P. Baucq, 1931–39.

Sphinx. *Test.* Megarock Records. MRRCD 020. Compact disc. 1994.

Spiel, Paul M. *Die neue Sphinx: 500 Räthsel für Alt und Jung.* Leipzig, 1877.

Staatliche Museen zu Berlin. *Ägyptisches Museum.* Mainz: Verlag Philipp von Zabern, 1991.

Statius. *Thebaid.* 2 vols. Translated by J. H. Mozley. Cambridge: Harvard University Press, 1928 [91–92 AD].

Steinhardt, Julius. *Schwarze Sphinx: Schicksale und Wandlungen.* Berlin: Paul Parey Verlag, 1927.

Stolz, Mary. *Zekmet the Stone Carver: A Tale of Ancient Egypt.* New York: Harcourt Brace, 1988.

Stolzenberg, Daniel, ed. *The Great Art of Knowing: The Baroque Encyclopedia of Athanasius Kircher.* Stanford: Stanford University Libraries, 2001.

Storz, J. F., H. R. Bhat, and T. H. Kunz. "Genetic Consequences of Polygeny and Social Structure in an Indian Fruit Bat." *Journal of Organic Evolution* 55, no. 6 (2002): 1224.

Straw, Syd. "Sphinx." *Surprise.* Virgin Records America. 7 91266-2. Compact disc. 1989.

Sturdy, Carole. "Questioning the Sphinx: An Experience of Working in a Women's Organization." In *Living with the Sphinx: Papers from the Women's Therapy Centre,* edited by Sheila Ernst and Marie Maguire, 30–48. London: Women's Press, 1987.

Suetonius, Gaius. *The Lives of the Caesars.* 2 vols. Translated by J. C. Rolfe. Cambridge: Harvard University Press, 1914 [circa 120 AD].

Symonds, John. *Oedipus and the Sphinx.* Vol. 15 of *Plays.* London: Pindar Press, 1994.

Taranow, Gerda. *Sarah Bernhardt: The Art within the Legend.* Princeton: Princeton University Press, 1972.

Tasso, Torquato. *Gerusalemme liberata.* Edited by Fredi Chiappelli. Milan: Rusconi, 1982. Translated by Anthony Esolen as *Jerusalem Delivered* (Baltimore: Johns Hopkins University Press, 2000).

Tavard, George H. *Les anges.* Paris: Éditions du Cerf, 1971.

Tefnin, Roland. *La statuaire d'Hatshepsout: Portrait royal et politique sous la 18e Dynasty.* Monumenta Aegyptiaca 4. Brussels: Fondation Égyptologique Reine Élisabeth, 1979.

Tennyson, Alfred, Lord. "Tiresias." In *The Poems of Tennyson*, edited by Christopher Ricks, 568–74. London: Longman, 1969.

Tertullian. *Against Marcion*. In *The Ante-Nicean Fathers*, edited by A. Cleveland Coxe, 3:269–475. New York: Christian Literature Company, 1885 [circa 210 AD].

Tervarent, Guy de. *Attributs et symboles dans l'art profane*. Geneva: Droz, 1997.

Thevet, André. *Cosmographie de Levant*. Edited by Frank Lestringant. Geneva: Librarie Droz, 1985 [1556].

Thiemann, August. *Das Buch der Sphinx: Ein Rätselbuch mit 800 Rätseln und Scherzfragen*. Lahr in Baden: Verlag für Volkskunst und Volksbildung, Richard Keutel, 1926.

Thomas, D. M. *Sphinx*. New York: Viking, 1987 [1986].

Thomson, James. *"The City of Dreadful Night" and Other Poems*. London: Reeves & Turner, 1888 [1870, 1874].

Thoreau, Henry David. *Walden and Other Writings*. New York: Random House, 1937 [1854].

Thumann, Harry. "Sphinx." *Andromeda*. Philips. 6423 531. 33 rpm. 1982.

Time Machine. "Sphynx (The Witness)." *Eternity Ends*. Lucretia Records. NEMS 106. Compact disc. 1998.

Todorov, Tzvetan. *Theories of the Symbol*. Translated by Catherine Porter. Ithaca: Cornell University Press, 1982 [1977].

Tooke, Andrew. *The Pantheon, Representing the Fabulous Histories of the Heathen Gods and Most Illustrious Heroes*. 6th ed. London: Charles Harper, 1713.

Turgenev, Ivan. *Fathers and Sons*. Translated by Constance Garnett, revised by Ralph E. Matlaw. New York: W. W. Norton, 1966 [1862].

Twain, Mark. *Innocents Abroad*. In *"Innocents Abroad" and "Roughing It,"* 1–523. New York: Library of America, 1984 [1869].

Unamuno, Miguel de. *Del sentimiento trágico de la vida*. In *Obras completas*, 16: 125–451. Madrid: Afrodisio Aguado, 1958 [1912]. Translated by Anthony Kerrigan as *The Tragic Sense of Life in Men and Nations* (Princeton: Princeton University Press, 1972).

———. *La Esfinge*. In *Teatro completo y monodialogos, obras completas*, 5:201–71. Madrid: Escelicer, 1968.

Valentine, Edward Uffington, and S. Eccleston Harper. *The Red Sphinx: A Romance*. London: T. Fisher Unwin, 1907.

Valeriano Bolzani, Giovanni Pierio. *Hieroglyphica*. A facsimile of the 1602 Lyon edition. New York: Garland, 1976.

Valéry, Paul. *Cahiers*. 2 vols. Edited by Judith Robinson. Paris: Gallimard, 1974.

————. *Eupalinos; ou, L'architecte*. Paris: Gallimard, 1921. Translated by William McCausland Stewart as *Eupalinos; or, The Architect, Dialogues* (Princeton: Princeton University Press, 1956), 63–150.

————. *Monsieur Teste*. Paris: Gallimard, 1929. Translated by Jackson Mathews as *Monsieur Teste* (Princeton: Princeton University Press, 1973).

Van der Horst, Pieter Willem. *Chaeremon: Egyptian Priest and Stoic Philosopher*. Leiden: E. J. Brill, 1984.

Varda, Agnès, director. *Cléo de 5 à 7*. DVD. Criterion Collection, 1998 [1961].

Velikovsky, Immanuel. *Oedipus and Akhnaton*. Garden City NY: Doubleday, 1960.

Verne, Jules. *Le Sphinx des glaces*. Paris: J. Hetzel, 1897. Illustrations by George Roux.

Vernier, Valery. *Un Sphinx du demi-monde*. Paris: Libraire de la Sociétè des Gens de Lettres, 1886.

Villiers de L'Isle-Adam, Auguste. *Isis*. In *Œuvres Complètes*, 1:99–199, Edited by Alan Raitt and Pierre-Georges Castex. Paris: Gallimard, 1986 [1862].

Vilott, Rhondi. *Secret of the Sphinx*. Dragontales 14. New York: Signet, 1985.

The Vishnu Purāna. 2 vols. Translated by H. H. Wilson. Enlarged and arranged by Nag Sharan Singh. Delhi: Nag, 1980.

Vögelin, Friedrich Salomon. *Denkmaler des Weltgeschichte*. Basel: C. Krüsi, [1870].

Vogt, Rolf. *Psychoanalyse zwischen Mythos und Aufklärung; oder, Das Rätsel der Sphinx*. Frankfurt: Campus Verlag, 1986.

Vollenweider, Andreas. "Manto's Arrow and the Sphinx." *Book of Roses*. Columbia. CK 48601. Compact disc. 1991.

Voltaire. *Oedipus*. In *Œuvres complétes de Voltaire*, rev. ed., 1:5–117. Paris: Garnier, 1877 [1764].

von Daniken, Erich. *The Eyes of the Sphinx: The Newest Evidence of Extraterrestial Contact in Ancient Egypt*. New York: Berkley, 1996.

Von der Osten, Hans Henning. *Ancient Oriental Seals in the Collection of Mr. Edward T. Newell*. Chicago: University of Chicago Press, 1934.

Von Hornstein, Ferdinand. *Die Sphinx und der Sadist*. Potsdam: Müller & I. Kiepenheuer Verlag, 1930.

Von Zahn, Peter. *Schwarze Sphinx: Bericht von Rhein und Ruhr*. Hamburg: Rowohlt Verlag, 1949.

Vorse, Albert White. *Laughter of the Sphinx*. New York: D. Biddle, 1900.

Voss, Richard. *Sphinx.* Stuttgart: Adolf Bonz, 1913. Illustrations by Carl Liebich.

Vox, Carol [William Houghton Sprague Pearce]. *The Sphinx and the Mummy: A Book of Limericks.* New York: H. M. Caldwell, 1909.

Vyse, Colonel Howard. *Operations Carried on at the Pyramids of Gizeh in 1837, with an Account of a Voyage into Upper Egypt. And: Appendix to Operations Carried on at the Pyramids of Gizeh in 1837, containing a Survey by J. S. Perring, Esq., Civil Engineer, of the Pyramids at Abou Roash, and to the Southward, including those in the Faiyoum.* 3 vols. London: Fraser, 1840–42.

Wagner, Richard. *Das Judenthum in der Musik.* In *Schriften und Dichtungen,* 3rd ed., vol. 5. Leipzig: C. F. W. Siegel's Musikalienhandlung, 1871–83 [1850]. Translated by W. Ashton Ellis as *Judaism in Music and Other Essays* (Lincoln: University of Nebraska Press, 1995).

———. *Oper und Drama.* Vols. 3 and 4 of *Schriften und Dichtungen,* 3rd ed. Leipzig: C. F. W. Siegel's Musikalienhandlung, 1871–83 [1851]. Translated by W. Ashton Ellis as *Opera and Drama* (Lincoln: University of Nebraska Press, 1995).

Waite, Arthur Edward. *A New Encyclopedia of Freemasonry.* 2 vols. Hyde Park NJ: University Books, 1970 [1920].

Walch, Caroline C. *Doctor Sphinx.* New York: F. Tennyson Neely, 1898.

Wallace, Susan E. *The Repose in Egypt: A Medley.* New York: John B. Alden, 1888.

Wang, Wen, Frédéric G. Brunet, Eviatar Nevo, and Manyuan Long. "Origin of *Sphinx,* a Young Chimeric RNA Gene in *Drosophila Melanogaster.*" *Proceedings of the National Academy of Science, USA* 99, no. 7 (2002): 4448–53.

Wansleben, Johann Michael. *Sammlung der merkwurdigsten Reisen in den Orient.* Jena: C. H. Cuno, 1792–1803.

Watson, Sydney. *What the Stars Held; or, The Secret of the "Sphinx."* London: William Nicholson & Sons, 1900.

W. B. and E. P. *A Helpe to Discourse; or, A Miscellany of Merriment. Consisting of witty, Philosophicall and Astronomicall Questions and Answers.* 5th ed. London: G. Eld, for Leonard Becket, 1623.

Wegner, Max. *Die Musensarkophage.* Berlin: Gebr. Mann, 1966.

Weissberg, Liliane. "Circulating Images: Notes on the Photographic Exchange." In *Writing the Image after Roland Barthes,* edited by Jean-Michel Rabaté, 109–31. Philadelphia: University of Pennsylvania Press, 1997.

Wells, Carolyn. *At the Sign of the Sphinx.* New York: Duffield, 1906 [1896].

Wells, H. G. *The Time Machine*. In *Seven Famous Novels by H. G. Wells*, 3–66. New York: Alfred Knopf, 1934 [1895].

West, John Anthony. *The Serpent in the Sky: The High Wisdom of Ancient Egypt*. New York: HarperCollins, 1979.

White, Arthur Silva. *From Sphinx to Oracle: Through the Libyan Desert to the Oasis of Jupiter Ammon*. London: Hurst & Blackett, 1899.

Wilde, Oscar. *The Sphinx*. Decorations by Charles Ricketts. London: Elkin Mathews & John Lane, 1894.

Wilkinson, Richard H. *The Complete Temples of Ancient Egypt*. New York: Thames & Hudson, 2000.

Williams, Jay G. *The Riddle of the Sphinx: Thoughts about the Human Enigma*. Lanham MD: University Press of America, 1990.

Wilson, Colin. *From Atlantis to the Sphinx*. Australia: Random House, 1997.

Wilson, Elizabeth. *The Sphinx in the City: Urban Life, the Control of Disorder, and Women*. London: Virago Press, 1991.

Withers, Percy. *Egypt of Yesterday and Today*. New York: Frederick A. Stokes, 1910.

Witt, R. E. *Isis in the Ancient World*. Baltimore: Johns Hopkins University Press, 1997 [1971].

Wittels, Fritz. *Sigmund Freud: His Personality, His Teaching, and His School*. Translated by Eden and Cedar Paul. New York: Dodd, Mead, 1924 [1923].

Wittgenstein, Ludwig. *Wittgenstein's Lectures: Cambridge 1930–1932*, edited by Desmond Lee, 28. Chicago: University of Chicago Press, 1982.

Wolff, Theodor. *Die lächelnde Sphinx, von großen und kleinen von ernsten und heiteren Problemen*. Prague: Academia Verlagsbuchhandlung, 1937.

Woodcott, Keith [John Brunner]. *The Martian Sphinx*. New York: Ace Books, 1965.

Wyndham, Violet. *The Sphinx and Her Circle*. London: André Deutsch, 1963.

Wynn, Walter. *The Sphinx Unveiled*. London: Williams & Norgate, 1928.

Yanni. "The Sphynx." *Port of Mystery*. Windham Hill Recordings. WHCD 11241. Compact disc. 1997 [1989].

Yeats, William Butler. "The Second Coming." In *The Variorum Edition of the Poems of W. B. Yeats*, edited by Peter Alt and Russell K. Alspach, 401–2. New York: Macmillan, 1940 [1920].

Zivie-Coche, Christiane. *Sphinx! Le Père la terreur: Histoire d'une statue*. Paris: Éditions Noêsis, 1997. Translated by David Lorton as *Sphinx: History of a Monument* (Ithaca: Cornell University Press, 2002).

Zola, Emile. *La curée*. Paris: Flammarion, 1970 [1872]. Translated by A. Teixeira de Mattos as *The Kill* (London: Elek Books, 1957).

Zuchtschwerdt, Friedrich. *Sphinx und Clio; oder, Sammlung der besten und neuesten Rätsel, Charaden, Logogriphen und Anagramman*. Berlin: Petsch & Winkler, 1812.

———. *Sphinx und Harmonia; oder, Rätsel, Charaden, Logogriphen und Anagramman*. Berlin: C. G. Petsch, 1813.

B4. World War I Memorial, Kuringai Chase, New South Wales.

Index

Aaron, 105
Abdel-Latif, 62
Abraham, 43, 44
Achilles, 199
Adam, 46
Adamson, Joy, 230n10
Adler, Alfred, 238n6
Aelian, 218n17
Africa, 117, 157–59
Ahl, Frederick, 228n31
Alain, 168
Albright, W. F., 12
Alciati, Andrea, 171
Aldersmith, H., 33
Alexander, Hartley Burr, 23
Alexander the Great, 4, 62, 181, 190
Alexandria, 45, 187
Alley Oop, 167, 244n50
Al Sager, Mohammed, 222n19
Amasi, 78
Ambrose, Saint, 130
Amenhotep I, 171
Amenhotep III, 171, 189
Ammenemes I, 171
Ammenemes II, 171
Ammenemes III, 171, 245n63
Andrew, Saint, 43
angels, 12–16, 51, 94, 219nn27–28, 220n29
Anguillara, Giovani Andrea dell', 71
anguish, 160
Annesley, Maude, 230n8
Anouilh, Jean, 231n21
Antigone, 86, 116
Antinous, 22
Antonius Pius, 22, 178
anxiety, 160
Apollo, 41, 42, 75, 108, 116, 146, 168, 183, 200, 240n35
Apollodorus, 2, 71, 74, 101, 137, 201, 202, 226n1
Araaraart, 33, 222n23

Aragon, Louis, 130, 237n44
Aratus, 48
Aristophanes, 100–101
Aristotle, 101, 104, 154, 179
Asclepius, 43
Ashby, N. B., 179
Assigni, Marius d', 218n16
Astarte, 168, 245n55
atheism, 160
Athena, 58, 196, 249n121
Athenaeus, 128, 186
Atlantis, 34, 222n27
Augustus Caesar, xviii, 171, 245n60
Aulus Gellius, 184
Ausonius of Bordeaux, 101
Aven Vaschia, 87, 190, 229n41, 247n82
Averroës, 154

Bacon, Sir Francis, xvii, 78, 182
Bagwell, William, 75–76
Bakunin, Michael, 161
Balzac, Honoré de, 123
Baraize, Emile, 31
Barbarin, Georges, 34, 225n24
Barberino, Cardinal Francisco, 86
Bar-Cepha, 12
Barthes, Roland, 245n56
Bartholomaeus, 98
Bataille, Henri, 128
Batman, 218n13
Bauchau, Henry, 117–18, 202
Baudelaire, Charles, 15, 169, 238n1, 247n88
Baur, Theodore, 83
Bauval, Robert, 222n27, 223n31
Becher, Johann Joachim, 86
Bela IV, 246n72
Bell, Clare, 230n10
Benjamin, Walter, 71
Berloquin, Pierre, 77, 228n23
Berman, Louis, 37–38
Bernhardt, Sarah, 35, 201

Besant, Annie, 106
Bibesco, Princess Marthe, 91, 122
Bion, Wilfred, 149
Bird, Robert, 77
Bishop, Michael, 166
Bismarck, Otto von, 164
Black Sabbath, 111
Blanchot, Maurice, 71
Blavatsky, Madame Helena Petrovna, 165
Blismon, Ana-gramme, 76
Bloemink, Barbara, 248n100
Blumenberg, Hans, 251n22
Boccaccio, Giovanni, 4
Bonfils, Félix, 56–57
boredom, 160
Borges, Jorge Luis, 147–48, 155
Boullaye-le-Gouz, 24
Bourget, Paul, 128
Bouvet, Marguerite, 104–5
Brand New Heavies, 111
Breton, André, 128
Briey, Renaud de, Comte, 157–58
Briggs, L. B. R., 77
Brontë, Charlotte, 105
Brosi, Sybille, 220n36, 230n10, 235–36n25
Brough, Brothers, 228n35
Brown, John, 71
Brownell, Henry Howard, 101
Browning, Elizabeth Barrett, 175
Brunton, Paul, 22, 106
Bulfinch, Thomas, 4, 98
Burden, Bob, 218n13
Burleigh, George Shepard, 162
Burton, Robert, 186, 200
Busoni, Ferruccio, 109
Byron, George, Lord, 88

Cacciatore, 28–29
Cadmus, 147, 183
Caligula, 171
Calvin, 143
capitalism, 161
Carew, Henry, 8
Carlyle, Thomas, 178, 184
Carr, John Dickson, 132–33
Carrington, Hereward, 218n18

Carroll, Leon, 110
Cartland, Barbara, 123–24
Cassiodorus, Aurelius, 184
Cassion, John, 219n26
Casson, Lionel, 12
Castleman, Henry C., 110
cats, 3, 91, 95–96, 120
Caviglia, Giovanni, 21, 29
Cayce, Edgar, 33, 154
Cebes of Thebes, 104
Cecilie, Crown Princess of Prussia, 53
Cendrars, Blaise, 132
Centofanti, Silvestro, 71, 183
Chaeremon, 188
Chamberlain, N. H., 122, 224n5
Champaigne, Philippe de, 177
Champollion, Jean François, 10
chance, 161
Chantpleure, Guy, 175
Charles, L. M. H., 239n24
Chekhov, Anton, 115
Cheops. *See* Khufu
Chephren. *See* Kafre
Cherubim, 12–15, 44, 51, 219n27
Chilling Tales, 35
Chimera, 98–100
Chius, Jacobus, 12
Chosson, François, 165
Chrysippus, 41, 116, 200
Cicero, 24
Clarke, Arthur C., 166
Claudel, Camille, 165
Claudius, 171
Clearchus, 101
Clement of Alexandria, 45–48
Clement of Rome, 224n11
Cleopatra, 4, 50, 120–21, 156, 172, 181, 234n13
Clio, 168
Cocteau, Jean, 71, 110, 117, 132
Coleman, Ornette, 110
Colette, 132
Collier, Robert, 72
Colrat, Raymond, 226n35, 243–44n37
comic books, 8–9, 35, 167, 208, 218n13, 244n50
Conrad, Joseph, 71

consolation, 162, 163
Conti, Natale, 98, 101, 231n22, 250n1
contraries, 162
Cook, Robin, 230n8, 244n50
Cooke, Rose Terry, 143
Cooper, Gary, 132
Corelli, Marie, 127, 236n31
Corinna, 199, 250n3
Corneille, Pierre, 71
Cortot, Alfred, 233n54
Costandinos, Alec, 110
Craig, W. M., 27, 103
Creon, 3, 116, 183
Cromwell, Oliver, 143
Crowley, Aleister, 196
Crowley, John, 117
curse, 162, 200
Cymbeline, 178
Cyrus the Great, 181

Danby, Frank, 175
Dante Alighieri, 143
Darwin, Charles, 37, 179
David, 15
Davidson, D., 33
Davis, Jefferson, 67
Deacon, Gladys, Duchess of Marlborough,
    91, 165
de Beauvoir, Simone, 128
Debussy, Claude, 187
Dekobra, Maurice, 181, 247n85
Delaney, Samuel, 244n47
Delcourt, Marie, 84, 145, 251n17
Delsol, Lysianne, 185
Demisch, Heinz, 12, 219n26, 221n12, 229n1,
    230n10, 241n2, 245n55, 246n81, 249n121,
    250n1
De Quincey, Thomas, 71, 79, 100, 155
Derrida, Jacques, 154
Descartes, René, 162, 243n35
Dessenne, André, 12, 245n54
Dickens, Charles, 75, 77
Dick Tracy, 218n13
Diderot, Denis, 26
Dietrich, Marlene, 132
Dijkstra, Brad, 220n36

Diocletian, 171
Diodorus of Sicily, 100, 184, 226n1
Direx, Benard, 26
Disraeli, Benjamin, 149
Djedefre, 171, 221n7
dogma, 163
dogs, 100–101, 191
Doherty, Robert, 244n46
Doll Man, 218n13
Domitian, 171
Donaghe, M. Virginia, 34, 223n29
Donnelly, Ignatius, 249n107
Doré, Gustave, 14, 15
doubt, 163
Douglas, Lord Alfred, 6
dreams, 21–22, 73, 91, 137–38, 150, 238n4,
    250
Dreyer, Hans P., 224n4
Dryden, John, 102, 183
Du Bois, W. E. B., 72, 157–59, 243n24
Du Camp, Maxime, 29
Dumas, Alexandre, 177, 246n71
Dumézil, Georges, 100
Dummer, H. Boylston, 67
Dylan, Bob, 117

Echidna, 100, 143
Eden, Garden of, 12
Edmunds, Lowell, 71, 78, 238n8
Egypt, 21, 23, 43, 120, 141, 178, 200; Sphinx
    as symbol of, 163
Eichler, Fritz, 90–93
Eldridge, Paul, 106
Electra, 116
Elizabeth I, 143
El-Makrizi, 62
Elson, A. W., 2
Emerson, Ralph Waldo, 69, 155, 169, 178,
    209
Emerson, Ru, 228n34
Eminescu, Mihai, 197
emptiness, 164
Enel [pseudonym of Scariatin], 105, 106,
    249n107
Enescu, Georges, 205
Enoch, 15

Ephesus, 44, 91, 188
Erasmus, Desiderius, 186, 228n35
Erlenbusch, Hans, 175, 235n18
Ernst, B. M., 248n98
Esmael, Feisal A., 251n30
eternity, 164
Euripides, 74, 86, 116, 199
evolution, 164
Ezekiel, 219n27

fame, 164–65
Fantastic Four, 9
Farrakhan, Louis, 159
Farrington, Marie Lesquoy, 10, 224n4
Fawcett, Farah, 165
Ferdinand III, 86
Feuillet, Octave, 201
Fitzgerald, F. Scott, 117
Flaubert, Gustave, 6, 29, 157, 160, 209
Fleg, Edmond, 205
Flemming, Harford, 175
Fliess, Wilhelm, 238n7
Fogg, William Perry, 6
Follett, Ken, 8
Forrest, Leon, 220n33
fortune, 165
Foscolo, Ugo, 71
Fould, Wilhelmine, 92
Fragerolle, Georges, 48, 50, 169
France, Anatole, 15
Frankau, Julia, 230n8
Frazer, Sir James, 140
Freemasons, 162, 179, 239n24
Freud, Sigmund, 56, 80, 137–40, 145–47, 149,
   164
Friedreich, J. B., 228n22
Friesner, Esther M., 120, 202, 227n7
Fuller, Roy, 149
future, 166–68

Gable, Clark, 132
Gaffarel, Jacob, 12
Galatea, 92
Galton, Sir Francis, 37
Gamal-ed-Din Abu Garfa El-Idrissi, 36
Garbo, Greta, 165

García Lorca, Federico, 185
Gardner, Martin, 77, 228n23
Garreta, Anne, 233n55
Gautier, Théophile, 103, 160, 169, 191,
   230n13
Gautruche, Pierre, 231n24
Gay, Peter, 137
Gazaeus, Procopius, 12
Gérôme, Jean-Léon, 62–64, 80
Geryon, 98
Gibbes, Jacob A., 86
Gibbon, Edward, 200
Gide, André, 43, 75
Ginzberg, Louis, 219n28
Godwin, Joscelyn, 229n42
Goebbels, Paul Joseph, 178
Goethe, Johann Wolfgang von, 1, 4, 154, 210
Goodall, E., 102–3
Goold, Marshall, 187
Gorgias Leontinus, 47
Goupil & Co., 63, 80
Goux, Jean-Joseph, 100, 122, 205
Grafton, Anthony, 229n42
Grant, Cary, 132
Greener, Leslie, 221n14
Griffith, P. M., 106–7
Grimal, Nicolas, 218n15, 221n7, 245n59,
   248n101
Group μ, 154
Grün, Max, 245n65
Gubel, E., 239n15
Guerber, Helene A., 205
Gügler, Joseph Heinrich Alois, 162

Hadrian, 171, 177
Haggard, H. Rider, 126–27, 236n28
Hamilton, Edith, 4, 201–2
Hancock, Graham, 222n27, 223n31
Harper, S. Eccleston, 232n51
Harpocrates, 196
Harpocration, 12
Harris, John R., 229n42
Harry Potter, 227n3
Hassan, Selim, 31, 36, 221n6, 222nn20–21,
   223n33, 226n33, 245n55
Hathor, 168, 190, 245n55

Hatshepsut, 171, 172, 173, 246n66
Hauptmann, Carl, 155–56
Hawass, Zahi, 180, 218n19, 221n8, 222n22
Hawks, Francis L., 222n18
Hay, John, 245n65
Heath-Stubbs, John Francis Alexander, 10
Heberer von Bretten, Michael, 16
Hecube, 206
Hegel, G. W. F., xviii, 5, 51, 77, 139, 153, 154, 164, 191, 227n19
Heidfeld, Johannes, 75, 227n21
Heine, Heinrich, 91–92, 185
Heka, 172
Hera, 116, 200
Hercules, 4, 46, 141, 199, 205
Heri, François, 165
Hermant, Abel, 127, 206, 207
hermaphroditism, 16, 101, 220n33
Hermes Trismegistus, 21, 43
Herod, 43
Herodotus, 129, 180, 237n39
Hesiod, 5, 100
history, 168, 179
Hitler, Adolf, 178
Hofmannsthal, Hugo von, 109, 183, 203
Holt, Erika, 225n24
Homer, 46, 84
homosexuality, 141–42
Horemakhet, Great Sphinx of Giza, 2, 3, 5–11, 52–68, 162, 166, 167, 171, 180, 191, 199; age of, 3, 23, 32; construction of, 10; defaced, 56, 62; erosion of, 188, 222n37; excavated, 21–22, 29–31; as female, 10, 12, 16, 101; as monster, 6, 8–10, 35; Roman repair of, 22, 58; size of, 22; speaks, 51, 105–6, 163, 164, 168, 181, 209
Horney, Karen, 238n6
Horus, 168, 196
Howard, Richard, 118
Hudson, William Henry, 244n40
Hughes, Ted, 206
Hugo, Victor, 60, 78, 122, 130, 156, 163, 168, 181, 182, 247n88
Humbert, Jean-Marcel, 220n31, 225n21, 234n13, 249n117
Hume, Fergus, 230n8

Hus, Alain, 245n53
Husserl, Edmund, 154
Huysmans, Joris, 98, 230n15
Hyginus, 2, 201, 230n18
Hypatia, 45

Ibsen, Henrik, 165
ice, 169–71, 245n57
iconoclasm, 62
Ida, Countess Hahn-Hahn, 51
ignorance, 64, 171
incest, 100, 116–17, 142–43
Incredible Hulk, 218n13
Ingres, Dominique, 16, 79–83
introspection, 147–49
Ionesco, Eugène, 78
Iron Maiden, 111
Isaac, 44
Isis, 3, 45, 121, 168
Iverson, Erik, 229n39

Jacob, 44
Jacob, Max, 132
James, Henry, 122
James, William, 163, 246n75
Jarry, Alfred, 15
Jary, Michael, 110
Jean, Duke of Berry, 184
Jeddy, H. P., 94–95
Jeffers, James A., 34, 224n4, 225n24
Jefferson, Thomas, 67, 261
Jerome, Saint, 45
Jesus Christ, 3, 33, 43–45, 48–51, 72, 154, 164, 222n25, 224n4, 224n6, 225n24
Jocasta, 3, 41–42, 116, 143
John, Saint, 43, 51, 91, 242n12
Joncières, Léonce de, 89, 120–21
Jones, Ernest, 238n6
Jones, Sir William, 34
Jordan, Charlotte Brewster, 77
Jordan, Paul, 221n8, 222nn18–19, 231n30, 245n55, 249n113
Joseph, father of Jesus, 48–50
Joseph, son of Jacob, 16, 45
Joseph-Renaud, J., 232n51
Joyce, James, 210

Julius Caesar, 37, 62, 172
Jung, Carl, 139, 140, 142, 143, 145, 240n28

Kafka, Franz, 155
Kafre (Chephren), 10, 23, 32, 171, 180
Kaplan, Stuart R., 244n44, 249n120
Kazantzakis, Nikos, 225n16
Kelly, Ethel Knight, 105, 175
Kena Upanishad, 154
Kerényi, Karl, 71, 240n35
Khnopff, Ferdnand, 16
Khufu, 32, 52, 180
Kierkegaard, Søren, 122
Kimchi [David Kimhi], 12
King, Robert, 110
King Tut, 32, 246n72
Kinglake, Alexander W., 106
Kircher, Athanasius, xvii, 16, 24–25, 86–88,
    100, 180, 190, 221n13, 229nn40–42
Kirchwey, Karl, 245n57
Klein, Étienne, 183
Klein, Melanie, 142, 146, 149
Kochno, Boris, 110
Koerner, Ernst, 29–30
Kortabinsky, V., 13
Kossak, Wojciech, 65
Kunitz, Stanley, 135

Lacan, Jacques, 238n4
Laistner, Ludwig, 140
Laius, 3, 41–42, 116, 143, 183, 200
Lanciarini, Giuseppe, 127
Lasus Hermioneus, 101
Latona, 22
Lawrence, David Herbert, 71, 75, 120
Lear, Amanda, 110
Lee, Nathaniel, 102
Le Gallienne, Richard, 117
Lehner, Mark Edward, 180, 217n1, 218n19,
    221n2, 221n8, 221n14, 221n16, 222n22,
    231n30
Leiris, Michel, 132
Lemestre, Marthe [Madame Sphinx, Mar-
    toune], 130, 132
Lemuria, 34
L'Engle, Madeleine, 44, 202

Leoncavallo, Ruggiero, 110
Lepsius, Richard, 29
Lesky, Albin, 226n1, 232n47
Leucius Charinus, 43
Lévi, Éliphas, 196
Levinas, Emmanuel, 154
Lévi-Strauss, Claude, 142, 145
Lewis, Wyndham, 38
Leyhausen, Paul, 95–96
Leysen, Sylvain, 249n109
Liddy, G. Gordon, 184
Limat, Maurice, 244n46
Lindsay, David, 150
lions, 8, 10, 12, 16, 95, 129, 156, 218n17, 234n7
Liriopë, 147
London, Jack, 171
Los Angeles Public Library, 23–24
Loti, Pierre, 175
Louis XVI, 91
love, 115, 122–24, 127–28, 129, 132–33
Lowell, James Russell, 64, 103
Loye, David, 166
Lucas, St. John, 44
Ludwig, Emil, 62
Luther, Martin, 171
Luxor, 5, 222n19
Luxor Casino, Nevada, 53, 161
Lydgate, John, 101, 205

MacLeish, Archibald, 106
Madame Sphinx. *See* Lemestre, Marthe
Madenié, Pierre, 165
magic, 172, 174, 184, 230n9
Malatesti, Antonio, 77–78
Mamelukes, 62
Mandeville, Bernard, 98
Mann, Thomas, 16, 221n2
Marcellus, comte de, 101
Marcus Aurelius, 22, 196
Marie Antoinette, 91
Mariette, Auguste, 32
Mark, Saint, 45
marriage, 122, 175
Martineau, Harriet, 6
Mary, Saint, 45, 48–50, 91
Maspero, Gaston, 29, 32, 54

Massenet, Jules, 109
Masterton, Graham, 113, 120, 202
Matthias, 43
May, Rollo, 147
Meinke, Hanns, 228n26
melancholy, 175
Melville, Herman, 56, 64
Memnon, 199
memory, 175
menace, 177
Mendelssohn, Felix, 108, 232n48
Menes, 105
Mentuhotpe VII, 171, 245n59
Menzl, C. A., 28–29
Merope, 41
Merson, Luc Olivier, 48–50
Metternich, Clemens von, 134
Michelet, Jules, 168, 177, 246n71
Mickey Mouse, 218n13, 231n21
Miller, Henry, 130, 244n42
Milton, John, 106, 154
Mirandola, Pico de, 23
Mishna, 154
Mittis, 207
Mohammed, Sheik, 62
money, 36, 58, 59, 147, 176–78, 246n72
Moreau, Gustave, 16, 96, 97
Moret, Jean-Marc, 205, 220n33, 228n33, 229n1, 230n7, 232n45, 250n2
Morris, F. O., 195
Moses, 5, 15, 46, 51, 105, 139, 153
mother, 142–43
Mott, Francis John, 143
Muhammed Alī, 21
Munch, Edvard, 16
Murtada ibn al-Afif, 129
Muses, 47, 108
music, 106–11, 150

Nag Hammadi library, 43
Napoleon III, 165, 172
Napoleon Bonaparte, xviii, 21, 27, 37, 50, 62–67, 159, 165, 172, 190, 200
Narasingh, 34
Narcissus, 147
Nasser, Gamel Abdel, 165

National Socialism, 178
natural law, 179
natural selection, 179
nature, 178
Naylor, Colin, 214
Nero, 22, 143, 235n20
Nessos, 199
New Warriors, 208, 218n13
Nichols, Robert, 127
Nicholas I, 189
Nico, 111
Niemeyer, Anton, 77
Nietzsche, Friedrich, 37, 46, 154, 179, 186, 205, 244n43, 247n89
Nightingale, Florence, 37
Nile, 180, 181, 190
Nin, Anaïs, 130
Nitocris, 129, 181
Norry, Charles, 27
Nova, 218n13
Novalis, 78, 115

O'Connell, Robert L., 186
Odysseus, 46–47, 225nn15–16
Oedipus, xvii, 17, 46–47, 56, 58, 60, 62, 71–88, 96, 97, 104, 108, 110, 122, 137, 139, 202, 203, 209, 252; has sex with the Sphinx, 118; as killer of the Sphinx, 199, 204–6; as legend, 2, 41–44, 109, 116, 141, 142, 186, 206, 208; in opera, 109–10; as self-recognition, 147–49; as Sphinx, 79; as stupid, 44, 84–88, 117, 206; as thief, 183
Oedipus complex, 128, 139–40, 142–43, 145, 238n6, 238n8
O. Henry, 101
Oleaster, 12
Orestes, 116
Orff, Carl, 110
Orthus, 100, 143
Oscott, Francesco Luciano, 222n23
Ovid, 200, 202

Page, 27
Pagnin, 12
Paiva, Mona, 130, 131
Palaephatus, 183

Paradin, Claude, 245n61
Paris, 15, 95, 128, 130–32, 202, 216
Parkes, Michael, 84, 85, 228n32
Pasolini, Paolo, 73
Paul, M., 76, 77
Paulsen, Friedrich, 246n75
Pausanias, 73, 143, 184, 200
Payen, Jean-Pierre, 165
Peck, Sheldon, 157
Peirce, Charles Sanders, 74
Péju, Pierre, 231n31
Péladan, Le Sar Joséphin, 78, 105, 125–26,
    190, 203, 235n24
Pelops, 200
Perec, Georges, 206
Perino del Vaga, 123
Perseus, 205
Petrie, William M. Flinders, 164
Pfuhl, Ernst, 221n12
Phidias, 91
Philo of Alexandria, 8, 21, 45
Phix, Sphinx of Thebes, 3–6, 199–209; as
    killer, xvii, 5, 91, 92, 102, 199; as musical,
    108–11; psychoanalysis of, 139–45, 147,
    149–50, 160; as punishment, 200, 233n3;
    as riddler, 3–4, 41–42, 71–76, 78–86,
    178, 179; as robber, 183–84; and sex with
    Oedipus, 118; suicide of, 3, 201–3; as test
    for marriage, 122–23, 175
Phoenix, 210, 251n31
Picinelli, Filippo, 129, 231n22
Pike, Albert, 162
Pindar, 46, 250n3
plague, 200–201, 250n9
Plato, 46, 231n32
Pliny the Elder, 8, 16, 22, 129
Plutarch, 23, 24, 48, 121
Pluto, 231n21
Pococke, Richard, 24
Poe, Edgar Allan, 245n57, 250n9
Polastron, Louise de, 91
Polydeuces, 41
Pond, William A., Jr., 110
Popy, Francis, 110
Pownall, David, 166–67
Pradus, 12

Prestre, W. A., 157
pride, 181
Proclus, 23
progress, 181
Propp, Vladimir, 234n6
prostitution, 128–32
Proust, Marcel, 221n12
Proverbs, 46, 129–30
Psellus, Michael, 249n109
Puccini, Giacomo, 109
Purcell, Henry, 108
Pygmalion, 92
pyramids, 5, 6, 33, 52–55, 127, 129, 180, 188
Pythagoras, 47

Rā, 168
Rabelais, François, 210
Radzilvilius, 24
Ramses I, 171
Ramses II, the Great, 8, 171, 218n15
Rank, Otto, 16, 142–43, 160
Rawie, Henry, 179
Reade, Charles, 121, 234n14
Redon, Odilon, 17
regression, 182
Rehn, Jens, 245n57
Reik, Theodor, 141
Rennliw, A. M., 175
Repp, Ed Earl, 244n46
Repplier, Agnes, 50, 230n10
revolution, 182
Rhodopis (Rhodope), 50, 129, 237n40
Richelieu, Cardinal, 177, 246n71
riddle books, 75–78
the Riddler, 218n13
Rilke, Rainer Maria, 36–37
Rimbaud, Arthur, 164–65
Robert, Carl, 141, 202, 233n3
Robin, Liliane, 230n8
Róheim, Géza, 140
Ronell, Avital, 84, 232n42
Roosevelt, Franklin Delano, 165
Roosevelt, Theodore, 66–67, 172, 226n40
Rops, Félicien, 16, 124, 235–36n25
Rosegger, Hans Ludwig, 220n37
Rostand, Maurice, 35, 36, 106, 122

Roux, George, 170
Rowling, J. K., 227n3
Rozenfeld, 60–61
Rubenstein, Ida, 35
Rüdisühli, I. L., 10–11
Rukeyser, Muriel, 17
Rus, P. J., 245n55

Saim-ed-Dahr, 62
Saltus, Francis, 168
Sanderson, John, 24
Sandys, George, 129, 157
Sargent, John Singer, 98, 99
Sarna, Nahum, 12
Satan, 98
Sauget, Henri, 110
Savage, M. J., 179
Schepenupet II, 171
Schiller, Ferdinand Canning Scott, 142, 153, 180
Schmid, Julius, 237n37
Schmidt, Bernhard, 143
Schmidt, Dan, 8
Schmied, Wieland, 78
Schoch, Robert M., 222n27
Schumann, Clara, 110
Schumann, Robert, 110
Schuré, Éduoard, 51, 105, 163, 222n27
Schwabach, Kurt, 110
Schweitzer, Ursula, 59, 245n59
science, 182–83
Scott, Cyril, 110
sculpture, 89–93
Segal, Charles, 108
Seneca, 71, 111, 145, 200, 201
Septimius Severus, 22
Serapis, 45
Serres, Michel, 3
Sesotris I, 171, 245n59
Sethos I, 171, 245n63
sex, 111, 115–26, 129–32
Sextus Aurelius Victor, 120
Shakespeare, William, 50, 108, 224n6
Sharp, 24–25
Shaw, George Bernard, 172
Shawqi, Ahmad, 163

Shelley, Percy Bysshe, 98
Siamun, 171
siblings, 115–17
Sicard, François Léon, 204
Sirens, 46–47, 108, 120, 251n22
Snoopy, 231n21
Socrates, 153, 231n32
Sollers, Philippe, 206
Solomon, 154
Somtow, S. P., 167
Sophocles, 4, 71, 101, 108, 110, 111, 139, 141, 145, 183, 200, 201, 206, 209, 238n8, 240n32
Sosso, Lorenzo, 249n109
Soupault, Philippe, 237n44
Southey, Robert, 34
Spencer, Theodore, 251n31
Spenser, Edmund, 203
Sphinxes: and animal names, 194; bull, 15, 218–19n25; in music, 110–11; and place names, 191–93; and trademarks, 192, 196. *See also* Horemakhet, Great Sphinx of Giza; Phix, Sphinx of Thebes
stars, 36–37
Statius, 78, 202
Steinhardt, Julius, 157
Stevens, Alfred, 130, 131
Stoltz, Mary, 222n23
Stolzenberg, Daniel, 229n42
Stratton, H. H., 31
Stravinsky, Igor, 110
Straw, Syd, 111
Stuck, Franz von, 16, 119, 229n5
Sturdy, Carole, 149
Suetonius, 245n61
suicide, 150, 201–5
sun, xvii, 3, 6, 22, 36, 88, 116, 128, 177, 183, 190
Superman, 167, 218n13
Symonds, John, 71

Taharqa, 171
Talleyrand, Charles Maurice de, 164
Tansey, Mark, 33
tarot, 105, 165, 196, 249n120
Tarzan, 167, 218n13
Tasso, Torquato, 98

Tatian, 46
Tefnin, Roland, 229n2
Tennyson, Alfred, Lord, 202
terrorism, 8
Tertullian, 219n27
theft, 171, 183–84
Thiemann, August, 214
Theodoret, 12
Theophilus, 46
Theosophy, 10, 51, 106
Theseus, 205
Thevet, André, 24
Thomas, D. M., 189, 237n36
Thomson, James, 15–16
Thoreau, Henry David, 147
Thoth, 196
Thumman, Harry, 110
Thutmose I, 171, 245n63
Thutmose II, 171
Thutmose III, 171
Thutmose IV, 21–22, 29, 171
Tiberius, 171
Tiffany Company, 185, 248n100
time, 184–85
Time Machine, 111
Tiresius, 147, 200, 251n19
tobacco, 185
Tonkin, Barbara A., 95–96
Tooke, Andrew, 98, 231n22
tourism, 29, 54, 64
tradition, 186
Trajan, 178
Turgenev, Ivan, 117
Tutankhamun (King Tut), 32, 246n72
Tutu, 45, 101, 224n8
Twain, Mark, 16, 58, 64, 175, 220n35
Typhon, 3, 100

Uchida, Mitsuko, 233n54
Unamuno, Miguel de, 60, 149, 155, 160,
    240n39

Valentine, Edward Uffington, 232n51
Valeriano Bolzani, Giovanni Pierio, 232n33
Valéry, Paul, 19, 39, 160

vanity, 155
Varda, Agnès, 121
Varése, Edgard, 108–9
Vedder, Elihu, 32–33
Velikovsky, Immanuel, 228n29
Velvet Underground, 111
Vermeer, Jan, 164
Verne, Jules, 169–71, 184, 245n57
Vernier, Valery, 175
Verus, 22
Vignola, Amédée, 48, 50, 169
Villapandus, 12
Villiers de L'Isle-Adam, Auguste, 121–22
Vilott, Rhondi, 71, 167
Vishnu, 34, 238n50
Vogt, Rolf, 239n18
Vollenweider, Andreas, 111
Voltaire, 71, 111, 171
von Daniken, Erich, 222n27
Von Hornstein, Ferdinand, 15
Von Zahn, Peter, 243n23
Vorse, Albert White, 171
Vox, Carol [pseudonym of William Pearce],
    67
Vyse, Howard, 29, 32, 222nn17–18

Wagner, Richard, 109–10, 153
Wallace, Susan E., 50
Wallis, T., 26
Wansleben, Johann Michael, 62
war, 64, 155, 156, 186, 286
Warren, Harry, 110
Washington, George, 67
waste, 187
water, 187–88
Watson, Sydney, 190
Weber, Carl Maria von, 109
Wegner, Max, 232n44, 245n56
Weissberg, Liliane, 240n34
Wells, Carolyn, 77
Wells, H. G., 166, 201, 244n48
West, John Anthony, 10, 249n112
White, Arthur Silva, 137
White, H. C., 30–31
Wilde, Oscar, 37, 48, 100, 101, 110, 118, 182

Wilhelm, Crown Prince of Prussia, 53
Williams, Jay G., 249n109
Wilson, Colin, 188
Wilson, Elizabeth, 132
Wirth, Oswald, 165, 196
wisdom, 188
Withers, Percy, 104
Witt, R. E., 245n55
Wittels, Fritz, 239n12
Wittgenstein, Ludwig, 151
Wolff, Theodor, 77
Wonders of the World, 161, 188
Wonder Woman, 218n13
Woodcott, Keith [pseudonym of John Brunner], 166

Wyndham, Violet, 250n11
Wynn, Walter, 33, 101, 224n4, 225n24

Xena, 84

Yanni, 111
Yeats, William Butler, 209

Zangakis, 54–55
Zeus, 5, 46, 91, 188
Zivie-Coche, Christiane, 22
zodiac, 189, 249nn112–14
Zola, Emile, 116–17, 124, 235n24, 245n65
Zoroaster, 87
Zuchtschwerdt, Friedrich, 77

In the *Texts and Contexts* series

Affective Genealogies
Psychoanalysis, Postmodernism, and the "Jewish Question"
after Auschwitz
By Elizabeth J. Bellamy

Impossible Missions?
German Economic, Military, and Humanitarian Efforts
in Africa
By Nina Berman

Sojourners
The Return of German Jews and the Question of Identity
By John Borneman and Jeffrey M. Peck

Serenity in Crisis
A Preface to Paul de Man, 1939–1960
By Ortwin de Graef

Titanic Light
Paul de Man's Post-Romanticism, 1960–1969
By Ortwin de Graef

The Future of a Negation
Reflections on the Question of Genocide
By Alain Finkielkraut
Translated by Mary Byrd Kelly

The Imaginary Jew
By Alain Finkielkraut
Translated by Kevin O'Neill and David Suchoff

The Wisdom of Love
By Alain Finkielkraut
Translated by Kevin O'Neill and David Suchoff

The House of Joshua
Meditations on Family and Place
By Mindy Thompson Fullilove

Inscribing the Other
By Sander L. Gilman

Antisemitism, Misogyny, and the Logic of
Cultural Difference
Cesare Lombroso and Matilde Serao
By Nancy A. Harrowitz

Opera
Desire, Disease, Death
By Linda Hutcheon and Michael Hutcheon

Man of Ashes
By Salomon Isacovici and Juan Manuel Rodríguez
Translated by Dick Gerdes

Between Redemption and Doom
The Strains of German-Jewish Modernism
By Noah Isenberg

Poetic Process
By W. G. Kudszus

Keepers of the Motherland
German Texts by Jewish Women Writers
By Dagmar C. G. Lorenz

Madness and Art
The Life and Works of Adolf Wölfli
By Walter Morgenthaler
Translated and with an introduction by
Aaron H. Esman in collaboration with Elka Spoerri

The Nation without Art
Examining Modern Discourses on Jewish Art
By Margaret Olin

Organic Memory
History and the Body in the Late Nineteenth and
Early Twentieth Centuries
By Laura Otis

Book of the Sphinx
By Willis Goth Regier

Crack Wars
Literature, Addiction, Mania
By Avital Ronell

Finitude's Score
Essays for the End of the Millennium
By Avital Ronell

Herbarium / Verbarium
The Discourse of Flowers
By Claudette Sartiliot

Atlas of a Tropical Germany
Essays on Politics and Culture, 1990–1998
By Zafer Şenocak
Translated and with an introduction by Leslie A. Adelson

The Inveterate Dreamer
Essays and Conversations on Jewish Culture
By Ilan Stavans

Budapest Diary
In Search of the Motherbook
By Susan Rubin Suleiman

Rahel Levin Varnhagen
The Life and Work of a German Jewish Intellectual
By Heidi Thomann Tewarson

The Jews and Germany
From the "Judeo-German Symbiosis" to the Memory of Auschwitz
By Enzo Traverso
Translated by Daniel Weissbort

Richard Wagner and the Anti-Semitic Imagination
By Marc A. Weiner

Undertones of Insurrection
Music, Politics, and the Social Sphere in the Modern German Narrative
By Marc A. Weiner

The Mirror and the Word
Modernism, Literary Theory, and Georg Trakl
By Eric B. Williams